INTERNATIONAL TOURISM MANAGEMENT

Bholanath Dutta

Himalaya Publishing House
ISO 9001 : 2015 CERTIFIED

First Edition : 2010
Reprint : 2023

Published by : Mrs. Meena Pandey
for **HIMALAYA PUBLISHING HOUSE PVT. LTD.,**
"Ramdoot", Dr. Bhalerao Marg, Girgaon, Mumbai - 400 004.
Phone: 022-23860170, 23863863; **Fax:** 022-23877178
E-mail: himpub@bharatmail.co.in; **Website:** www.himpub.com

Branch Offices :

New Delhi : "Pooja Apartments", 4-B, Murari Lal Street, Ansari Road, Darya Ganj, New Delhi - 110 002. Phone: 011-23270392, 23278631; Fax: 011-23256286

Nagpur : Kundanlal Chandak Industrial Estate, Ghat Road, Nagpur - 440 018. Phone: 0712-2721215, 2721216

Bengaluru : Plot No. 91-33, 2nd Main Road, Seshadripuram, Behind Nataraja Theatre, Bengaluru - 560 020. Phone: 080-41138821; Mobile: 09379847017, 09379847005

Hyderabad : No. 3-4-184, Lingampally, Besides Raghavendra Swamy Matham, Kachiguda, Hyderabad - 500 027. Phone: 040-27560041, 27550139

Chennai : No. 34/44, Motilal Street, T. Nagar, Chennai - 600 017. Mobile: 09380460419

Pune : "Laksha" Apartment, First Floor, No. 527, Mehunpura, Shaniwarpeth (Near Prabhat Theatre), Pune - 411 030. Phone: 020-24496323, 24496333; Mobile: 09370579333

Cuttack : Plot No. 5F-755/4, Sector-9, CDA Markat Nagar, Cuttack - 753 014, Odisha. Mobile: 09338746007

Kolkata : 3, S.M. Bose Road, Near Gate No. 5, Agarpara Railway Station, North 24 Parganas, West Bengal - 700 109. Mobile: 09674536325

DTP by : Prerana Enterprises, Mumbai

Printed at : Trinity Academy, Mumbai. On behalf of HPH

To

My Parents

Shri Jatindranath Dutta

Smt. Jharna Dutta

&

My loving wife and best friend

Paramita

PREFACE

Tourism is a service industry, which has been growing at a fast rate to be one of the biggest industries in the world. According to WTO (World Tourism Organization) in 1995, there were more than 5000 million tourists and they generated more than 350 billion dollars and in the same year travel and tourism produced direct and indirect employment for more than 200 million people, which accounts for 11% of the global workforce. Next to the oil and automobile industry, tourism has gained its place in the world's top 3 industries. In this way, we see that tourism is a great economic force, as a source of foreign exchange and catalyst of development; hence, governments of developed countries of the modern world have realized the importance of tourism.

Tourism plays an important role in the economic development of many parts of the country and world.

The Hospitality industry is a rapidly growing industry in our country and in many parts of the world, since there has been a growth in the travel business which ultimately leads to the hotel industry boom in order to cater to the people traveling away from home for their comfortable stay, food and beverage.

Today, the benefits of tourism are not to be judged in terms of economic benefits only. Tourism provides social, cultural and educational benefits as well. There are huge opportunities lying for the qualified professional in this field. This book has been written to address the various aspects of tourism in global context.

The author will be highly grateful to those who will find out the various ways to improve the book further. The author will feel himself amply satisfied if this book can meet the demand of the students.

The author requests teaching professors, students and practitioners to send their comments and valuable suggestion for improvement of this book in the coming years. Please post your suggestions to: *bhola_dutta@yahoo.com.*

Bengaluru, 2010 **_Bholanath Dutta_**

ACKNOWLEDGEMENTS

While preparing the manuscript, the author takes the help from some foreign books and inserts the idea, opinion and data, etc., in order to create attractions to the students and clarify critical concepts. The author expresses his heartiest thanks and gratitude as well as indebtedness to the authors and publishers of those books.

In order to get the book ready for the students, all employees of Himalaya Publishing House have performed such a tremendous job for which no thanks for their contribution will be enough

I feel great pleasure in expressing my profound gratitude to Dr. K.C. Sabita Ramamurthy – President, CMR Jananadhara Trust (CMRJT), Shri K.C. Ramamurthy (IPS – Retd.), Chairman – CMRJT, Shri Jayadeep (CEO-CMRJT), Ms. Tristha Ramamurthy (Vice-President- CMRJT), Dr. KVS Anand Babu – Principal, CMRIT, Dr. L Sudarshan Reddy – Vice-Principal, CMRIT, Dr. Col. (Retd.) Mukesh Kumar V, Director, PG Studies, CMRIT, Prof. K. Ravi – Director, Career Guidance & Placement Bureau, CMRIT, Prof. Sundar Raj Vijaynagar, Prof. M.B. Lobo and all my esteemed colleagues in CMRIT for their incessant guidance, stimulation and encouragement in my academic endeavor.

Last but not the least, the silent support received from Mrs. Paramita Dutta, my wife, my parents (Shri Jatindranath Dutta & Smt. Jharna Dutta), in-laws (Shri Dipak Chaudhri & Smt. Keya Chaudhuri), who stand behind all of my even or odd situations to convert any distress into delight, desire unconditional recognition.

Bengaluru, 2010 ***Bholanath Dutta***

Contents

1

INTRODUCTION TO INTERNATIONAL TOURISM MANAGEMENT

Chapter Outline

- *Introduction*
- *Definition*
- *Globalization and Tourism*
- *Tourism and Globalization*
- *Tourism Industry*
- *Challenges*
- *Demand and Origin Factors*
- *Resource Factors*
- *Contemporary Trends in International Tourist*
- *Impact of Tourism on World Economy*
- *UNWTO Vision on World Tourism – 2020.*

Learning Objective

At the conclusion of this lesson you should be able to understand:

- *The importance of tourism industry in national growth*
- *The impact of globalization on tourism*
- *Major challenges to tourism*
- *Various demand and origin factors*
- *Different resource factors in tourism*
- *The contemporary trends in international tourist*
- *UNWTO vision world tourism-2020*
- *Impact of tourism on world economy*

"More than ever before people want to travel. The more people travel, the more they understand the world and one another."

— *Geoffrey J.W. Kent,*
Chairman, World Travel & Tourism Council, Chairman & CEO, Abercrombie & Kent

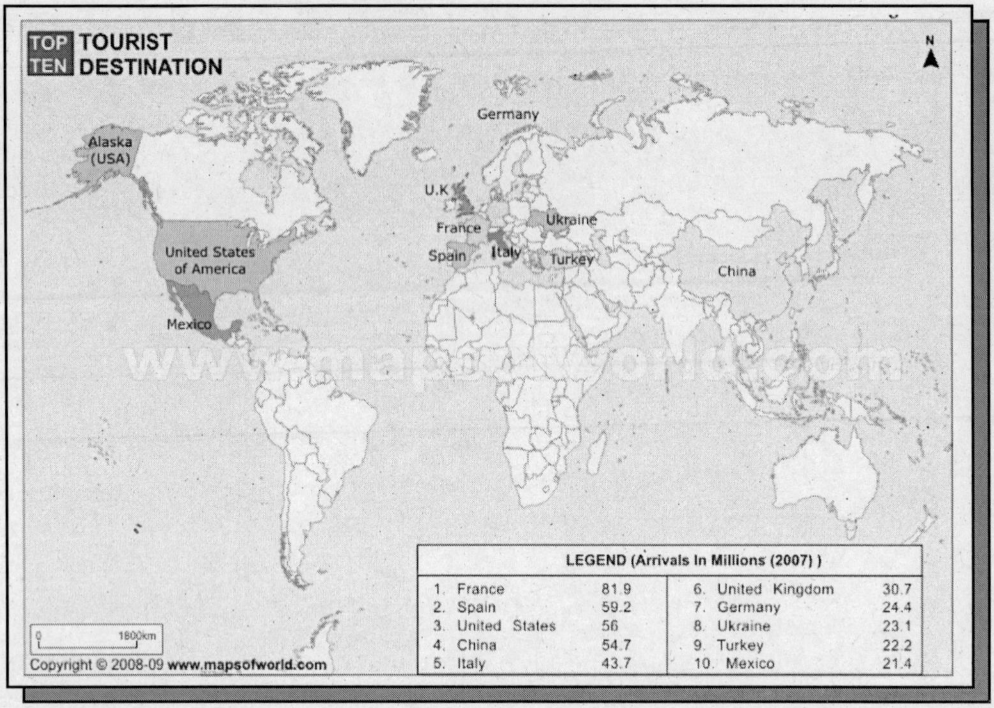

INTRODUCTION

Tourism is considered a smokeless industry; it is more environmentally friendly than other industries. Tourism brings immense benefits to a country. Foreign exchange earnings, tax earnings for government, employment opportunities, development of the local economy of tourism centres, perpetuation of cultural heritage, creation of social assets like tourism attractions, preservation of arts and handicrafts, broad based investment in transport, hostel and restaurant industries, international understanding, etc., are some of the salient benefits derived from tourism. Lured by these, every country vies with each other to woo more tourists.

Tourism industry involves the movement of people, in contrast with other industries where the products are trans-shipped. Movement of people is conditioned by certain factors that influence movement of people are discretionary income, discretionary time, discretionary mobility and desire and drive.

People have been travelling from one place to another since the primitive age when they were living in a small group and did hunting and gathering for their daily life. The movement of people has become clearer when nation-states emerged. They were moving within or across borders for various purposes such as travel, trade, migration, spread of cultural, and dissemination of knowledge and understanding (Amartya Sen); hence, contributing to the development of human civilization.

As for recreation purpose, a lot of wealthy middle class people in Roman era were visiting Pompeii and Herculaneum, seaside resorts, to escape from hot summer in Rome (William, 1998). Thus, tourism is not the recent phenomenon.

In this 21st century, tourism is growing very fast and plays an important role in the world economy. According to Tourism Highlight 2006 Edition, published by World Tourism Organization, international tourist arrivals and receipts worldwide in 2005 was approximately 800 millions and $680 billion respectively despite terrorism in US and Europe, tsunami in some part of Asia, SAR in China and Southeast Asia, and rising oil price.

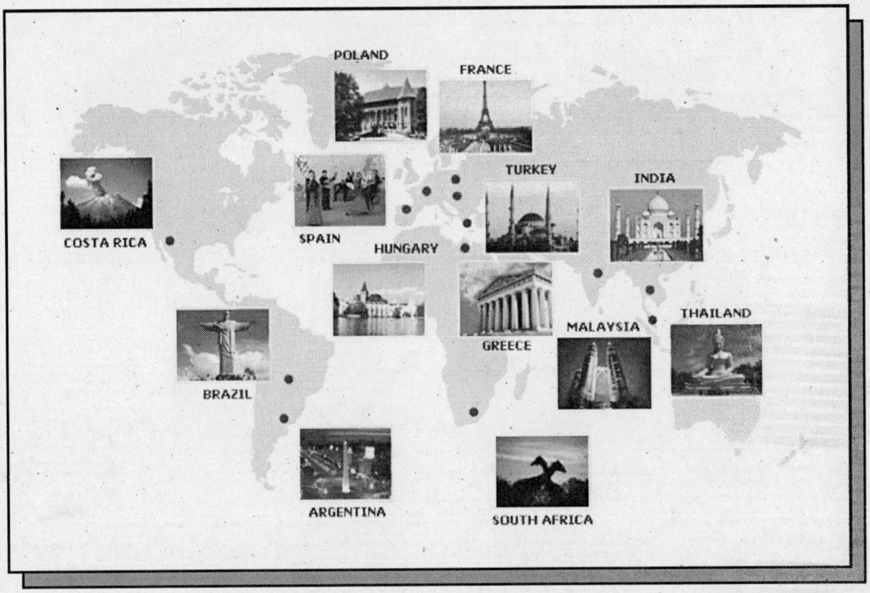

Fig. 1.1. Major tourist attractions of few countries

DEFINITION

Since tourism has been developing very rapidly from time to time and particularly in the 21st century, it is better to search for more definitions to reflect the current situation and to understand its present characteristics. The characteristics of tourism in the 18th century are, of course, different from what it is now in the 21st century. According to World Tourism Organization (2002), 'Tourism' is defined as "the activities of persons travelling to and staying in places outside their usual environment for not more than one consecutive year for leisure, business and other purposes not related to the exercise of an activity remunerated from within the place visited." This definition identifies clearly the activities and length of stay in the destination outside the usual environment where people use to be. However, to match the definition of tourism in the context of Cambodia, which is a small developing country, we should see it from different perspective. Donald G. Reid's definition of 'tourism' based on economic perspective was very right for Cambodia. He asserted that 'for nation-state, especially in the developing world, tourism is defined by the issues of economic growth and employment, which are of paramount concern' (Donald G. Reid, 2003).

To sum up, tourism has been changing progressively according to the development of technology and the development of industry sector. Thus, its definition also has been upgrading to reflect the real situation. It is not just as simple as the movement of people and their length of stay in the destination away from their environment. In developing country like Cambodia, tourism means more than travelling. Tourism is the engine of economic growth and employment creation for the people.

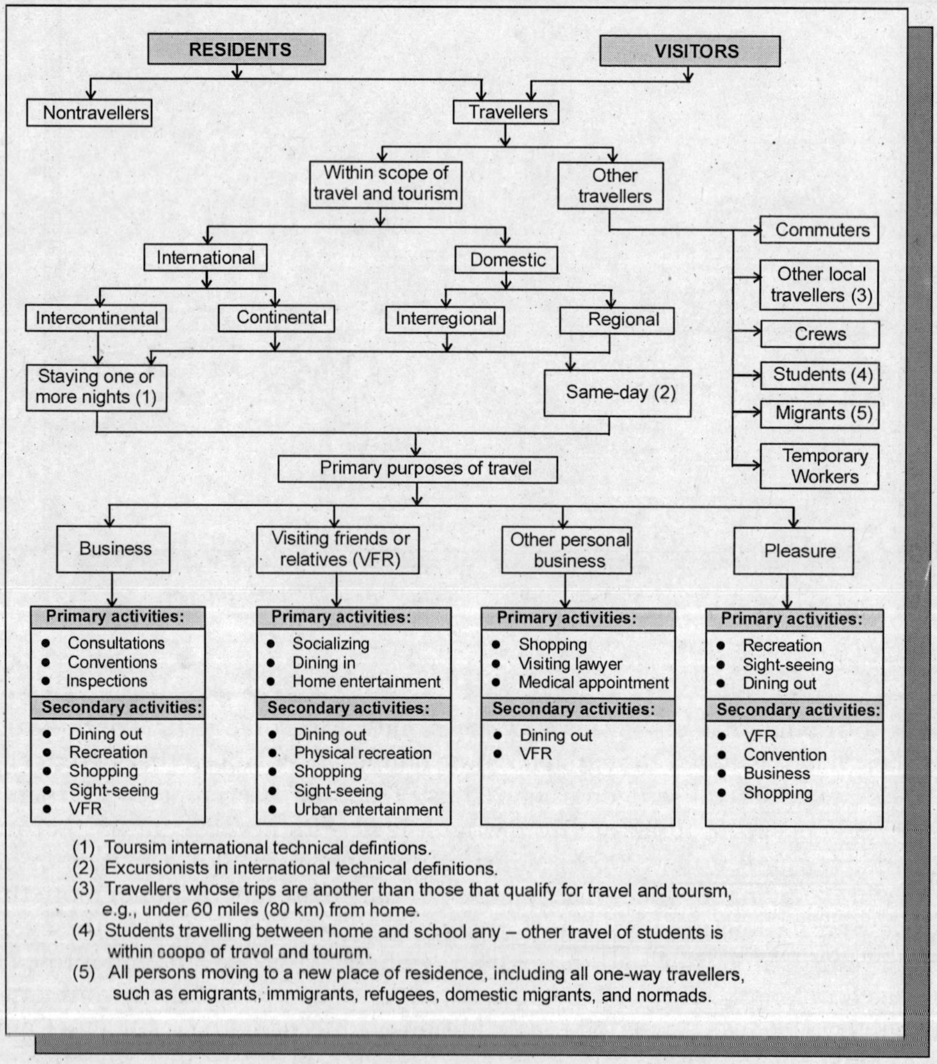

(**Source:** *Tourism-Principles, Practices, Philosophies,* by Charles R. Goeldner & G.R. Brent Ritchie)

Fig.1.2. Different types of travellers

TRAVELLER TERMINOLOGY FOR INTERNATIONAL TOURISM

Underlying the conceptualization of tourism is the overall concept of traveller, defined as "any person on a trip between two or more countries or between two or more localities within his/her country of usual residence." All types of travellers engaged in tourism are described as visitors, a term that constitutes the basic concept of the entire system of tourism statistics. Visitors are persons who travel to a country other than the one in which they generally reside for a period not exceeding twelve months, whose main purpose is other than the exercise of an activity remunerated from within the place visited.

GLOBALIZATION AND TOURISM

The term 'Globalization' has been given various definitions by different international organizations, scholars and other entities. According to the two giant world financial institutions, World Bank and International Monetary Fund (IMF), 'Globalization' is mainly focusing on the process of integrating the world economy: particularly, through international trade and financial flows. While economist scholar, Amartya Sen, sees globalization as a movement of people through travel, trade, migration; thus, contributes to the spread of culture and dissemination of knowledge and understanding throughout entire world. We can see the evidences of globalization in our today's world through movement of people within border, between borders, or across continents, as well as the movement of goods and services between countries; especially, garment and electronic products. And the movement of capital investments of multi-national and trans-national corporations from developed countries to developing countries.

Globalization and tourism seems to be inter-related. On one hand, globalization can contribute to the growth of tourism sector through free movement of almost anything; on the other hand, tourism can spread and foster the movement of globalization.

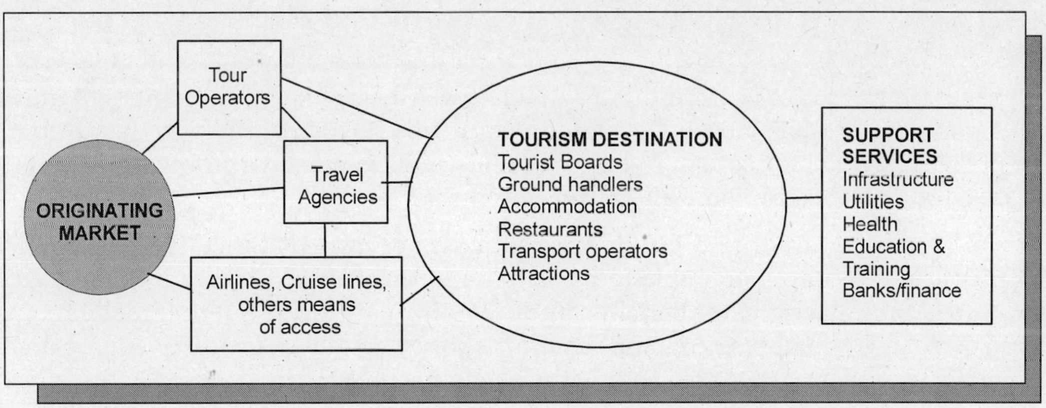

Fig.1.3. The structure of international tourism industry

TRAVEL & TOURISM ECONOMY EMPLOYMENT 2004-2013 ('000 of Jobs Created)	
Top Ten Countries	
1. China	11,493
2. Indonesia	4,192
3. Mexico	3,914
4. India	3,845
5. CIS'	2,221
6. Brazil	1,854
7. United States	1,559
8. Bangladesh	1,104
9. Spain	971
10. Pakistan	968

TRAVEL & TOURISM DEMAND 2004-2013 (% Annualized Real Growth)	
Top Ten Countries	
1. Angola	9.5
2. Mexico	9.5
3. Turkey	9.2
4. China	8.9
5. India	8.8
6. Botswana	8.5
7. Laos	8.4
8. Malaysia	8.2
9. Hong Kong	8.1
10. Vanuatu	7.8

*(**Source:** WTTC)*

Fig.1.4. Travel & tourism economic development

TOURISM AND GLOBALIZATION

Tourism is a major world industry that is a well-established component of the most recent pattern of globalization. Developing countries have been able to use tourism in their policies as a viable economic sector to facilitate development; however, their options may be circumscribed by some globalization pressures.

As a result of the rapid fall in the real costs of long-distance travel, developing regions worldwide have been able to participate in the growth of international tourism. There is a potential for greater benefits for developing countries, but market shares are a source of globalization pressure. Market shares vary strongly from one county to another and within very short periods, reflecting the economic or security crises affecting different countries or regions. According to the International Labour Organization, although tourism is a global industry, its structural characteristics show that the majority of tourism receipts still accrue to the Americas and Europe, because major destinations in those regions have had the time, resources and demand needed to develop their tourism industries. Understanding the economic and social dynamics of the globalization of the tourism industry and the need for fast responses are major issues for tourism growth.

Historical perspective of world tourism

The substantial growth of the tourism activity clearly marks tourism as one of the most remarkable economic and social phenomena of the past century. The number of international arrivals shows an evolution from a mere 25 million international arrivals in 1950 to an estimated 806 milion in 2005, corresponding to an average annual growth rate of 6.5%

International Tourist Arrivals, 1950-2005*

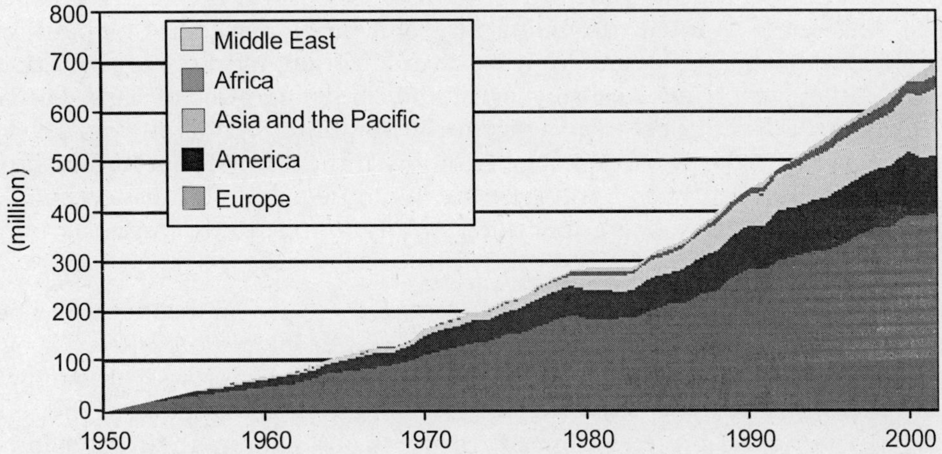

During this period; development was particularly strong in Asia and the Pacific (13% on average a year) and in the Middle East (10%) while the Americas (5%) and Europe (6%), grew at a slower pace and slightly below the world's average growth. New destinations are steadily increasing their market share while more mature regions such as Europe and the Americas tend to have less dynamic growth. Europe's world share declined by over 10 percentage points since 1950 whereas the Americas lost 13 percentage points. Though the Americas'; performance has been most affected by the declines suffered in the past years, the fact is that its annual average grwoth rate for the period 1950-2000 was 5.8%. also bellow the average for the world (6.8%).

Europe and the Americas were the main tourist-receiving regions between 1950 and 2000. Both regions represented a joint market share of over 95 per cent in 1950, 82% forty years later and 76% in 2000.

*(**Source:** UNWTO Report)*

The globalization of travel and tourism services, including information technologies, as well as the internationalization of hotel and other tourism-related enterprises, has been driving recent developments in the tourism industry. The changing global market for tourism services as well as the impact of technological and educational progress in the tourism industry has influenced employment and human resources development, even in countries with a large number of small and medium-sized local tourism enterprises.

Globalization has transformed the tourism product over time from domination by mass tourism to a diversified industry catering more for the individual needs of travellers. "New tourism" is the term used to define the transformed tourism product. This new tourism emerged from several interrelated trends in the global economy, such as overall economic growth and various other socioeconomic changes, government policies, the technological revolution and new management practices.

The concept of new tourism includes ideas and practices related to responsible, green, alternative and sustainable tourism. Globalization has transmitted these ideas and practices worldwide, thus making the tourism industry more diversified and putting pressure on developing countries to create targeted, niche markets. Competition has become stronger and is based increasingly on diversification, market segmentation and diagonal integration, which involves the merger and conglomeration of related business activities. An important source of tourism revenue is now based on identifying, developing and promoting niche markets. Market segmentation in the form of ecotourism, cultural tourism, cruise and adventure tourism is becoming more evident and successful. New niche markets are constantly being identified in an attempt to diversify the industry further.

The changing consumer preferences of international tourists constitute another aspect of globalization that is creating new challenges for developing countries. Providers of tourism services now try to gain a competitive advantage by catering for the individual needs of travellers. Tourists are actively changing the pace and direction of the tourism industry as they become more experienced travellers and change their behaviour and values. The increased travel experience, flexibility and independent nature of tourists has been generating demand for better quality, more value for money and greater flexibility in the travel experience.

The new tourism also reflects demographic changes as well as changing lifestyles, thus creating demand for more targeted and customized holidays since travellers now belong to a number of different lifestyle segments. The changing values of tourists are also generating demand for more environmentally conscious and nature-oriented holidays, which means that tourism providers have to pay more attention to the way people think, feel and behave. In recent years, the niche market has become a more important factor in the tourism industry, reflecting the need to diversify and customize the industry and ensure product sustainability. The main niche markets (sports travel, spas and health care, adventure and nature tourism, cultural tourism, theme parks, cruise ships, religious travel and others) hold great potential and are developing rapidly. The transformations that have created new tourism put pressure on basic ways of doing business and on government strategies and plans for national tourism development.

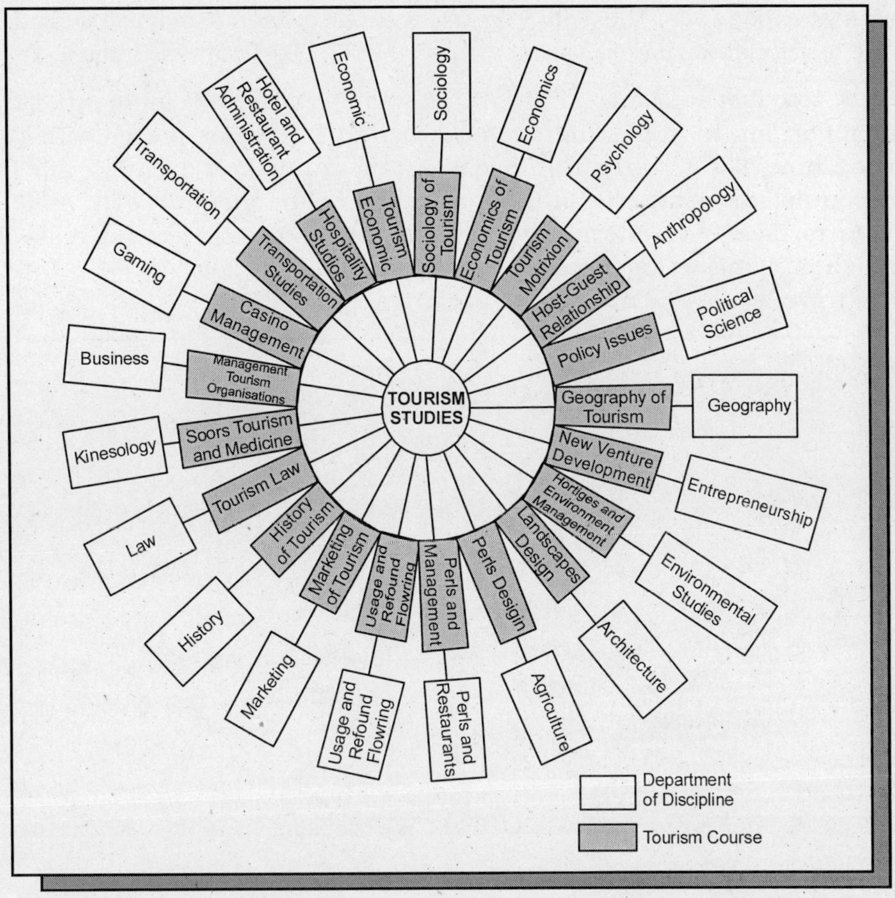

Fig.1.5. Disciplinary inputs to the tourism field. Adapted from Jafar Jafari, University of Wisconsin-Stout, Study of Tourism: Choices of Discipline and Approach

THE TOURISM INDUSTRY

European tourism can be said to originate with the medieval pilgrimage. Although undertaken primarily for religious reasons, the pilgrims in the Canterbury Tales saw the experience as a holiday (the term itself being derived from the 'holy day' and its associated leisure activities). Pilgrimages created a variety of tourist aspects that still exist – bringing back souvenirs, obtaining credit with foreign banks (in medieval times utilizing international networks established by the Lombards), and making use of space available on existing forms of transport (such as the use of medieval English wine ships bound for Vigo by pilgrims to Santiago de Compostela). Religious and secular pilgrimages are still prevalent in modern tourism – such as to Lourdes or Knock in Ireland, Graceland and the grave of Jim Morrison in Père Lachaise Cemetery.

During the 17th century, it became fashionable in England to undertake a Grand Tour. The sons of the nobility and gentry were sent upon an extended tour of Europe as an educational experience. The 18th century was the golden age of the Grand Tour, and many of the fashionable visitors were painted at Rome by Pompeo Batoni.

Health tourism has long existed, but it was not until the eighteenth century that it became important. In England, it was associated with spas, places with supposedly health-giving mineral waters, treating diseases from gout to liver disorders and bronchitis. The most popular resorts were Bath, Cheltenham, Buxton, Harrogate and Tunbridge Wells. Visits to take 'the waters' also allowed the visitors to attend balls and other entertainments. Continental Spas such as Carlsbad (Karlovy Vary) attracted many fashionable travellers by the nineteenth century.

Fig.1.6. Health Tourism

Leisure Travel

Leisure travel was associated with the industrialization of United Kingdom – the first European country to promote leisure time to the increasing industrial population. Initially, this applied to the owners of the machinery of production, the economic oligarchy, the factory owners, and the traders. These comprised the new middle class. Cox & Kings were the first official travel company to be formed in 1758. Later, the working class could take advantage of leisure time.

The British origin of this new industry is reflected in many place names. At Nice, France, one of the first and best-established holiday resorts on the French Riviera, the long esplanade along the seafront is known to this day as the Promenade des Anglais; in many other historic resorts in continental Europe, old well-established palace hotels have names like the Hotel Bristol, the Hotel Carlton or the Hotel Majestic - reflecting the dominance of English customers.

Many tourists do leisure tourism in the tropics both in the summer and winter. It is often done in places such as Cuba, The Dominican Republic, Thailand, North Queensland in Australia and Florida in the United States.

Fig.1.7. Leisure Tourism

Winter Tourism

Winter sports were largely invented by the British leisured classes, initially at the Swiss village of Zermatt (Valais), and St Moritz in 1864. The first packaged winter sports holidays took place in 1902 at Adelboden, Switzerland. Winter sports were a natural answer for a leisured class looking for amusement during the coldest season.Major ski resorts are located in various mainland European countries, Canada, the United States, Australia, New Zealand, Japan, Korea, Chile and Argentina.

Fig.1.8. Winter Tourism

Mass tourism

Mass travel could only develop with improvements in technology allowed the transport of large numbers of people in a short space of time to places of leisure interest, and greater numbers of people began to enjoy the benefits of leisure time.

Fig.1.9. Mass Tourism

Adjectival Tourism

Adjectival tourism refers to the numerous niche or speciality travel forms of tourism that have emerged over the years, each with its own adjective. Many of these have come into common use by the tourism industry academics. Others are emerging concepts that may or may gain popular usage. Examples of the more common niche tourism markets include:

Fig.1.10. Adjectival Tourism

- ☹ Aboriginal tourism (also Tribal tourism and Native American tourism)
- ☹ Adventure tourism (or Adventure travel usually outdoors)
- ☹ Alternative tourism
- ☹ Backpack tourism (or Youth Backpack tourism, see Backpacking (travel))
- ☹ Battlefield tourism
- ☹ Border tourism (or Cross-Border Tourism)
- ☹ Business tourism (or Business travel)
- ☹ Celebrity tourism (including Celebrity Cruises)
- ☹ Community based tourism (or Community supported tourism)
- ☹ Cruise tourism (see Cruise ship)
- ☹ Culinary tourism
- ☹ Disaster tourism
- ☹ Dark tourism
- ☹ Dive tourism (see SCUBA diving)
- ☹ Ecotourism (or Ecotourism in some countries)
- ☹ Educational tourism (or Edutourism, see below)
- ☹ Ethnic tourism
- ☹ Event tourism (or Special Event tourism, including Festivals)
- ☹ Extreme tourism (or Shock tourism)
- ☹ FIT - Free Independent Traveller (or Fully Independent Travel)
- ☹ Geopark tourism (geology-based)
- ☹ Geotourism (related to sustainable tourism)
- ☹ Girlfriend Getaway (all female trip)
- ☹ GIT - Group Inclusive Travel (see Group (travel))
- ☹ Golf tourism
- ☹ Grief tourism (related to Thanatourism)
- ☹ Health tourism (or Wellness tourism; overlap with Medical tourism and New Age tourism)
- ☹ Heritage tourism
- ☹ Incentive travel (gift vacations for employees)
- ☹ Island tourism
- ☹ Honeymoon (or Second Honeymoon)
- ☹ Mass tourism
- ☹ Medical tourism
- ☹ MICE - Meetings, Incentive Travel, Conventions and Exhibitions (or Meetings, Incentives, Conferencing, Exhibitions)

- ☹ Mountain tourism
- ☹ New Age tourism
- ☹ Nightlife tourism (also Entertainment tourism)
- ☹ Package tourism
- ☹ Photography (or Photo) tourism
- ☹ Religious tourism (including Pilgrimage)
- ☹ Reunion tourism
- ☹ Roots tourism (or Genealogy related tourism)
- ☹ Rural tourism
- ☹ Second Home tourism
- ☹ Sex tourism
- ☹ Shopping tourism
- ☹ Space tourism
- ☹ Sports tourism
- ☹ SSS - Sun, Sand and Surf (also Sun, Surf and Sex)
- ☹ Sustainable tourism
- ☹ Thanatourism (meaning death related tourism)
- ☹ Urban tourism
- ☹ VFR - Visiting Friends and Relatives
- ☹ Volunteer tourism (or Volunteer travel)
- ☹ War tourism
- ☹ Winter (Sports) tourism (see below)

A much-visited spot is the Mount Rushmore National Memorial in the Black Hills of South Dakota. The famous faces of four U.S. presidents measure 60 feet from forehead to chin and look over a setting of pine, spruce, birch, and aspen, *Photoby South Dakota Tourism*

There has been an upmarket trend in the tourism over the last few decades, especially in Europe where international travel for short breaks is common. Tourists have higher levels of disposable income and greater leisure time and they are also better-educated and have more sophisticated tastes. There is now a demand for a better quality products, which has resulted in a fragmenting of the mass market for beach vacations; people want more specialised versions, such as Club 18-30, quieter resorts, family-oriented holidays, or niche market-targeted destination hotels.

The developments in technology and transport infrastructure, such as jumbo jets and low-cost airlines, and more accessible airports have made many types of tourism more affordable. There have also been changes in lifestyle, such as retiree-age people who sustain year round tourism. This is facilitated by internet sales of tourism products. Some sites have now started to offer dynamic packaging, in which an inclusive price is quoted for a tailor-made package requested by the customer upon impulse.

There have been a few setbacks in tourism, such as the September 11, 2001 attacks and terrorist threats to tourist destinations such as Bali and European cities. Some of the tourist destinations, including the beach resorts of Cancún have lost popularity due to shifting tastes. In this context, the excessive building and environmental destruction often associated with traditional "sun and beach" tourism may contribute to a destination's saturation and subsequent decline. Spain's Costa Brava, a popular 1960s and 1970s beach location is now facing a crisis in its tourism industry.

On December 26, 2004 a tsunami, caused by the 2004 Indian Ocean earthquake hit Asian countries bordering the Indian Ocean, and also the Maldives. Thousands of lives were lost and many tourists died. This, together with the vast clean-up operation in place, has stopped or severely hampered tourism to the area.

The terms tourism and travel are sometimes used interchangeably. In this context travel has a similar definition to tourism, but implies a more purposeful journey. The terms tourism and tourist are sometimes used pejoratively, to imply a shallow interest in the cultures or locations visited by tourists.

Educational Tourism

Educational tourism developed because of the growing popularity of teaching and learning of knowledge, and enhancing technical competency outside the classroom environment. In the educational tourism, the main focus of the tour or leisure activity includes visitation of another country to learn about the culture of the visited country (Student Exchange Program and Study Tour) or to work and apply their learning inside the classroom in different environment (International Practicum Training Program).

Fig.1.11. Educational Tourism

Other Developments

- ☹ Emerging Adjectival Tourism Terms
- ☹ Atrocity tourism (also War, Disaster, etc., above)
- ☹ Hot-Spot tourism (places of current armed conflict)
- ☹ Staycation (very popular term in summer 2008)
- ☹ Babymoon (a pre-birth honeymoon)
- ☹ Celebration Vacations (travel to celebrate a special event)
- ☹ Creative tourism (tourist participation in destination arts) (see below)
- ☹ Graffiti tourism (travel to commit graffiti)
- ☹ Libel tourism
- ☹ Mancation (an all male trip)
- ☹ Momcation (for mothers)
- ☹ Purposeful tourism (also Meaningful Tourism, related to Volunteer travel)
- ☹ Tummy Tuck Travel (Medical tourism for plastic surgery)

Creative tourism Creative tourism has existed as a form of cultural tourism since the early beginnings of tourism itself. Its European roots date back to the time of the Grand Tour, which saw the sons of aristocratic families traveling for the purpose of (mostly interactive) educational experiences. More recently, creative tourism has been given its own name by Crispin Raymond and Greg Richards, who as a member of the Association for Tourism and Leisure Education (ATLAS) has directed a number of projects for the European Commission, including cultural tourism, crafts tourism or sustainable tourism. They have defined "creative tourism" as tourism related to the active participation of travellers in the culture of the host community, through interactive workshops and informal learning experiences.

Meanwhile, the concept of creative tourism has been picked up by high-profile organizations such as UNESCO, who through the Creative Cities Network have endorsed creative tourism as an engaged, authentic experience that promotes an active understanding of the specific cultural features of a place.

More recently, creative tourism has gained popularity as a form of cultural tourism, drawing on active participation by travellers in the culture of the host communities they visit. Several countries offer examples of this type of tourism development, including the United Kingdom, Spain, Italy and New Zealand.

Dark Tourism

One emerging area of special interest tourism has been identified by Lennon and Foley (2000) as "dark" tourism. This type of tourism involves visits to "dark" sites such as battlegrounds, scenes of horrific crimes or acts of genocide, for example concentration camps. Dark tourism poses severe ethical and moral dilemmas: should these sites be available for visitation and, if so, what should the nature of the publicity involved be. Dark tourism remains a small niche market driven by varied motivations, such as mourning, remembrance, macabre curiosity or even entertainment. Its early origins are rooted in fairgrounds and medieval fairs.

Fig.1.12. Dark Tourism

The World Tourism Organization (UNWTO) forecasts that international tourism will continue growing at the average annual rate of 4 %. By 2020 Europe will remain the most popular destination, but its share will drop from 60% in 1995 to 46%. Long-haul will grow slightly faster than intraregional travel and by 2020 its share will increase from 18% in 1995 to 24%.

With the advent of e-commerce, tourism products have become one of the most traded items on the internet. Tourism products and services have been made available through intermediaries, although tourism providers (hotels, airlines, etc.) can sell their services directly. This has put pressure on intermediaries from both on-line and traditional shops.

It has been suggested there is a strong correlation between Tourism expenditure per capita and the degree to which countries play in the global context. Not only as a result of the important economic contribution of the tourism industry, but also as an indicator of the degree of confidence with which global citizens leverage the resources of the globe for the benefit of their local economies. This is why any projections of growth in tourism may serve as an indication of the relative influence that each country will exercise in the future.

Space tourism is expected to "take off" in the first quarter of the 21st century, although compared with traditional destinations the number of tourists in orbit will remain low until technologies such as a space elevator make space travel cheap.

Fig.1.13. Space Tourism

Technological improvement is likely to make possible air-ship hotels, based either on solar-powered airplanes or large dirigibles. Underwater hotels, such as Hydropolis, expected to open in Dubai in 2009, will be built. On the ocean, tourists will be welcomed by ever larger cruise ships and perhaps floating cities.

CHALLENGES

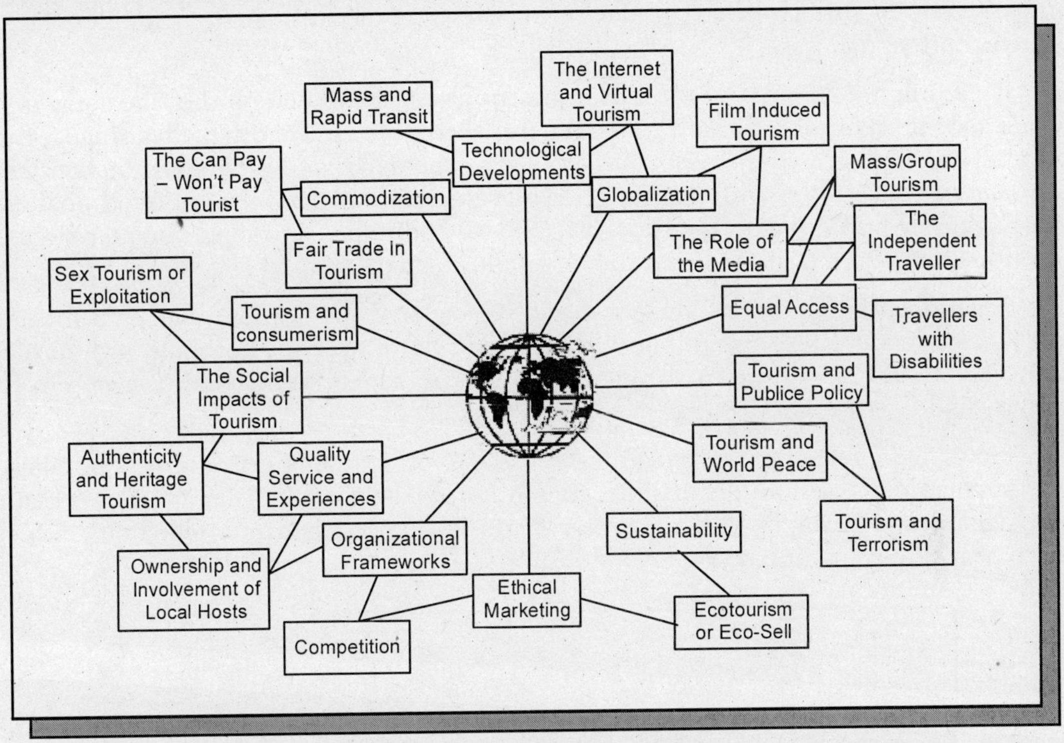

Fig.1.14. Challenges to Tourism

The local population — However, with growing concern for global warming, the industry will be in an introspective in coming years, trying to find out solutions locally that could moderate its contribution to the global warming.

The challenges would be of sustainable tourism, using indigenous methods to meet the energy needs or even reducing emission of greenhouse gases at the individual or community level.

It could be also moving towards responsible tourism that will benefit the stakeholders of the industry, local community and the tourists as well.

To create awareness about global warming; the World Tourism Day 2008 is being observed with a theme "Tourism: Responding to the Challenge of Climate Change" here on Saturday with specific focus on sustainable tourism involving local responses to mitigate causes that leads to global warming.

The World Tourism Day is commemorated on September 27 each year, coinciding with the anniversary of the adoption of the United Nations World Tourism Organisation (UNWTO) statutes on that day in 1970. The World Tourism Day was designated by the UNWTO General Assembly.

Different diverse businesses jointly form this industry *(transportation, hotels, infrastructure, aviation etc.)*, and a balanced development of all these different businesses and high coordination amongst all the participants is a prerequisite for enhancing competitiveness of this industry and creating this 'fine blend' of such 'polar elements' is a tough challenge in itself.

If we talk about Indian Tourism Industry, it can be called as the "industry of big paradoxes", first, on one hand it has almost unbeatable competitive advantages, huge potential and high growth rates *(in terms of - generating foreign exchange, growth rates, & employment generation)*, and on the other hand, inspite of above mentioned positives, Indian Tourism and Hospitality Industry is still way behind even from its small neighbors in South-East Asia, not to mention the large counterparts like China.

Second paradox is that, on one hand, in order to be competitive, this industry needs the cooperation of both public and private sector players as both play a vital role in it, and on the other hand, cut throat competition also exists between the two in this industry itself.

Finally, the 'offering' of this industry is also paradoxical. For India, where 'history' is an important attraction for tourists, this industry has to offer 'history', but it cannot loose sight of modernization either, in other words, Indian Tourism and Hospitality Industry has to be a 'historian' and a 'futurist' simultaneously.

The Great Pyramids of Egypt are the sole remaining wonder of the Seven Wonders of the Ancient World. *Photo courtesy of United Nations.*

DEMAND AND ORIGIN FACTORS

Discretionary Income refers to that part of income left after meeting the essential outgo. DI is freely spendable at the discretion of the recipient. The size of DI of the people influences the decision to go on a tour, the choice of destination, the duration of tour and the like. The DI of the people is a function of the level of development of the country and its population. Accordingly, the third world countries have only a less percentage of people with DI. On the contrary the regions like North America, Canada, Western and Eastern Europe, West Asia, Australia, New Zealand, Fiji and the Pacific Islands have a larger population with DI.

DI has certain competing claimants. It may be spent on tourism activities or invested in income earning assets. Research suggests DI are more likely to be spent on tourism.

Discretionary Time is another prerequisite for tourism. It is the time at the disposal of the individual with discretion. It is 24 hours less the time one needs to spend in office, factory or farm. In the past people were yoked to their avocations almost all the time. Rural households had virtually no DT as they were tied to the farm operations and maintenance of farm animals, in addition to the home chores. Now things have been changing. The privilege of the modern society is that it has more DT. The average work week of factory workers in the USA got scaled down from 70 hours in the 1860s to almost one-half. This is a universal trend. With the labour–saving devices that are invented and introduced to replace humans, the work-time is apt to go down further and further, five-day work-week is also common. Religious and Government declared holidays are there. Earned leave and medical leave facilities exist. Paid vacations are enjoyed by certain sections of employed people. The entire off-season is DT for the farmers and farm-workers. So, DT is on the increase. With rise in DT, tourism and leisure–activities bloom, for people cannot just while away time brooking the corridors of home all the time. People have wanderlust. Given DI and DT, they prefer travel and tour than staying home. The aged populations have lots of DT. Incidentally, they have more wealth, DI too. The aged Americans are the most moneyed people and are having large DT. Such segments of demography contain lots of potentials for tourism growth.

Discretionary Mobility comes next. Freedom to move from place to place and country to country is essential for growth of tourisms. Within a nation there is more DM, generally speaking. However, internal disturbances might damage this mobility. Across countries, Visa and Passport requirements cause discretionary mobility difficult. Till recently some communist countries did not allow inflow and outflow of people. Now the global village syndrome is very much in vogue.

Desire and drive, on the part of people to travel and tour are vital. Even with all the three discretionary factors referred to above be present, the absence of the 'urge' to go on a tour halts the growth of tourism. The desire and drive factors, are not, fortunately lacking in people. Travel is educative, it makes one more knowledgeable; it enhances ones social status; it means faster conclusions of business dealings; its pleasure is simply superb. These personal values of travel, coupled with the promotional pull injected in by the host countries, make and maintain the 'urge'.

DESTINATION & RESOURCE FACTORS

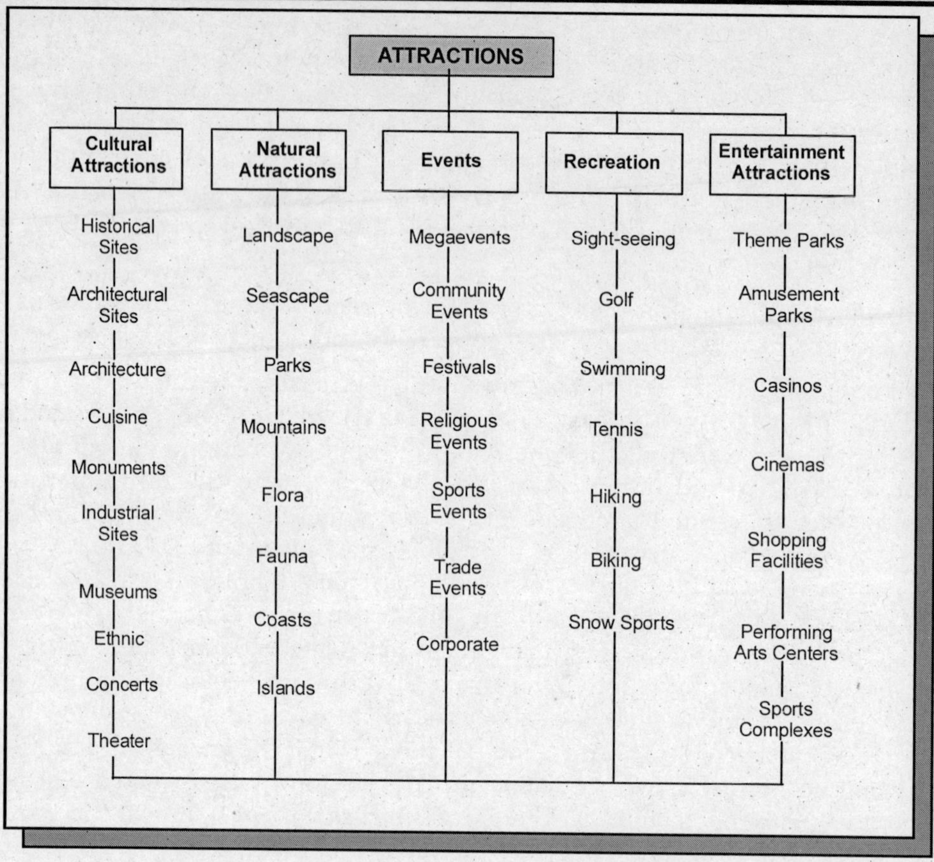

Fig.1.15. Different types of attractions

Attractions are the essential requisites for tourism growth. A place without sufficient tourism attractions will not receive tourists; in spite of that it has other facilities. Religious entre, historical resorts, ancient and modern cities, wildlife sanctuaries, bird sanctuaries, water, surface and space sports, fountains, dams, parks, concerts, conventions, conferences, festivals, celebrations, exhibitions, flower shows, adventure pursuits etc attract tourist. Diverse tourism attractions are necessary, as the interest of tourists is varied.

Such diverse interests make possible the growth of diverse tourism such as religious tourism, resort tourism, sport tourism, business tourism, adventure tourism, pleasure tourism, social tourism, ethnic tourism, health tourism, youth tourism, mass tourism, air tourism, rail tourism, road tourism etc.

Tourism attractions need not necessarily be beautiful, pleasing, aesthetic and socially acceptable; these can be ugly, unpleasant or socially unacceptable. War devastations, ghettos, gambling and even prostitution might serve as major tourism attractions. Renowned personalities associated with a destination are also enough attractions.

There are ample scopes for innovations in tourism industry. Take the example of Singapore, it is making lot of innovations: some instances are worth mentioning i.e. Underwater world – an aquatic wonderland, Butterfly Park, World Insectariums, discovery island (a top-notch resort island), Garden of the Orient etc.

For generations, travellers have flocked to the Great Wall of China. At least 2600 years old and some 3946 miles long, it is the only man-made structure on earth visible to the naked eye from the moon. *Photo courtesy of the China National Tourist Office*

Accessibility of tourism destinations/centres is another essential condition for tourism development. The size, the quality and the variety of means of transportation matter much. Transportation is an integral part of tourism, since tourism is about being elsewhere. First , for the foreign tourists travel to and from a tourism destination is to be well arranged. Second, within a country, the tourists, foreign and domestic, need transportation to various tourism centres. Third, movement of tourists to various tourism attractions at a tourist centre need to be provided for.

Air tourism is mostly confined to travel between countries and a small extent between tourism centres. For those who can afford money, but not time air tourism is a bonanza. However, travel between tourism centres is better made through rail, road or water, as the case may be.

Railway fare better, except on one count, the speed. In Europe, a new generation of streamlined, super swift, comfortable and ecologically-friendly trains has been developed. France introduced trains with an average speed of 300 KM ph in 1989, West Germany introduced with an average speed of 250 KMph in 1991, Italy has introduced 300 KMph trains, Spain has introduced 480 KMph in 1992 and so on. There are various promotional ventures also adopted by the Railways. The 'palace on wheels' – luxurious excursion train service between Delhi and Jaipur meant for foreign tourist. 'Hotels on Wheels'- the deluxe train service with complete air-conditioning vestibule lounge, prayer room, deluxe sleeperettes, etc., in the Calcutta-Gaya-Varanasi-Gorakhpur section means for the Buddhist tourist are some notable promotional-cum-transportational service of the railways.

Roadways are of paramount importance for mobility of tourists to and from contiguous tourist centers. Road transport normally complements the services of other modes. To take the tourists to and from airports, sea sports or railway stations, road transport is the only means. Besides, roadways are becoming popular as the primary means of transport for the tourism industry. Whatever the stage of development of other modes of transport, road transport will always continue to play a significant role in the development of tourism.

Waterways for tourism are still in their infancy, in spite of the technological advancements in the form of hydrofoils and hovercrafts and potential areas-backwaters of Kerala, Ocean systems between Gulf and India, Between Bombay and Goa and between some ports on the Eastern Coast are available. Tourists tired of overland modes for a change might prefer passenger water transport at least for short distance destinations.

Accommodations facilities are the places where tourists stop traveling and become guests. The level of guest satisfaction achieved by an area's accommodation facilities will in a large measure, determine the total success of the tourism programme. The weary tourists after day long wandering needs rest by night only to recuperate themselves adequately to bear the next day's programme. So getting a good night's sleep is important. The success of tourism industry depends on the availability and quality of accommodation has changed over time. Variety is preferred to stereotype. Hotels of different sorts, motels, guest houses, private hotels, establishment with bed and breakfast only, camp sites, paying guest accommodation, youth hostels, yatri niwas, etc., are today available. Among these hotels are most important because of their variety, versatility and volume.

Atmosphere, congenial and warm is last but not the least determinant to tourism. Courteous warm welcome and reverential care for tourists make appositive perception of tourism atmosphere. A tourist comes into contact with variety of service personnel the travel agency personnel, the tour operations, hoteliers, the transporters , the customs authorities, the tourism information personnel, the restaurateurs, the tourist guides, the shop personnel etc. Every encounter is a human transaction where quality is important. The hospitality is a very important factor which matters a lot.

The internal and external security conditions of a destination are vital determinants of tourist. War, internal disturbances, floods, droughts, epidemics, etc., are enemies of tourism.

The Taj Mahal in Agra, India, is a favorite travel destination along the Asian Highway. The Asian Highway was initiated in 1958 and funded by the National Governments in Asia. *Photo courtesy of the United Nations*

CONTEMPORARY TRENDS IN INTERNATIONAL TOURIST MOVEMENTS

Travel and tourism will grow to new heights in the 21st century as it becomes more accessible to a larger cross section of the global population. This will result in commensurate economic opportunities for developed and emerging destinations around the world. It will also create major challenges, not only in attracting and serving increased tourism demand, but also in mitigating the numerous potential negative externalities that will emerge as a result of tourism's rapid growth. Successful destinations will strike a balance in developing their tourism industries by monitoring international trends, engaging tourism stakeholders, ensuring that the benefits of tourism outweigh any potential negative impacts and pledging a more equitable distribution of tourism revenue. There is good reason for countries to focus on honing their abilities in tourism: it is a big business. According to the UNWTO, 846 million international visitor arrivals generated US$735 billion (US$2 billion/day) in tourism revenue in 2006. Tourism represents 35 percent the world's export of services and over 70 percent in the Least Developed Countries. The UNWTO predicts that international tourism demand will double by 2020 to an astronomical 1.6 billion visitors generating nearly US$2 trillion in economic activity. Currently, the tourism industry is characterized by a variety of issues and trends, which present a range of inherent threats and opportunities. These include, but are not necessarily limited to.

There has been an increase in the perception of terrorist threats in many countries most graphically embodied in the Bali bombings in 2002 and 2005. There have also been subsequent terrorism scares and attacks in London, Glasgow, Madrid, Bangkok and other destinations. Well intended safety and security procedures and regulations are creating traveller inconvenience in the form of longer lines at airports and stricter visa policies and standards.

The notable growth of China into one of the largest source markets in the Asia Pacific region has become a primary focus of the world's tourism industry. Chinese nationals have been increasingly visiting international destinations; a trend the industry widely agrees will continue to increase in the foreseeable future. Equally phenomenal growth is also evident from the Indian outbound market.

New destination branding campaigns from relative newcomers such as India, South Korea, New Zealand, Egypt, South Africa, Vietnam, Eastern Europe and the Philippines have been recently launched, adding increased competition to mainstay destinations such as Australia, Singapore, Thailand and Malaysia.

Technology such as the internet has made booking travel-related products easy and convenient, empowering the consumer to be less reliant upon the traditional tourism supply chain. This disintermediation opens many possibilities for consumer-direct marketing and distribution.

In what many refer to as the emergence of a Leisure Society, tourism is seen as a basic right – as opposed to an activity for a privileged few - and has become widely accessible for a more diverse global demographic. The rise of low-cost airlines and cut-rate travel deals is fuelling a new wave of demand for tourism in the new millennium. A similar boom last occurred in the early 1970s with the launch of the Boeing 747 and other technological advancements in transport creating a wave of mass international tourism demand by increasing affordability and access.

The emergence of sub-regional cooperative agreements in which neighboring countries jointly market multi-nation itineraries in an attempt to increase the value and synergy for the tourist and the participating economies is on the rise. Demand is rapidly increasing for niche tourism products that are customised to satisfy the tastes of an increasingly discerning traveller, particularly among business and affluent leisure travellers. Many of these new niches are narrowly defined, but should not be overlooked.

An increased awareness and consciousness among travellers of the social and environmental impacts of tourism which is fuelling a rapidly increasing interest in responsible, sustainable and green tourism.

WTO estimated in its study "Tourism 2020 Vision", published in 2000, that while in the 1990's the market share of Europe's Inbound Tourism represented 60%, due to the ever-increasing levels of destination competition outside the region, this percentage is expected to decrease to 46% by 2020. The analysis shows that while Europe will remain the world's largest tourist receiving region by some considerable margin, it is losing its market share. The reason is that Europe continues to grow but at a slower pace compared to other regions: for the period 1995-2020, Europe's growth rate is foreseen to be of 3% while other regions such as East Asia and the Pacific or South Asia are expected to grow during this period by 6.5% and 6.2% respectively.

Tourism since September 11

The second perspective we need to look at is related to the unprecedented situation affecting international tourism in the last 2-3 years. We often cite 11 September 2001, the day of the terrorist attacks in the United States as a reference date signaling change in international tourism. In fact several factors influenced a dynamic that on one hand accelerated trends already existing in the tourism industry but on the other brought new issues to the fore.

Since late 2001, world tourism has been be characterized by:

- A global economic downturn which affected all major economies at the same time;
- A general uncertainty after the attacks in New York and Washington followed by two wars, in Afghanistan and Iraq, and other terrorist attacks, like the one in Djerba or Bali, specifically targeting tourists.
- Unexpected crises like the outbreak of SARS, which had a dramatic impact on international travel, particularly in Asia

There is a new attitude of "wait and see", resulting in late bookings;

- Trips are closer to home, to familiar destinations and there is sensitivity to price;
- Business travels are cut: they are less and cheaper;

Changes in tourist behaviour

- ☹ Individual (not organised) travel/do it yourself => internet, low cost airlines
- ☹ Travel by car/coach/train instead of plane
- ☹ Accommodation other than hotel (apartments, country houses, etc.)
- ☹ Visiting family, friends and relatives (VFR)
- ☹ Travel is organised individually, instead of going for the "organised trips": do it yourself through Internet, low cost airlines;
- ☹ For transportation, consumers prefer to travel by car, coach or train, instead of using planes;
- ☹ With regard to accommodation, apartments, country houses or similar are used instead of hotels;
- ☹ In terms of purpose of travel, consumers prefer to choose as destinations visits to family, friends or relatives (VFR).

Let's now have a look at the recent tourism trends. Preliminary estimates for the year 2003 show that worldwide the number of international tourists decreased by just over 1% to 694 million, corresponding to a contraction by some 8.6 million arrivals on the 2002 volume of 703 million. This result is closely linked to the unexpected drop by 12 million arrivals suffered by Asia and the Pacific due by the SARS panic, the Iraqi conflict and the persistent weak economy.

Although conditions improved considerably as the year progressed the recovery was not sufficient to result in growth for all destinations. In 2002 the number of international tourist arrivals had grown globally by 2.7%, after a decrease of 0.5 % in 2001. Therefore, twice since 11 September 2001, international tourism, measured by the number of international travellers, has recorded a negative growth. However, if we compare the current number of international arrivals with the exceptional "millennium" year worldwide there is still a net increase of 7 millions arrivals in 2003 over the year 2000.

The WTO panel of some 180 tourism experts from over 90 countries confirms a clear positive trend for international tourism in 2004. On a five-point scale ranging from 1 (much worse) to 5 (much better), the panel attributes an average score of 4.0, corresponding to better, to expected performance in 2004 as compared to 2003.

2004 Positive Prospects:

- ☹ Recovery of major economies
- ☹ Consumers' confidence returns: pent-up demand
- ☹ Increased ability to respond to crises
- ☹ Rebound of long-haul traffic to Europe
- ☹ New markets: China

For 2004, prospects are generally optimistic based essentially on the positive signs of recovery from the economies of U.S., Japan and Western Europe and on the moderation of world geopolitical conflicts. As consumer's confidence returns, the unsatisfied demand from previous year will positively influence the market. While there is some fear of resurgence of SARS or other epidemic, most experts consider that the countries involved will be ready to react rapidly and effectively.

Europe should benefit in 2004 of some rebound in long haul traffic, in particular from the U.S and possibly from Asia in view of the better economic performance in Japan. China is considered as a huge potential market for 2004 and beyond as an increasing number of European destinations have obtained the ADS *(Approved Destination Status).*

A strong Euro is likely to continue stimulating traffic from the Euro zone countries. This element is likely to favour destinations outside the current Euro land, like the Czech Republic. As a new EU member, your country will probably profit in terms of image from a bigger international exposure and in terms of immediate flows from improved access border facilities from source markets in the EU. While a few countries joining the EU and which are more dependent of traditional generating markets from Eastern Europe, may suffer from the more complex visa procedures from this area, for the Czech Republic, given the nationalities of its international tourists, this aspect should not constitute a serious obstacle.

Other aspects are favourable to the further development of tourism in the Czech Republic. In January 2002 WTO participated here in Prague to the conference "Central Europe and the Czech Republic Safe tourist destinations". The Czech tourist authorities that organized this event had seen clearly the importance of safety in today's tourism, and the country enjoys today an excellent reputation concerning safety of visitors.

CONCLUSION

A CALL TO ACTION FOR NEW TOURISM

GOVERNMENTS SHOULD:

- Show leadership by defining coherent and streamlined management structures that can efficiently drive New Tourism.
- Elevate Travel & Tourism to strategic national level with senior level policy-making.
- Factor Travel & Toursim into all policies and decision-making, to promote growth that respects both business needs and the well-being of citizens.

INDUSTRY SHOULD:

- Adapt strategic thinking so as to develop tourism with benefits for everyone.
- Extend and divesify product offerings to improve yields and social value.
- Spearhead innovative management and help spread best practice through corporate social responsibility.

ALL STAKEHOLDERS SHOULD:

- Cooperate identifying opportunities for growth.
- Focus on building Travel and Tourism that opens up prospects for people–from employment to development.
- Work together to remove impediments to growth–from infrastructure shortcoming to pollution, and from outdated legislation to unmet health and security concerns.

Source: *WTTC*

BENEFITS AND COSTS OF TOURISM

Tourism brings both economic and noneconomic benefits and costs to host communities. Some of the considerable economic impacts and benefits were described in the preceding section. There are additional areas of benefits that have not received much research attention. These relate to the benefits occurring to the traveller, such as the contribution of pleasure travel to rest and relaxation, the educational benefit, the understanding of other people and cultures, and the physical and mental well-being of the traveller.

There is no question that tourism delivers benefits, but tourism is not perfect. Even advocates for tourism such as your authors (we have been accused of being cheer-leaders for tourism) acknowledge that tourism is not an unqualified blessing. There are costs and benefits, and they do not accrue equally. Many of the social costs incurred are difficult or impossible to measure. Books such as The Golden Hordes, Tourism: Blessing or Blight, and the Holiday Makers (see the Selected References) point out some of the unpleasant aspects of tourism. Improperly planned and developed tourism can create problems. The demands of tourism may come into confiict with the needs and wishes of local residents. Thoughtless development, inappropriate development, overdevelopment, or unfinished development can easily damage the environment.

Tourism has been blamed for polluting beaches; raising the price of labor, land, goods, and so on; spoiling the countryside; contaminating the values of native people; crowding; congestion; noise; litter; crime; loss of privacy; creating social tensions; environmental deterioration; lack of control over a destination's future; and low-paid seasonal employment. These problems are common to many forms of development and in many cases represent dissatisfaction with the *status quo* or overdevelopment. They emphasize the need for a coordinated overall economic development plan, of which tourism will be one part.

We must accept that tourism is neither a blessing nor blight, neither poison nor panacea. Tourism can bring great benefits, but it can also bring social problems. The world has experience in how to increase the benefits of tourism and at least some experience in how to lessen social problems. What has to be done is to balance the benefits and costs to come up with the best cost/benefit result.

Tourism students and executives must have a clear understanding of both the positive and the negative impacts of tourism on the quality of life of a nation, a province or state, or a community. What are the positive aspects? The negative aspects? We need a balance sheet. First we look at the plus side of the ledger; tourism:

- Provides employment opportunities, both skilled and unskilled, because it is a labor-intensive industry

- ☹ Generates a supply of needed foreign exchange
- ☹ Increases incomes
- ☹ Creates increased gross national product
- ☹ Can be built on existing infrastructure
- ☹ Develops an infrastructure that will also help stimulate local commerce and industry
- ☹ Can be developed with local products and resources
- ☹ Helps to diversify the economy
- ☹ Tends to be one of the most compatible economic development activities available to an area, complementing other economic activities
- ☹ Spreads development
- ☹ Has a high multiplier impact
- ☹ Increases governmental revenues
- ☹ Broadens educational and cultural horizons and improves feelings of self-worth
- ☹ Improves the quality of life related to a higher level of income and improved standards of living
- ☹ Reinforces preservation of heritage and tradition
- ☹ Justifies environmental protection and improvement
- ☹ Provides employment for artists, musicians, and other performing artists because of visitor interest in local culture, thereby enhancing the cultural heritage
- ☹ Provides tourist and recreational facilities that may be used by a local population
- ☹ Breaks down language barriers, sociocultural barriers, class barriers, racial barriers, political barriers, and religious barriers
- ☹ Creates a favorable worldwide image for a destination
- ☹ Promotes a global community
- ☹ Promotes international understanding and peace

On the minus side of the ledger we find a number of problems that can be created by tourism, especially by its overdevelopment:

- ☹ Develops excess demand for resources
- ☹ Creates the difficulties of seasonality
- ☹ Causes inflation
- ☹ Can result in unbalanced economic development
- ☹ Creates social problems
- ☹ Degrades the natural physical environment and creates pollution
- ☹ Degrades the cultural environment

- ☹ Increases the incidence of crime, prostitution, and gambling
- ☹ Increases vulnerability to economic and political changes
- ☹ Threatens family structure
- ☹ Commercializes culture, religion and the arts
- ☹ Creates conflicts in the host society
- ☹ Contributes to disease, economic fluctuation, and transportation problems

Like all change, tourism exacts a price. However, it is here, it is huge, and it needs to be planned and managed. The challenge is to get the right balance, which is to have the benefits outweigh the costs and take steps to lessen the unfavorable impacts that are a part of change. Tourism development must be a part of overall economic development and must be done in a manner that is sustainable.

TOURISM AND THE WORLD ECONOMY

International tourism receipts represented in 2003 approximately 6 per cent of worldwide exports of goods and services (as expressed in US$). When considering service exports exclusively, the share of tourism exports increases to nearly 30 per cent.

2003

World Exports of merchandise and commercial services (Balance of Payments, Goods and Services Credit)

	US$ billion	*Share (%)*	*Share (%)*
Total	**9,089**	**100**	
Merchandise exports	7,294	80	
Agricultural products	674	7	
Mining products	960	11	
Manufactures	5,437	60	
Other	223	2	
Commercial Services	**1,795**	**20**	**100**
Transportation	405	4	23
Travel	525	6	29
Other	865	10	48

Source : *World Trade Organization, World Tourism Organization*

Tourism demand depends above all strongly on the economic conditions in major generating markets. When economies grow, levels of disposable income will usually also rise. A relatively large part of discretionary income will typically be spent on tourism, in particular in the case of emerging economies. A tightening of the economic situation on the other hand, will often result in a decrease or trading down of tourism spending. In general, the growth of international tourism arrivals significantly outpaces growth of economic output as measured in Gross Domestic Product (GDP). In years when world economic growth exceeds 4 per cent, the growth of tourism volume tends to be higher. When GDP growth falls below 2 per cent, tourism growth tends to be even lower. In and GDP at 3.5 per cent, i.e. tourism grew on average 1.3 times faster than GDP. the period 1975-2000 tourism increased at an average rate of 4.6 per cent a year.

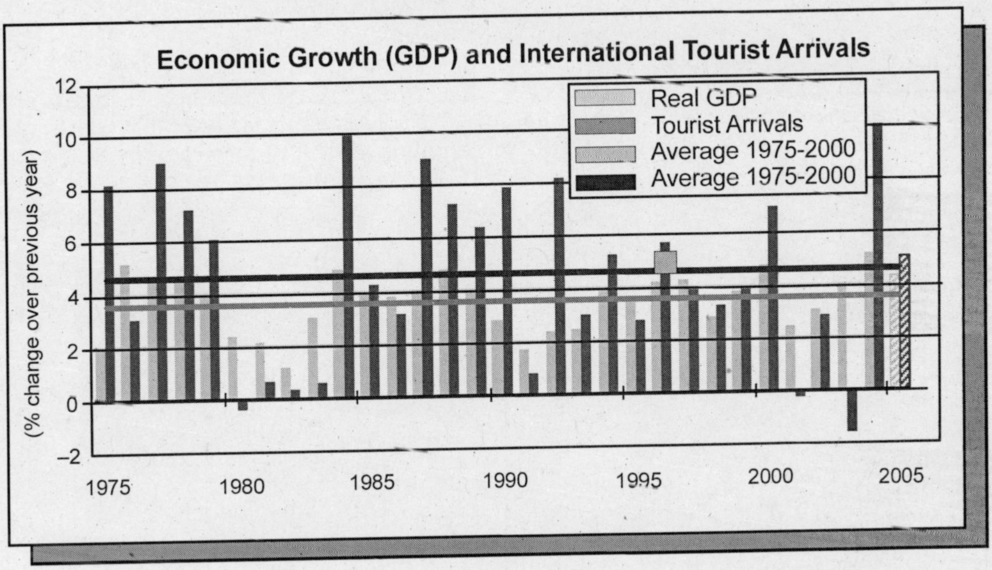

Source: *World Tourism Organization; International Monetary Fund*

(**Source:** *UNWTO Report)*

Exhibit- Source: WTTC

GROSS DOMESTIC PRODUCT

Which countries are expected to produce the largest amount (absolute terms) of Travel & Tourism Economy GDP in 2009?

Economy GDP	2009 US$ bn
(1) United States	1,356.9
(2) Japan	479.3
(3) China	449.3
(4) France	278.2
(5) Germany	267.3
(6) Span	251.5
(7) Italy	212.5
(8) United Kingdom	200.1
(9) Mexico	133.8
(10) Canada	110.4

Which countries are expected to produce the largest amount (absolute terms) of Travel & Tourism Economy GDP in 2019?

Economy GDP	2019 US$ bn
(1) United States	2,358.0
(2) China	1,597.0
(3) Japan	588.6
(4) United Kingdom	406.3
(5) France	390.6
(6) Span	380.5
(7) Germany	368.9
(8) Russian Federation	366.4
(9) Italy	285.0
(10) Mexico	276.9

Which countries are expected to produce the largest amount (absolute terms) of Travel & Tourism Economy GDP in 2009?

Economy GDP	2009 % of Total GDP
(1) Antigua & Barbuda	73.5
(2) Seychelles	72.6
(3) Macau	69.9
(4) Aruba	67.1
(5) Angola	65.8
(6) Maldives	59.7
(7) Bahamas	50.0
(8) Barbados	39.0
(9) Vanuatu	37.5
(10) US Virgin Islands	37.4

Which countries are expected to produce the largest amount (absolute terms) of Travel & Tourism Economy GDP in 2019?

Economy GDP	2019 % of Total GDP
(1) Antigua & Barbuda	76.3
(2) Macau	70.7
(3) Aruba	68.2
(4) Angola	58.4
(5) Seychelles	57.0
(6) Bahamas	51.7
(7) Maldives	47.9
(8) Vanuatu	47.3
(9) St Lucla	42.1
(10) Barbados	40.6

Which countries are expected to grow their Travel & Tourism Economy GDP the fastes in 2009?

Economy GDP	2009 Real Growth, %
(1) Montenegro	9.7
(2) Zambia	7.6
(3) Malawi	5.9
(4) New Zealand	5.3
(5) Ghana	4.9
(6) Namibia	4.5
(7) Moldava	4.1
(8) Syria	4.0
(9) Seychelles	3.9
(10) Togo	3.7

Which countries are expected to grow their Travel & Tourism Economy GDP the fastes from 2010-19?

Economy GDP	10 Yr. Real Growth Annualised, %
(1) Montenegro	9.2
(2) Zambia	7.9
(3) Malawi	7.8
(4) New Zealand	7.7
(5) Ghana	7.7
(6) Namibia	7.2
(7) Moldava	7.0
(8) Syria	7.0
(9) Seychelles	6.9
(10) Togo	6.9

Which countries are expected to produce the largest amount (absolute terms) of Travel & Tourism Direct Industry GDP in 2009?

Direct Industry GDP	2009 US$ bn
(1) United States	503.4
(2) Japan	177.6
(3) China	107.3
(4) France	103.6
(5) Span	93.7
(6) Italy	85.8
(7) United Kingdom	76.2
(8) Germany	72.6
(9) Mexico	44.8
(10) Australia	36.9

Which countries are expected to produce the largest amount (absolute terms) of Travel & Tourism Direct Industry GDP in 2019?

Direct Industry GDP	2019 US$ bn
(1) United States	843.8
(2) China	431.8
(3) Japan	214.3
(4) United Kingdom	148.9
(5) France	145.3
(6) Span	134.1
(7) Italy	116.0
(8) Germany	95.8
(9) Mexico	86.9
(10) Australia	64.1

Which countries are expected to produce the largest amount (absolute terms) of Travel & Tourism Direct Industry GDP in 2009?

Direct Industry GDP	2009 % of Total GDP
(1) Seychelles	37.5
(2) Maldives	28.5
(3) Macau	27.1
(4) Aruba	18.0
(5) Angola	17.8
(6) Antigua & Barbuda	15.5
(7) British Virgin Islands	15.5
(8) Cape Verde	15.2
(9) Bahamas	14.9
(10) Vanuatu	14.3

Which countries are expected to produce the largest amount (absolute terms) of Travel & Tourism Direct Industry GDP in 2019?

Direct Industry GDP	2019 % of Total GDP
(1) Macau	28.3
(2) Seychelles	28.2
(3) Maldives	23.4
(4) Cape Verde	20.7
(5) Montenegro	19.2
(6) Vanuatu	19.1
(7) Aruba	18.1
(8) Antigua & Barbuda	17.8
(9) Angola	17.4
(10) British Virgin Islands	15.7

Which countries are expected to grow their Travel & Tourism Direct Industry GDP the fastes in 2009?

Direct Industry GDP	2009 Real Growth, %
(1) Trinidad and Tobago	16.7
(2) Libya	9.6
(3) Brunei	8.9
(4) Iran	8.2
(5) Norway	7.8
(6) Zambia	6.9
(7) Namibia	6.8
(8) Montenegro	6.2
(9) New Zealand	6.2
(10) Seychelles	5.4

Which countries are expected to grow their Travel & Tourism Direct Industry GDP the fastes from 2010-2019?

Economy GDP	10 Yr. Real Growth Annualised, %
(1) Namibia	10.6
(2) China	10.6
(3) Angola	9.4
(4) Chad	8.7
(5) Oman	8.3
(6) Gabon	7.9
(7) Cape Verde	7.9
(8) Libya	7.8
(9) Moldova	7.5
(10) Montenegro	7.4

EMPLOYMENT

Which countries are expected to generate the largest amount (absolute terms) of Travel & Tourism Economy Employment in 2009?

T & T Economy Employment	2009 '000 jobs
(1) China	60,841
(2) India	31,105
(3) United States	13,850
(4) Indonesia	6,743
(5) Japan	6,507
(6) Mexico	5,631
(7) Brazil	5,562
(8) Vietman	4,862
(9) Thailand	4,040
(10) Russian Federation	3,794

Which countries are expected to generate the largest amount (absolute terms) of Travel & Tourism Economy Employment in 2010?

T & T Economy Employment	2019 '000 jobs
(1) China	83,519
(2) India	40,037
(3) United States	15,552
(4) Indonesia	8,262
(5) Brazil	7,505
(6) Japan	6,895
(7) Mexico	6,865
(8) Vietnam	5,675
(9) Thailand	5,667
(10) Philippines	4,222

Which countries are expected to generate the largest amount (relative terms) of Travel & Tourism Economy Employment in 2009?

T & T Economy Employment	2009 % of Total Employment
(1) Seychelles	86.9
(2) Antigua & Barbuda	80.6
(3) Aruba	78.6
(4) Angola	67.6
(5) Macau	65.3
(6) Bahamas	60.4
(7) Maldives	51.5
(8) British Virgin Islands	50.6
(9) US Virgin Islands	44.8
(10) Barbados	43.7

Which countries are expected to generate the largest amount (relative terms) of Travel & Tourism Economy Employment in 2019?

T & T Economy Employment	2019 % of Total Employment
(1) Antigua & Barbuda	85.9
(2) Aruba	79.6
(3) Seychelles	70.2
(4) Macau	69.6
(5) Bahamas	62.7
(6) Angola	61.3
(7) British Virgin Islands	50.6
(8) Barbados	46.2
(9) Vanuatu	42.6
(10) US Virgin Islands	42.6

Which countries are expected to grow their Travel & Tourism Economy Employment the fastes in 2009?

T & T Economy Employment	2009 Growth, %
(1) Montenegro	7.5
(2) Syria	4.6
(3) Seychelles	4.3
(4) Namibia	3.9
(5) Togo	3.3
(6) Slovak Republic	2.9
(7) New Zealand	2.7
(8) Zambia	2.5
(9) Ghana	2.5
(10) Zimbabwe	2.4

Which countries are expected to grow their Travel & Tourism Economy Employment the fastes in 2010-2019?

T & T Economy Employment	10 Yr. Real Growth Annualised, %
(1) Oman	5.8
(2) Syria	5.5
(3) Vanuatu	5.4
(4) Namibia	5.3
(5) Cape Verde	5.1
(6) Qatar	5.0
(7) Chad	4.8
(8) Saudi Arabia	4.6
(9) Bahrain	4.5
(10) Gabon	4.3

Which countries are expected to generate the largest amount (absolute terms) of Travel & Tourism Direct Industry Employment in 2009?

Direct Industry Employment	2009 '000 jobs
(1) China	18,052
(2) India	12,875
(3) United States	5,194
(4) Japan	2,526
(5) Brazil	2,243
(6) Indonesia	2,044
(7) Thailand	1,862
(8) Mexico	1,731
(9) Egypt	1,529
(10) Vietman	1,374

Which countries are expected to generate the largest amount (absolute terms) of Travel & Tourism Direct Industry Employment in 2010?

Direct Industry Employment	2019 '000 jobs
(1) China	27,066.6
(2) India	15,952.2
(3) Maxico	5,710.6
(4) Brazil	2,963.6
(5) Japan	2,649.5
(6) Indonesia	2,613.8
(7) Thailand	2,202.7
(8) Mexico	1,954.1
(9) Egypt	1,857.9
(10) Philippines	1,586.3

Which countries are expected to generate the largest amount (relative terms) of Travel & Tourism Direct Industry Employment in 2009?

Direct Industry Employment	2009 % of Total Employment
(1) Seychelles	47.8
(2) Macau	34.2
(3) Aruba	25.3
(4) Maldives	25.0
(5) Antigua & Barbuda	21.7
(6) British Virgin Islands	21.7
(7) Bahamas	20.9
(8) Angola	20.6
(9) Other Oceania	16.6
(10) US Virgin Islands	15.5

Which countries are expected to generate the largest amount (relative terms) of Travel & Tourism Direct Industry Employment in 2019?

Direct Industry Employment	2019 % of Total Employment
(1) Seychelles	37.7
(2) Macau	34.5
(3) Aruba	25.3
(4) Antigua & Barbuda	25.0
(5) British Virgin Islands	21.9
(6) Bahamas	21.9
(7) Maldives	20.5
(8) Angola	20.2
(9) Cape Verde	19.0
(10) Other Oceania	18.0

Which countries are expected to grow their Travel & Tourism Direct Industry Employment the fastes in 2009?

Direct Industry Employment	2009 Growth, %
(1) Iran	8.3
(2) Brunei	7.0
(3) Libya	6.8
(4) Venezuella	5.7
(5) Namibia	5.6
(6) Syria	5.3
(7) Seychelles	4.8
(8) New Zealand	4.0
(9) Montenegro	4.0
(10) Russian Federation	3.9

Which countries are expected to grow their Travel & Tourism Direct Industry Employment the fastes in 2010-2019?

Direct Industry Employment	10 Yr. Real Growth Annualised, %
(1) Namibia	7.5
(2) Gabon	7.4
(3) Chad	6.5
(4) Oman	6.2
(5) Syria	6.0
(6) Vanuatu	6.0
(7) Cape Verde	5.3
(8) Qatar	5.1
(9) Caracas	5.1
(10) Bahrain	5.0

DEMAND

Which countries are expected to total the largest amount (absolute terms) of Travel & Tourism Demand in 2009?

Travel & Tourism Demand	2009 US$ bn
(1) United States	1,640.3
(2) Japan	556.1
(3) China	526.6
(4) Germany	438.4
(5) France	378.1
(6) Spain	310.0
(7) United Kingdom	307.2
(8) Italy	281.0
(9) Canada	176.8
(10) Mexico	158.2

Which countries are expected to total the largest amount (absolute terms) of Travel & Tourism Demand in 2019?

Travel & Tourism Demand	2019 US$ bn
(1) United States	2,961.2
(2) China	1,880.5
(3) Japan	709.4
(4) Germany	673.9
(5) United Kingdom	616.0
(6) France	550.6
(7) Russian Federation	490.7
(8) Spain	485.2
(9) Italy	388.9
(10) Mexico	335.4

Which countries are expected to generate the largest amount (relative terms) of Travel & Tourism Demand in 2009?

Travel & Tourism Demand	2009 % of Total Final Expenditure
(1) Macau	59.2
(2) Antigua & Barbuda	47.4
(3) Bahamas	38.8
(4) Maldives	37.1
(5) Seychelles	35.8
(6) Aruba	33.8
(7) Angola	32.0
(8) St Lucia	29.8
(9) British Virgin Islands	28.2
(10) Barbados	27.9

Which countries are expected to generate the largest amount (relative terms) of Travel & Tourism Demand in 2019?

Travel & Tourism Demand	2019 % of Total Final Expenditure
(1) Macau	56.7
(2) Antigua & Barbuda	51.0
(3) Bahamas	39.1
(4) Aruba	36.2
(5) Angola	33.9
(6) Vanuatu	33.6
(7) St Lucia	32.7
(8) Maldives	31.8
(9) Seychelles	31.0
(10) Barbados	30.0

Which countries are expected to grow their Travel & Tourism Demand the fastes in 2009?

Travel & Tourism Demand	2009 Greal Growth, %
(1) Sao Tome and Principle	9.7
(2) Montenegro	8.2
(3) Papua New Guinea	6.8
(4) Cote d'Ivoire	6.5
(5) Tanzania	5.9
(6) Syria	5.4
(7) Lesotho	5.2
(8) New Zealand	5.2
(9) Bahrain	5.1
(10) Reunion	5.0

Which countries are expected to grow their Travel & Tourism Demand the fastes in 2010-2019?

Travel & Tourism Demand	10 Yr. Real Growth Annualised, %
(1) Sao Tome and Principle	20.1
(2) China	9.2
(3) India	8.2
(4) Malawi	7.2
(5) Cape Verde	7.1
(6) Vietnam	7.1
(7) Libya	7.0
(8) Montenegro	7.0
(9) Namibia	7.0
(10) Zimbabwe	6.9

VISITOR EXPORT EARNINGS

Which countries are expected to earn the largest amount (absolute terms) of Travel & Tourism Visitor Exports in 2009?

Visitor Exports	2009 US$ bn
(1) United States	157.9
(2) Spain	66.3
(3) France	57.0
(4) China	52.1
(5) Germany	47.6
(6) Italy	47.2
(7) United Kingdom	42.2
(8) Australia	26.3
(9) United Arab Emirates	22.7
(10) Austria	22.5

Which countries are expected to earn the largest amount (absolute terms) of Travel & Tourism Visitor Exports in 2019?

Visitor Exports	2019 US$ bn
(1) United States	304.5
(2) China	168.3
(3) Spain	101.4
(4) France	91.3
(5) United Kingdom	84.1
(6) Germany	81.4
(7) Italy	66.9
(8) Hong Kong	48.3
(9) Australia	46.2
(10) Thailand	44.8

Which countries are expected to earn the largest amount (absolute terms) of Travel & Tourism Visitor Exports in 2009?

Visitor Exports	2009 % of Total GDP
(1) Guadaloupe	80.2
(2) Angola	76.1
(3) Macau	71.2
(4) Cape Verde	68.7
(5) Antigua & Barbuda	67.1
(6) Vanuatu	64.2
(7) St Lucla	62.0
(8) Bahamas	60.7
(9) Maldives	60.3
(10) Grenada	57.9

Which countries are expected to earn the largest amount (absolute terms) of Travel & Tourism Visitor Exports in 2019?

Visitor Exports	2019 % of Total Exports
(1) Macau	76.9
(2) Antigua & Barbuda	73.1
(3) Angola	71.7
(4) Cape Verde	70.0
(5) Vanuatu	64.5
(6) St Lucla	59.6
(7) Gaudalupe	58.6
(8) Bahamas	57.5
(9) Other Oceania	55.4
(10) St Vincent and the Grenadines	52.0

Which countries are expected to grow their Travel & Tourism Visitor Exports fastes in 2009?

Visitor Exports	2009 Real Growth, %
(1) New Zealand	17.5
(2) Qatar	17.0
(3) Brunei	15.6
(4) Trinidad and Tobago	14.5
(5) Luxembourg	9.6
(6) Poland	9.3
(7) Venezuela	8.4
(8) Brazil	8.0
(9) United Kingdom	7.3
(10) Uruguay	6.9

Which countries are expected to grow their Travel & Tourism Visitor Exports fastes in 2010-2019?

Visitor Exports	2019 Annualised Real Growth, %
(1) Montenegro	10.1
(2) Namibia	9.6
(3) Sierra Leone	9.0
(4) Oman	8.8
(5) China	8.1
(6) Cape Verde	8.1
(7) Japan	7.9
(8) Venezuela	7.9
(9) Paraguay	7.8
(10) Congo	7.8

INVESTMENT

Which countries are expected to spend the largest amount (absolute terms) of Travel & Tourism Capital Investment in 2009?

Capital Investment	2009 US$ bn
(1) United States	262.3
(2) China	165.4
(3) Japan	65.2
(4) Spain	60.0
(5) Italy	39.3
(6) France	38.3
(7) Russian Federation	36.5
(8) Germany	32.8
(9) United Kingdom	31.0
(10) Australia	30.9

Which countries are expected to spend the largest amount (absolute terms) of Travel & Tourism Capital Investment in 2019?

Capital Investment	2019 US$ bn
(1) United States	505.8
(2) China	487.2
(3) Russian Federation	179.0
(4) Spain	97.4
(5) India	94.5
(6) Japan	82.6
(7) United Kingdom	66.8
(8) Mexico	64.3
(9) Australia	61.7
(10) Italy	52.2

Which countries are expected to spend the largest amount (relative terms) of Travel & Tourism Capital Investment in 2009?

Capital Investment	2009 % of Total Capital Investment
(1) Macau	75.7
(2) Other Oceania	75.1
(3) Aruba	69.5
(4) Barbados	58.1
(5) Antigua & Barbuda	52.2
(6) Angola	47.7
(7) US Virgin Islands	47.5
(8) United Arab Emirates	46.5
(9) Bahamas	43.4
(10) British Virgin Islands	43.2

Which countries are expected to spend the largest amount (relative terms) of Travel & Tourism Capital Investment in 2019?

Capital Investment	2019 % of Total Capital Investment
(1) Other Oceania	73.6
(2) Aruba	72.3
(3) Macau	70.0
(4) Barbados	58.9
(5) Antigua & Barbuda	54.4
(6) US Virgin Islands	48.7
(7) Angola	47.2
(8) United Arab Emirates	46.5
(9) Bahamas	44.0
(10) Vanuatu	43.4

Which countries are expected to grow their Travel & Tourism Capital Investment the fastes in 2009?

Capital Investment	2009 Real Growth, %
(1) Montenegro	19.4
(2) Trinidad and Tobago	15.5
(3) Libya	14.3
(4) Macau	11.4
(5) Egypt	11.2
(6) Kazakhstan	10.7
(7) Oman	9.1
(8) Chad	8.7
(9) Lebanon	8.5
(10) Cape Verde	8.2

Which countries are expected to grow their Travel & Tourism Capital Investment the fastes in 2010-2019?

Capital Investment	10 Yr. Real Growth Annualised, %
(1) Sao Tome and Principle	21.0
(2) Angola	11.6
(3) India	8.8
(4) Russian Federation	8.5
(5) Malawi	7.9
(6) Korea, Republic of	7.7
(7) Thailand	7.5
(8) Singapore	7.5
(9) China	7.2
(10) Finland	7.1

PERSONAL TRAVEL AND TOURISM

Which countries are expected to spend the largest amount (absolute terms) of Personal Travel & Tourism in 2009?

Personal Travel & Tourism	2009 US$ bn
(1) United States	814.9
(2) Japan	294.6
(3) Germany	176.4
(4) China	166.2
(5) United Kingdom	161.6
(6) France	155.5
(7) Italy	115.4
(8) Spain	112.8
(9) Mexico	77.5
(10) Canada	73.0

Which countries are expected to spend the largest amount (absolute terms) of Personal Travel & Tourism in 2019?

Personal Travel & Tourism	2019 US$ bn
(1) United States	1,380.7
(2) China	717.8
(3) Japan	354.9
(4) United Kingdom	305.3
(5) Germany	240.8
(6) France	217.3
(7) Russian Federation	172.8
(8) Spain	171.0
(9) Italy	157.3
(10) Mexico	154.6

Which countries are expected to spend the largest amount (relative terms) of Personal Travel & Tourism in 2009?

Personal Travel & Tourism	2009 % of Total Personal Consumption
(1) British Virgin Islands	48.3
(2) Maldives	31.9
(3) Qatar	21.1
(4) Macau	20.5
(5) Bahamas	20.3
(6) Luxembourg	19.1
(7) Lebanon	18.1
(8) Aruba	17.7
(9) Antigua & Barbuda	17.7
(10) Switzerland	17.0

Which countries are expected to spend the largest amount (relative terms) of Personal Travel & Tourism in 2019?

Personal Travel & Tourism	2019 % of Total Personal Consumption
(1) British Virgin Islands	47.2
(2) Maldives	34.9
(3) Qatar	23.1
(4) Bahamas	20.9
(5) Lebanon	20.6
(6) Luxembourg	20.3
(7) Antigua & Barbuda	19.6
(8) Reunion	19.5
(9) Aruba	19.2
(10) Seychelles	18.7

Which countries are expected to grow their Personal Travel & Tourism the fastes in 2009?

Personal Travel & Tourism	2009 Real Growth, %
(1) Sao Toma and Principle	35.2
(2) Saudi Araba	25.6
(3) Bahrain	22.1
(4) Libya	20.5
(5) Macau	15.6
(6) Venezuela	14.9
(7) Alqena	13.6
(8) Trinidad and Tobago	13.2
(9) United Arab Emirates	13.2
(10) Sierra Leone	13.1

Which countries are expected to grow their Personal Travel & Tourism the fastes in 2010-19?

Personal Travel & Tourism 10 Yr. Real Growth	Annualised, %
(1) Sao Tome and Principle	27.5
(2) China	11.3
(3) Congo	11.2
(4) Angala	9.4
(5) Chad	9.1
(6) Cambodia	8.3
(7) Laos	8.2
(8) Soloman Islands	8.1
(9) Gabon	7.9
(10) Taiwan	7.8

BUSINESS TRAVEL

Which countries are expected to spend the largest amount (absolute terms) of Business Travel in 2009?

Business Travel	2009 US$ bn
(1) United States	169.1
(2) Japan	79.0
(3) China	61.8
(4) Germany	47.4
(5) France	37.2
(6) Italy	34.7
(7) United Kingdom	33.6
(8) Spain	17.8
(9) Canada	14.0
(10) Netherlands	13.9

Which countries are expected to spend the largest amount (absolute terms) of Business Travel in 2010?

Business Travel	2010 US$ bn
(1) United States	283.1
(2) China	233.6
(3) Japan	93.8
(4) United Kingdom	66.2
(5) Germany	63.7
(6) France	48.8
(7) Italy	43.9
(8) Brazil	29.3
(9) Russian Federation	29.2
(10) Spain	26.8

Which countries are expected to spend the largest amount (relative terms) of Business Travel in 2009?

Business Travel	2009 % of GDP
(1) Moldova	7.1
(2) Burundi	6.4
(3) Malawi	5.9
(4) Brunei	4.3
(5) Argentina	3.3
(6) Mongolia	3.0
(7) Antigua & Barbuda	2.9
(8) Aruba	2.9
(9) Iceland	2.8
(10) Bellize	2.8

Which countries are expected to spend the largest amount (relative terms) of Business Travel in 2019?

Business Travel	2010 % of GDP
(1) Malawi	6.0
(2) Moldova	5.8
(3) Burundi	5.2
(4) Brunei	4.3
(5) Argentina	3.2
(6) Mongolia	3.0
(7) Antigua & Barbuda	2.9
(8) Iceland	2.9
(9) Bellize	2.8
(10) Aruba	2.8

Which countries are expected to grow their Business Travel the fastes in 2009?

Business Travel	2009 Real Growth, %
(1) Trinidad and Tobago	19.4
(2) Macau	10.4
(3) Serbia	9.4
(4) Zambia	8.7
(5) Qatar	8.7
(6) United Arab Emirates	7.6
(7) Mongolia	7.6
(8) Libya	6.9
(9) Chad	6.6
(10) Madagascar	6.6

Which countries are expected to grow their Business Travel the fastes in 2010-2019?

Business Travel	10 Yr. Real Growth Annualised, %
(1) Sao Tome and Principle	21.1
(2) China	9.9
(3) Macau	9.3
(4) Angola	8.7
(5) India	7.6
(6) Malawi	7.2
(7) Ukraine	7.1
(8) Kazakhstan	7.0
(9) Libya	6.7
(10) Slovak Republic	6.7

GOVERNMENT EXPENDITURES

Which countries are expected to spend the largest amount (absolute terms) of Travel & Tourism Government Expenditures in 2009?

Government Expenditures	2009 US$ bn
(1) United States	129.3
(2) Japan	40.9
(3) China	26.9
(4) Spain	20.8
(5) France	19.9
(6) Italy	17.1
(7) United Kingdom	13.6
(8) Germany	13.2
(9) Canada	10.9
(10) Brazil	7.9

Which countries are expected to spend the largest amount (absolute terms) of Travel & Tourism Government Expenditures in 2019?

Government Expenditures	2019 US$ bn
(1) United States	207.9
(2) China	100.0
(3) Japan	50.2
(4) Spain	32.3
(5) United Kingdom	27.8
(6) France	26.3
(7) Russian Federation	21.2
(8) Italy	20.4
(9) Canada	18.2
(10) Germany	15.9

Which countries are expected to spend the largest amount (relative terms) of Travel & Tourism Government Expenditures in 2009?

Government Expenditures	2009 % of GDP
(1) Antigua & Barbuda	28.2
(2) Cayman Islands	28.1
(3) British Virgin Islands	27.1
(4) Seychelles	22.2
(5) Dominican Republic	21.3
(6) Gaudalupe	20.8
(7) US Virgin Islands	20.0
(8) Other Oceania	19.7
(9) Bermuda	17.8
(10) St Lucia	17.2

Which countries are expected to spend the largest amount (relative terms) of Travel & Tourism Government Expenditures in 2019?

Government Expenditures	2019 % of GDP
(1) Antigua & Barbuda	29.3
(2) Cayman Islands	29.3
(3) British Virgin Islands	28.3
(4) Seychelles	22.7
(5) Dominican Republic	22.4
(6) Gaudalupe	21.3
(7) US Virgin Islands	20.9
(8) Other Oceania	20.5
(9) Bermuda	18.4
(10) St Lucia	17.7

Which countries are expected to grow their Travel & Tourism Government Expenditures the fastes in 2009?

Government Expenditures	2009 Real Growth, %
(1) Trinidad and Tobago	20.8
(2) Albania	18.3
(3) Chad	16.2
(4) Malaysia	13.2
(5) India	12.9
(6) China	11.9
(7) Singapore	11.3
(8) Macedonia	11.1
(9) Papua New Guinea	10.0
(10) Mali	10.0

Which countries are expected to grow their Travel & Tourism Government Expenditures the fastes in 2010-2019?

Government Expenditures	10 Yr. Real Growth Annualised, %
(1) Sao Tome and Principle	23.7
(2) Libya	10.4
(3) China	9.7
(4) Algeria	9.1
(5) Qatar	8.2
(6) Congo	8.1
(7) Angola	8.1
(8) United Arab Emirates	8.0
(9) Cambodia	7.7
(10) Malawi	7.6

INDIA

KEY FACTS AT A GLANCE

THE 2009 TRAVEL & TOURISM ECONOMIC RESEARCH

2009 **10-year trend**

Gross Domestic Product (GDP)

6.0% The contribution of Travel & Tourism to Gross Domestic Product (GDP) in expected to any the name as 6% (INR 3,2394 bn per US$ 67.3 bn) in 2009 to 6.0% (INR 10274.1 bn are US$ 187.3 bn) by 2019.

Employment

6.4% The contribution of the Travel & Tourism Economy to employment in expected to time from 31,105,000 jobs in 2009, 6.4% of total employment, or 1 in every 15.6 jobs to 400,37,000 jobs, 7.2% of total employment or 1 in every 13.8 jobs by 2019.

Growth

0.2% Real GDP growth for the Travel & Tourism Economy in expected to be 0.2% in 2009 and to averages 7.7% per annum over the coming 10 years.

Exports

6.0% Export examines from international visition and tourism goods are expected to generation 6.0% of total exports (INR 811.9 bn or US$ 16.9 bn) in 2009, growing (nominal terms) to INR 2,819.0 bn or US$ 51.4 bn (4.1% of exal) in 2019.

World ranking (out of 181 countries)

14	144	5
ABSOLUTE	RELATIVE	GROWTH
—	contribution to national economy	forecast

Ranking in South Asia (out of 6 countries)

1	3	1
Absolute	Relative	Growth
—	contribution to national economy	forecast

INDIA
Travel & Tourism Gross Domestic Product
(2000 constant US$ bn)

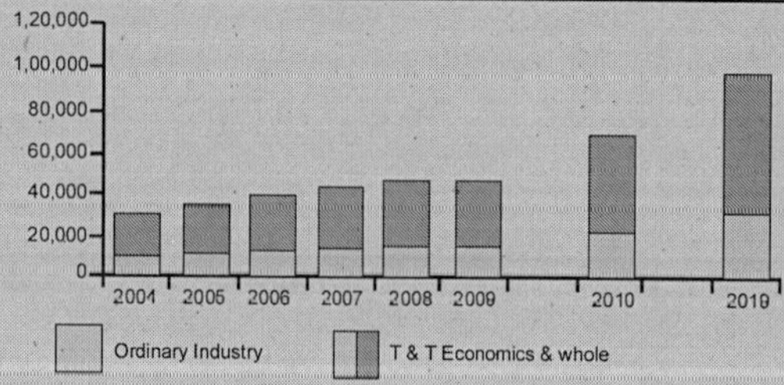

INDIA
Travel & Tourism Employment
(000 jobs)

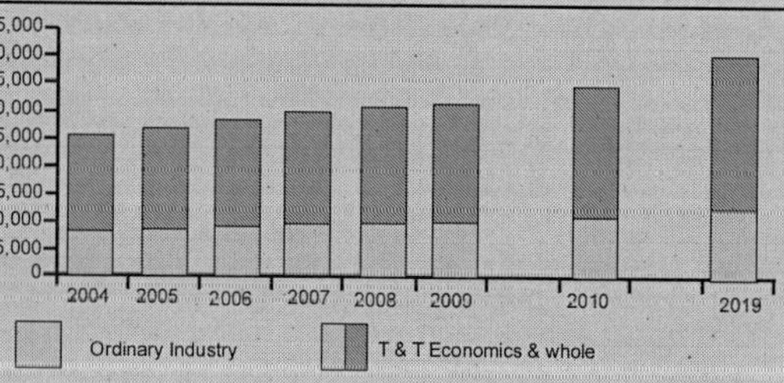

ECONOMIC SIGNIFICANCE OF TOURISM TO DEVELOPING COUNTRIES

Developing countries currently have only a minority share of the international tourism market (approximately 30 per cent) but their share is growing. International tourism arrivals in developing countries have grown by an average of 9.5 per cent per year since 1990, in aggregate across developing countries, compared to a growth of 4.6 per cent in arrivals worldwide. The tourism industry makes important contributions to the economies of developing countries, particularly to foreign exchange earnings, employment, and Gross Domestic Product (GDP). This is shown in Table 3 below. On average, international tourism receipts account for around 10 per cent of export revenues of developing countries. Tourism's contribution to GDP varies from 3–5 per cent in Nepal and Kenya to 25 per cent in Jamaica; contribution to employment is estimated at 6–7 per cent in India and South Africa. (Bennett, O; Roe, D; Ashley, C; Sustainable Tourism and Poverty Elimination Study)

Country (a)	*Is ITT an important economic sector? (b)*	*Have ITT arrivals grown significantly? (1990-1997) (c)*	*Percentage of population living on under IUS$ a day (d)*
India*	√		53
China*	√	√	22
Bangladesh*		√	na
Kenya*	√	Na	50
Pakistan*	na		12
Indonesia*	√	√	15
Nepal*	√	√	22
Nigeria*		√	29
Ethiopia*	√		34
Brazil*	√	√	29
Peru	√	√	49
Philippines	√	√	28
Mexico	√		15

ITT = International travel and tourism

n/a = data not available

(a) Countries identified by the World Bank - 1993 data (World Development Indices 1988) Listed according to their ranking as DFID bilateral and recipients (largest first)

(b) ITT receipts more than 5 per cent of exports or 2 per cent of GDP for 1996 – adapted from data from WTO 1998 and World Development Indices 1998.

(c) Percentage change between ITT arrivals for 1990 and 1997 – adapted from data from WTO 1997. International Tourism (e) Arrivals for 1997; WTO 1998.

(d) Percentage of population living under US$1/day – UNICEF 1999. World Development Indices 1998.

Fig.1.16. Significance of International Tourism

The economic significance of tourism varies greatly from country to country, with those economies most highly dependent on tourism tending to be small island states. In Fiji, for example, tourism is the largest source of foreign exchange and the most important commercial source of employment, providing over 26 per cent of export revenue and some 16 per cent of GDP. (Bennett, O; Roe, D; Ashley, C; Sustainable Tourism and Poverty Elimination Study).

Tourism data does not provide the full picture of its economic significance. Statistics cover the contribution of international tourism to national GDP. They hide the significance of domestic tourism (and may under-estimate regional tourists traveling by and), and the importance of tourism to a local economy. For example, tourism accounts for approximately 0.8 per cent of GDP in India, but it has been estimated that tourism (domestic and international) accounts for approximately half of economic activity in the hill region of Uttar Pradesh, popular for pilgrim trails. (Bennett, O; Roe, D; Ashley, C; Sustainable Tourism and Poverty Elimination Study).

Tourism 2020 Vision

Tourism 2020 Vision is the World Tourism Organization's long-term forecast and assessment of the development of tourism up to the first 20 years of the new millennium. An essential outcome of the *Tourism 2020 Vision* are quantitative forecasts covering a 25 years period, with 1995 as the base year and forecasts for 2010 and 2020. Although the evolution of tourism in the last few years has been irregular, UNWTO maintains its long-term forecast for the moment. The underlying structural trends of the forecast are believed not to have significantly changed. Experience shows that in the short term, periods of faster growth (1995, 1996, 2000) alternate with periods of slow growth (2001 to 2003).

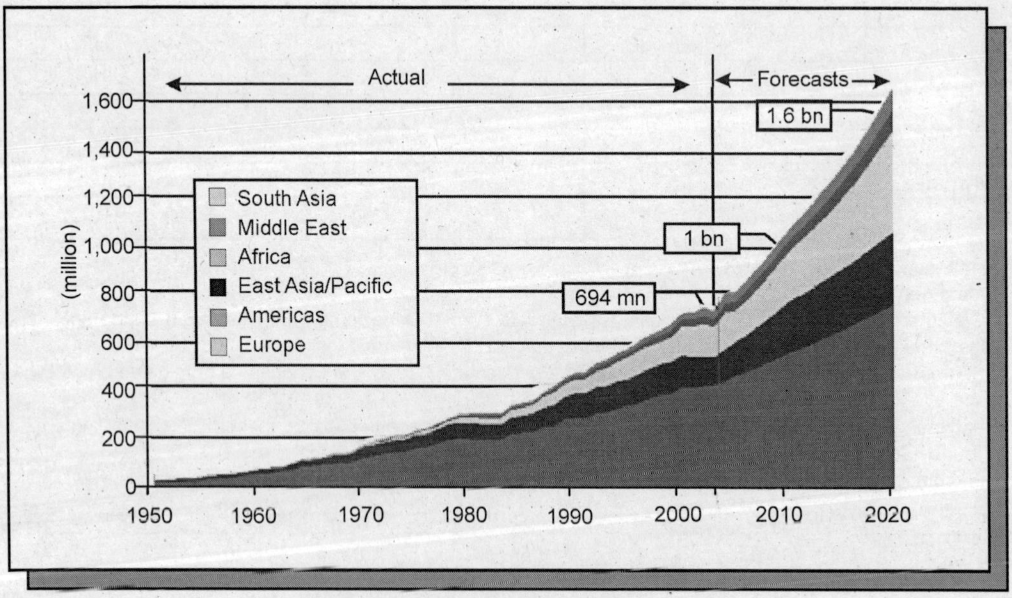

While the pace of growth till 2000 actually exceeded the *Tourism 2020 Vision* forecast, it is generally expected that the current slowdown will be compensated in the medium to long-term.

UNWTO's *Tourism 2020 Vision* forecasts that international arrivals are expected to reach nearly 1.6 billion by the year 2020. Of these worldwide arrivals in 2020, 1.2 billion will be intraregional and 378 million will be long-haul travellers. The total tourist arrivals by region shows that by 2020 the top three receiving regions will be Europe (717 million tourists), East Asia and the Pacific (397 million) and the Americas (282 million), followed by Africa, the Middle East and South Asia. East Asia and the Pacific, Asia, the Middle East and Africa are forecasted to record growth at rates of over 5% year, compared to the world average of 4.1%. The more mature regions Europe and Americas are anticipated to show lower than average growth rates. Europe will maintain the highest share of world arrivals, although there will be a decline from 60 per cent in 1995 to 46 per cent in 2020.

Long-haul travel worldwide will grow faster, at 5.4 per cent per year over the period 1995-2020, than intraregional travel, at 3.8 per cent. Consequently the ratio between intraregional and long-haul travel will shift from around 82:18 in 1995 to close to 76:24 in 2020.

	Base Year 1995	Forecasts 2010	2020	Market Share (%) 1995	2020	Average annual growth rate (%) 1995-2020
		(Million)				
World	565	1006	1561	100	100	4.1
Africa	20	47	77	3.6	5.0	5.5
Americas	110	190	282	19.3	18.1	3.8
East Asia and the Pacific	81	195	397	14.4	25.4	6.5
Europe	336	527	717	59.8	45.9	3.1
Middle East	14	36	69	2.2	4.4	6.7
South Asia	4	11	19	0.7	1.2	6.2

(**Source:** *UNWTO*)

LET US SUM UP

Strategic Marketing planning is the process of developing and maintaining a strategic fit between the organization's goals and capabilities and its changing marketing opportunities. It involves defining a clear company mission, setting supporting objectives, designing a sound business portfolio, and coordinating functional strategies.

The Strategic Planning tackles the following four issues i.e. purpose and mission, objectives, choice of businesses and course of action for achieving the objectives.

There are few concerned with strategic planning like strategic planning is concerned with the future or the long-term dynamics of the firm, it is concerned with growth, it is concerned with environment, the fit between the enterprise and its environment, it is concerned with the basket of businesses the firm should have. More specifically, it is concerned with the changes/ additions/ deletions to the firm's product-market posture etc.

Tourism industry involves the movement of people, in contrast with other industries where the products are transshipped. Movement of people is conditioned by certain factors that influence movement of people are discretionary income, discretionary time, discretionary mobility and desire and drive. DI, DT and DM are major drive behind the growth of tourism industry. Desire and drive, on the part of people to travel and tour are vital.

Attractions are the essential requisites for tourism growth. A place without sufficient tourism attractions will not receive tourists; in spite of that it has other facilities. Religious entre, historical resorts, ancient and modern cities, wildlife sanctuaries, bird sanctuaries, water, surface and space sports, fountains, dams , parks , concerts, conventions, conferences, festivals, celebrations, exhibitions, flower shows, adventure pursuits etc attract tourist. Diverse tourism attractions are necessary, as the interest of tourists is varied.

CHECK YOUR PROGRESS

(A) Fill in the Blanks

(i) The three levels of strategy in an organisation are ______________.

(ii) Strategic planning is concerned with the ______________ Term planning.

(iii) Organization's strategic posture includes a set of ______________.

(B) True/False

(i) Tourism industry is less environment friendly than other industry.

(ii) A place without sufficient tourism attractions will also receive good number of tourists.

(iii) Tourism attractions need not necessarily be beautiful.

(C) Fill in the Blanks

(i) DI stands for ______________.

(ii) DT stands for ______________.

(iii) DM stands for ______________.

(D) True/False

(i) Discovery island is a top notch resort island in Singapore.

(ii) The luxurious train 'Palace on Wheels' runs between Delhi and Jaipur.

(iii) European destinations have obtained the ADS.

LESSON AND ACTIVITY

(i) Draw a diagram of different levels of strategic planning in a company and briefly explain each component in the diagram.

(ii) How J & K crisis is shadowing the tourism industry there? Explain briefly and also suggest possible measures for solution of the problems.

KEY WORDS

Strategic Planning: The process of developing and maintaining a strategic fit between the organization's goals and capabilities and its changing marketing opportunities. It involves defining a clear company mission, setting supporting objectives, designing a sound business portfolio, and coordinating functional strategies.

Strategic Posture: organization's strategic posture include a set of goals and objectives, a statement of the philosophy and culture, the organization (of the firm), and the set of strategies that the organisation has adopted to achieve its goals and objectives.

Marketing Strategy: It includes differentiation/positioning/uniqueness.

Discretionary income: It refers to that part of income left after meeting the essential outgo. DI is freely spendable at the discretion of the recipient. The size of DI of the people influences the decision to go on a tour, the choice of destination, the duration of tour and the like. The DI of the people is a function of the level of development of the country and its population.

Discretionary time: It is another prerequisite for tourism. It is the time at the disposal of the individual with discretion. It is 24 hours less the time one needs to spend in office, factory or farm. In the past people were yoked to their avocations almost all the time. Rural households had virtually no DT as they were tied to the farm operations and maintenance of farm animals, in addition to the home chores. Now things have been changing. The privilege of the modern society is that it has more DT.

Discretionary mobility: Freedom to move from place to place and country to country is essential for growth of tourisms. Within a nation there is more DM, generally speaking. However, internal disturbances might damage this mobility. Across countries, Visa and Passport requirements cause discretionary mobility difficult. Till recently some communist countries did not allow inflow and outflow of people. Now the global village syndrome is very much in vogue.

QUESTIONS FOR DISCUSSION

(1) Define strategic marketing plan.

(2) Explain the components of marketing plan.

(3) What are issues related to strategic plan? Briefly explain.

(4) Explain the scope of marketing strategic plan.

(5) Explain the nature and importance of strategic marketing plan.

(6) Differentiate between strategy and tactics.

(7) Explain the factors that affect regional and global tourism industry.

(8) Write a short note on demand factors and resource factors.

(9) What are contemporary trends in international tourism movements? Explain briefly.

(10) Explain briefly the impact of "September 11" on tourism industry.

(11) How transportation facility has been improved over the years? What are the latest developments have happened? Explain briefly.

(12) Write short notes on *(i)* DI *(ii)* DT *(iii)* DM.

(13) List out the various benefits and costs of tourism.

(14) Explain the impact of tourism on world economy.

(15) Briefly explain various issues and challenges associated with international tourism.

(16) Write short notes on *(i)* health tourism *(ii)* SSS *(iii)* dark tourism *(iv)* leisure tourism *(v)* sex tourism.

(17) Explain different types of adjectival tourism with example.

(18) Explain the recent trends in world tourism.

(19) Narrate the vision of UNWTO on World Tourism – 2020.

CHECK YOUR PROGRESS: MODEL ANSWER

(A) *(i)* Corporate strategy, business unit strategy and functional strategy. *(ii)* Long. *(iii)* Goals and objectives.

(B) *(i)* F *(ii)* F *(iii)* T

(C) *(i)* Discretionary Income *(ii)* Discretionary Time *(iii)* Discretionary Mobility

(D) *(i)* T *(ii)* F *(iii)* T

❑ ❑ ❑

2

Emergence of Hotels, Aviation and Tourism

Chapter Outline

- *Introduction*
- *Historical Aspects*
- *Hotels*
- *Importance of Value Chain in Hotels*
- *Airline Connection*
- *Importance of Aviation Industry on Tourism Industry*

Learning Objective

At the conclusion of this lesson you should be able to understand:

- *Evolution of Hotel industry*
- *Importance of hotel in the growth of tourism industry*
- *Different types of hotels*
- *Value chain in tourism industry*
- *Evolution of Airlines*
- *Importance of aviation industry in tourism*

"I am not much an advocate for traveling, and I observe that men run away to other countries because they are not good in their own, and run back to their own because they pass for nothing in the new places. For the most part, only the light characters travel. Who are you that have no task to keep you at home?"

— Ralph Waldo Emerson (1803-1882)
U.S. poet, essayist and lecturer.

INTRODUCTION

Accommodation constitutes a vital and fundamental part of tourism. An adequate supply of accommodation suitably tailored to the requirements of the tourist market is one of the basic conditions of tourism development. The provision of accommodation facilities and their growth is regarded in a broader context as it contributes to the economy as a whole. In the promotion of tourism, of all the constituents of the tourist industry, accommodation sector constitute the most important segment and it has to play a distinctive role in the development of this expanding industry. This lesson will help you to understand the emergence and development of hotel and aviation industry and its impact on tourism industry.

HISTORICAL ASPECTS

The United Nations conference of International Travel and Tourism held in Rome in 1963 considered the problems relating to means for accommodation and acknowledged the essential importance of both traditional (hotels and motels) and supplementary (Camps, youth hostels etc) facilities for promoting the international tourism. The conference sought the help of respective governments to consider the possibility of including tourism projects relating to accommodation for eligible concessional loans through their financial institutions. It also recommended that governments should give sympathetic consideration to the possibility of granting special facilities and incentives for accommodation projects.

Later many countries have recognised the importance of accommodation and some of them provided the facilities like provision of hotel sites on liberal repayment terms, special concessions in the form of long term loans, liberal import licenses and taxation reliefs, contribution to the equity capital, cash grants for construction and renovation of Buildings etc.

Early History

The traveller, who leaves his home, requires accommodation at his destination and for journeys which cannot be completed in a single day. For this he needed overnight accommodation, perhaps inns may be such accommodation units. It is understood through history, in ancient time and during Roman Empire many inns found providing food and also entertainment to travellers. During fifteenth century, the travel to religious pilgrimage purposes in several countries of Europe made the Church to take major responsibility for accommodation. The facilities being provided by Inns were expanded. The English Common Law declared the 'Inn' to be a public house and imposed social responsibility of the inn-keeper for the well-being of the traveller. In United States of America another type of accommodation unit called 'tavern' become popular.

In India the concept of shelter for traveller is not new. The historical records are replete with mention/references of vihars, dharamsalas, saris, mosafirkhanas, etc. These establishments provided a home to all travellers. Hence, the demand for some kind of accommodation away from home is an important function of travel.

HOTELS

A hotel is an establishment that provides paid lodging, usually on a short-term basis. The provision of basic accommodation, in times past, consisting only of a room with a bed, a cupboard, a small table and a washstand has largely been replaced by rooms with modern facilities, including en-suite bathrooms and air conditioning or climate control. Additional common features found in hotel rooms are a telephone, an alarm clock, a television, and Internet connectivity; snack foods and drinks may be supplied in a mini-bar, and facilities for making hot drinks. Larger hotels may provide a number of additional guest facilities such as a restaurant, a swimming pool or childcare, and have conference and social function services.

Some hotels offer meals as part of a room and board arrangement. In the United Kingdom, a hotel is required by law to serve food and drinks to all guests within certain stated hours; to avoid this requirement it is not uncommon to come across private hotels which are not subject to this requirement. In Japan, capsule hotels provide a minimized amount of room space and shared facilities.

In Australia and Canada, hotel may also refer to a pub or bar. In India, the word may also refer to a restaurant since the best restaurants were always situated next to a good hotel.

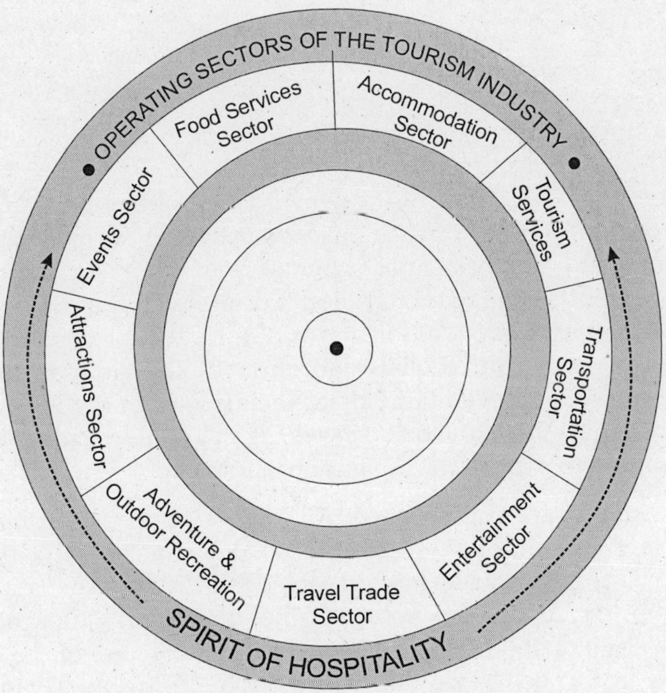

Fig. 2.1. Operating sector of tourism industry: Accommodation & Food Services

Etymology

The word hotel is derived from the French hotel (coming from hôte meaning host), which referred to a French version of a townhouse or any other building seeing frequent visitors, rather than a place offering accommodation.

Classification

The cost and quality of hotels are usually indicative of the range and type of services available. Due to the enormous increase in tourism worldwide during the last decades of the 20th century, standards, especially those of smaller establishments, have improved considerably. For the sake of greater comparability, rating systems have been introduced, with the one to five stars classification being most common and with higher star ratings indicating more luxury. Hotels are independently assessed in traditional systems and these rely heavily on the facilities provided. Some consider this disadvantageous to smaller hotels whose quality of accommodation could fall into one class but the lack of an item such as an elevator would prevent it from reaching a higher categorization. In some countries, there is an official body with standard criteria for classifying hotels, but in many others there is none. There have been attempts at unifying the classification system so that it becomes an internationally recognized and reliable standard but large differences exist in the quality of the accommodation and the food within one category of hotel, sometimes even in the same country. The American Automobile Association (AAA) and their affiliated bodies use diamonds instead of stars to express hotel and restaurant ratings levels.

Historic Hotels

Some hotels have gained their renown through tradition, by hosting significant events or persons, such as Schloss Cecilienhof in Potsdam, Germany, which derives its fame from the Potsdam Conference of the World War II allies Winston Churchill, Harry Truman and Joseph Stalin in 1945. The Taj Mahal Palace & Tower in Mumbai is one of India's most famous and historic hotels because of its association with the Indian independence movement. Some establishments have given name to a particular meal or beverage, as is the case with the Waldorf Astoria in New York City, United States where the Waldorf Salad was first created or the Hotel Sacher in Vienna, Austria, home of the Sachertorte. Others have achieved fame by association with dishes or cocktails created on their premises, such as the Hotel de Paris where the crêpe Suzette was invented or the Raffles Hotel in Singapore, where the Singapore Sling cocktail was devised.

A number of hotels have entered the public consciousness through popular culture, such as the Ritz Hotel in London, UK, through its association with Irving Berlin's song, 'Puttin' on the Ritz'. The Algonquin Hotel in New York City is famed as the meeting place of the literary group, the Algonquin Round Table, and Hotel Chelsea, also in New York City, has been the subject of a number of songs and the scene of the stabbing of Nancy Spungen (allegedly by her boyfriend Sid Vicious). The luxurious Grand Hotel Europe in Saint Petersburg, Russia achieved fame with its inclusion in the James Bond film Golden Eye.

Fig. 2.2. A Historic Hotel in France

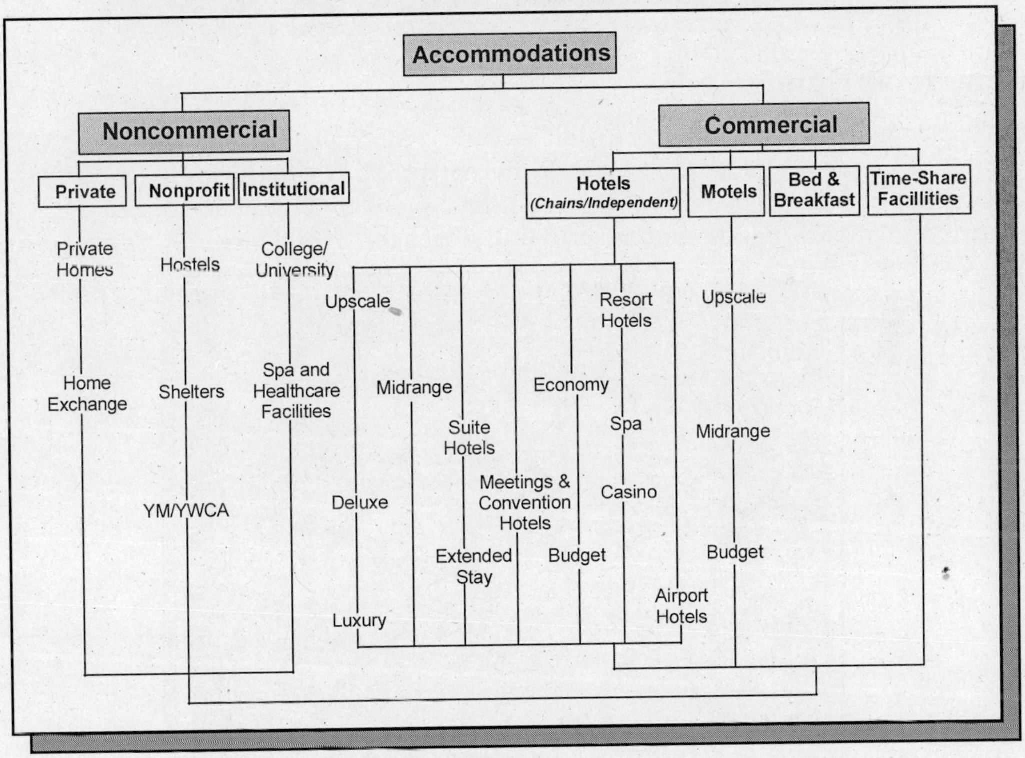

Fig. 2.3. Accommodation Structure

Resort Hotels

These cater to the needs of the holiday maker, the tourist and those who by reason of health desire a change of atmosphere. Resort hotels are located near the sea, mountain and other areas abounding in natural beauty. Rest, relaxation and entertainment are the key factors around which resorts are built.

Fig. 2.4. A Resort Hotel in Bangkok

Commercial Hotels

The commercial hotels direct their appeal primarily to the individual traveller as compared to international or resort hotel where the focus is on the group travel. As these hotels cater primarily to people who are visiting a place for commerce or business, these are located in important commercial and industrial centres of large towns and cities.

Fig. 2.5. Kai-Men-Zi Grand Hotel in China

Residential Hotels

These hotels can be described as department house complete with hotel service. These are often referred to as apartment hotels. The tariff of rooms in these hotels is charged on monthly, half-yearly or yearly basis and is charged for either furnished or unfurnished accommodation.

Fig. 2.6. A Residential Hotel

Floating Hotels

These hotels are located on the surface of the water. It may be on sea water, river or on a lake.

Fig.2.7. Queen Elizabeth Floating Hotel

Youth Hostel

It can be defined as a building which offers clean, moderate and inexpensive shelter to young people exploring their own country or other countries.

Fig. 2.8. City Central Youth Hotel Beijing

Pension

This accommodation is very popular in certain European countries. Pension is also described as a Private Hotel, a guest house or a boarding house. Catering facilities are optional and are usually restricted to the residents.

Fig. 2.9. Varkapu Pension Hotel - Budapest

Unusual Hotels

Many hotels can be considered destinations in themselves, by dint of unusual features of the lodging or its immediate environment:

Fig. 2.10. Ariau tower Hotel- Brazil

Tree House Hotels

Some hotels are built with living trees as structural elements, for example the Costa Rica Tree House in the Gandoca-Manzanillo Wildlife Refuge, Costa Rica; the Treetops Hotel in Aberdare National Park, Kenya; the Ariau Towers near Manaus, Brazil, on the Rio Negro in the Amazon; and Bayram's Tree Houses in Olympos, Turkey.

Fig. 2.11. Costa Rica Beach Tree House Hotel - Brazil

Cave Hotels

Desert Cave Hotel in Coober Pedy, South Australia and the Cuevas Pedro Antonio de Alarcón (named after the author) in Guadix, Spain, as well as several hotels in Cappadocia, Turkey, are notable for being built into natural cave formations, some with rooms underground.

Fig. 2.12. Cappadocia Elkep Evi Cave Hotel-URGUP- Cabbadocia-Turkey

Capsule Hotels

Capsule hotels are a type of economical hotel that are found in Japan.

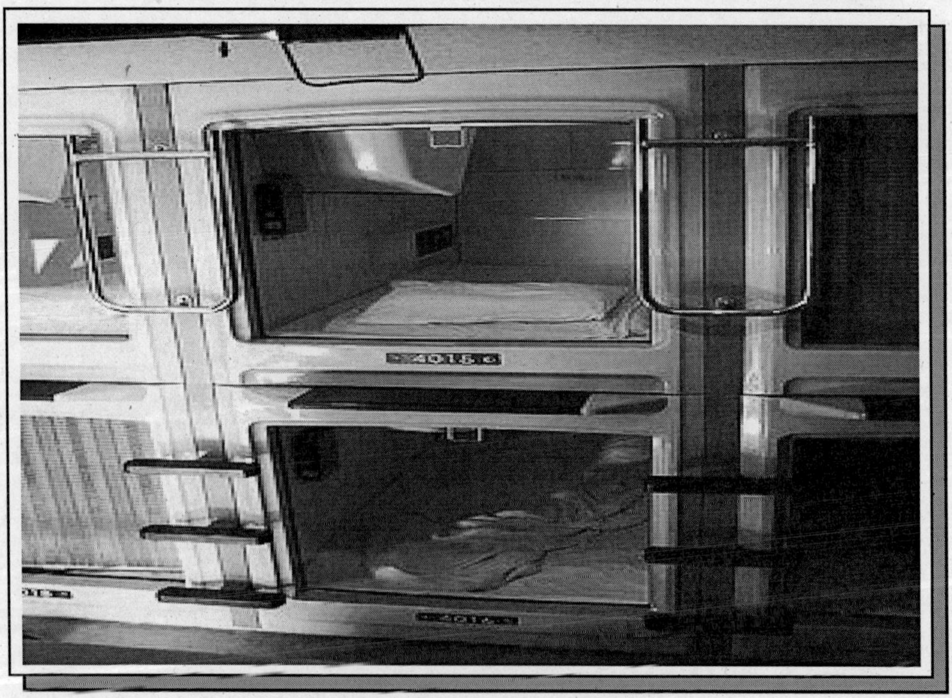

Fig. 2.13. Weird-Capsule- Hotel in Japan

Ice and Snow Hotels

The Ice Hotel in Jukkasjärvi, Sweden, and the Hotel de Glace in Duschenay,- Canada, melt every spring and are rebuilt each winter; the Mammut Snow Hotel in Finland is located within the walls of the Kemi snow castle; and the Lainio Snow Hotel is part of a snow village near Ylläs, Finland.

Fig.2.14. Sweden Ice Hotel

Garden Hotels

Garden hotels, famous for their gardens before they became hotels, include Gravetye Manor, the home of garden designer William Robinson, and Cliveden, designed by Charles Barry with a rose garden by Geoffrey Jellicoe.

Fig. 2.15. Dinahs Garden Hotel

Underwater Hotels

Some hotels have accommodation underwater, such as Utter Inn in Lake Mälaren, Sweden. Hydropolis, under construction in Dubai, will have suites on the bottom of the Persian Gulf, and Jules Undersea Lodge in Key Largo, Florida requires scuba diving to access its rooms.

Fig. 2.16. Hydropolis underwater hotel

Other Unusual Hotels

- The Library Hotel in New York City is unique in that each of its ten floors are assigned one category from the Dewey Decimal System.

Fig. 2.17. Library Hotel at New York

☹ The Burj al-Arab hotel in Dubai, United Arab Emirates, built on an artificial island, is structured in the shape of a boat's sail.

Fig. 2.18. Burj- Al-Arab Hotel – Inside

☹ The former ocean liner RMS Queen Mary in Long Beach, California uses its first-class staterooms as a hotel.

Fig. 2.19. Queens Mary

☹ The Jailhotel Löwengraben in Lucerne, Switzerland is a converted prison now used as a hotel.

❑ The Jail Hotel Lucerne

**

18 Lowengre Luceren CH-6004

Choose Dates

Check in: 14 Feb 2010

Check out: 16 Feb 2010

Go ▸

Other Popular Lucerne Hotel

- ☞ Hotel De La Paix Lucerne
- ☞ Des Balance Hotel Lucerne
- ☞ Best Western Krone Hotel Lucerne
- ☞ Hotel Schiller Lucerne
- ☞ Monopol Swiss Quality Hotel Lucerne

THE JAIL HOTEL LUCERNE DESCRIPTION

Switzerland's first prison propety, the The Jail Hotel Lucerne is a fun and youth-orientated property that is highly recommended for the budget traveller who likes to try something different.

LOCATION

Located right in the heart of the historical old town of Lucerne, Lowengraben Jail Hotel is only 10 minutes walking distance from the railway station and is close to the top tourist attractions such as the Kapellbrucke and Bucherer Watch Shop.

ROOMS

The hotel offers guestrooms that are simple in style, yet comfortable and are equipped with basic facilities.

RESTUARANT

You can begin your day with a cold continented buffet breakfast and later dine on a variety of dishes at the onsite restaurant that doubles as a bar in the evenings. Also, there is a separate restaurant serving Asian food at reasonable prices.

Fig. 2.20. The Jail Hotel Lucerne

☹ The Sheraton Doha Resort & Convention Hotel in Doha, Qatar is known as the Pyramid of the Gulf due to its pyramidal structure.

☹ The Liberty Hotel in Boston used to be the Charles Street Jail.

Motels

A motel is a hotel which is convenient for people who wish to be able to have quick access from their parked car to a hotel room.

Fig. 2.21. The Hollywood Motel

World Record Setting Hotels

Largest

The hotel with the greatest number of rooms is the MGM Grand Las Vegas in Las Vegas, United States, with a total of 6,852 rooms. In 2006, Guinness World Records listed the First World Hotel in Genting Highlands, Malaysia as the world's largest hotel with a total of 6,118 rooms.

Fig. 2.22. MGM Grand

Oldest

According to the Guinness Book of World Records, the oldest hotel still in operation is the Hoshi Ryokan, in the Awazu Onsen area of Komatsu, Japan which opened in 718.

Fig. 2.23. Hoshi Ryokan

Tallest

Burj Al Arab is the tallest building used exclusively as a hotel. However, the Rose Tower, also in Dubai, which has already topped Burj Al Arab's height at 333 m (1,090 ft), will take away this title upon its opening.

Living in Hotels

A number of public figures have notably chosen to take up semi-permanent or permanent residence in hotels.

IMPORTANCE OF VALUE CHAIN IN HOTEL

The global value chain in tourism takes the shape which is similar to that of a network whose influence reaches various areas of the economy starting from the tourist industry, through international transportation, to the banking sector and financial activities. The described network of relations and links is more of a form of interconnected chains oriented both horizontally (cooperation of enterprises and corporations, mutual relations, supra links and alliances within the industry represented by a given enterprise) and vertically (activities and relations among various companies, not necessarily from the same industry but involved in the creation of a product or service). One example is partnerships of large hotels with various enterprises such as airlines, travel agents, car rentals, credit card distributors, restaurants, shopping centres, etc. The primary role in this orientation is played by the companies creating a product, intermediaries and the consumer who is the last link in the value chain.

Recently, the concept of a global value chain has been gaining significance. This is caused by the growing concentration of capital in the hands of large concerns and the ever expanding scope of their influence and share of the tourism market. Related to this is a simultaneous decline in significance of small and medium-size enterprises in the tourism industry, which are unable to compete with powerful multinational groups. The most difficult situation is faced by those enterprises, e.g., hotels, which are held by private owners, operating on the market as independent entities, outside of any networks of relations or cooperation with hotel chains, travel agents or tourist operators. Such an enterprise must be able to cope with the all encompassing strong competition, relying on its own resources, competence and experience.

Such enterprises lose against their competitors who have the backing of other entities operating within industry networks. The benefits gained by enterprises taking part in the global value chain are priceless and provide considerable growth opportunities both for the enterprise concerned and for its environment.

Benefits of significance to the entities operating within hotel chains or cooperating networks:

- ☹ Enhanced brand image as a result of the ability to use the logo of a well-known international brand. This also indirectly leads to greater sales (more customers decide to use the offer of a hotel due to the quality of services being guaranteed by the international hotel brand);
- ☹ Significant reduction of certain expenses making up the company's fixed costs, resulting from the economies of scale (a chain often signs favourable contracts with selected suppliers of certain services or products necessary for daily operation of a hotel or restaurant. Such contracts make it possible to negotiate attractive terms of cooperation with the supplier for each entity within the chain);
- ☹ Expansion of sales markets thanks to a joint marketing and promotional policy, and participation in various global online reservation systems;
- ☹ Greater numbers of visiting foreign tourists and tourist groups organized by travel agents or tourism operators cooperating with a chain;
- ☹ Access to the headquarters' information resources on customers, market trends (which makes it possible to better match the quality of service to the customer and to choose better strategic solutions for company operation);
- ☹ Access to latest technologies and verified solutions;
- ☹ Access to professional training provided to the entire personnel, including management;
- ☹ Progress and encouragement of innovative behaviours at the enterprise.

From the perspective of benefits associated with being a member of a global value chain, a new force has been recently on the rise with the aim of posing a counterweight to large hotel groups. These are organizations affiliating independent entities operating in the tourism industry and local, regional and superregional hotel chains. Those organizations offer various support for the enterprises affiliated within such a chain, aimed to enhance their competitiveness in facing other entities from the sector, and especially international.

Competition. Recently, research has been initiated within an OECD project on the prospects of strengthening the role of small and medium-size enterprises in the global value chain. The first conclusions drawn on the basis of observations and preliminary research results confirm the advisability and the need of setting up local, regional alliances or local networks among small and medium enterprises operating to date in isolation in the increasingly competitive market. Such cooperation could help enhance the competitiveness of cooperating enterprises and strengthen their role in the global value chain. However, a broader analysis of the subject will not be possible until comprehensive research is conducted and conclusions are formulated on the basis of gathered materials. Perhaps, although this is the object of the research underway, such an analysis could lead to the formulation of a model of behaviour or a practical set of recommendations and proposed solutions helping small and medium tourism and hotel enterprises strengthen their market position in the sector.

AIRLINE CONNECTION

History

An airline provides air transport services for passengers or freight, generally with a recognized operating certificate or license. Airlines lease or own their aircraft with which to supply these services and may form partnerships or alliances with other airlines for mutual benefit.

Flight museums such as the Virginia Aviation Museum remind us what a short history the airplane has. *Photo by Cyane Lowdon, courtesy of the Science Museum of Virginia.*

Airlines vary from those with a single airplane carrying mail or cargo, through full-service international airlines operating many hundreds of airplanes. Airline services can be categorized as being intercontinental, intercontinental, or domestic and may be operated as scheduled services or charters.

DELAG, Deutsche Luftschiffahrts-Aktiengesellschaft (German: acronym for "German Airship Transport Corporation") was the world's first airline. It was founded on November 16, 1909 with government assistance, and operated airships manufactured by Zeppelin Corporation. Its headquarters were in Frankfurt. (Note: Americans, such as Rufus Porter and Frederick Marriott, attempted to start airlines in the mid-19th century, focusing on the New York-California route. Those attempts foundered due to such mishaps as the aircraft catching fire and the aircraft being ripped apart by spectators.) The five oldest non-dirigible airlines that still exist are Australia's Qantas, Netherland's KLM, Colombia's Avianca, Czech Republic's Czech Airlines and Mexico's Mexicana. KLM first flew in May 1920 while Qantas (for the Queensland and Northern Territory Aerial Services Limited) was founded in Queensland, Australia in late 1920.

INFLUENCE OF AVIATION ON TOURISM INDUSTRY

Tourism and Air Transport industry are complement to each other. Tourism depends on transportation to bring visitors, while the transportation industry depends on tourism to generate demand for its services. The growth in tourism industry directly reflects onto the air transportation. Over the last 25 years, the number of international tourists has more than doubled. The expansion of international tourism has a large impact on the discipline of transport geography.

Transport is the cause and the effect of the growth of tourism. To start with, the improved facilities have stimulated tourism, and the expansion of tourism has stimulated transport. Accessibility is the main function behind the basics of tourism transport. In order to access the areas that are mainly aimed, tourists will use any transportation mode. However, air transport is the main mode for international tourism. Air transport plays a dominant role in inter-regional movements of tourists, which normally entails travel over long-distance. Growth rates of international air traffic are pegged with growth rates of international tourism. Attractive package tours, competitive airfare attract more and more tourist day by days, therefore both the industry is expanding rapidly.

Transport policies and decisions of governments can make a big difference in the destinations available to tourists, for instance the Suvarnabhumi airport Bangkok, Thailand. Air transport is far advance than the transport mode. Air transport has revolutionized the geographical aspect of distances; the most remote areas can now be attained, any journey around the world can be measured in terms of hours of traveling. With jet that, can reach up to 1950 km/hrs, international tourism is no longer an on going adventure.

About 6.7 million jobs worldwide are in tourism industry directly supported by the spending of foreign visitors arriving by air. Taking into account both the overseas visors and work force employed it can be said that the Industry is giant in shape "The world's largest industry of Travel and Tourism". How big the airline industry and its market share are an example will give you a clear image - in a statistics it shown that, American Airlines saves US$40,000 in a year by eliminating one olive from each salad served in first class only.

U.S. AIRLINE INDUSTRY

Early Development

Tony Jannus conducted the United States' first scheduled commercial airline flight on 1 January 1914 for the Saint Petersburg-routes, Braniff Airways, American Airlines, Delta Air Lines, United Airlines (originally a division of Boeing), Trans World Airlines, Northwest Airlines, and Eastern Air Lines, to name a few.

US Airline Route Structure before World War II

Passenger service during the early 1920s was sporadic: most airlines at the time were focused on carrying bags of mail. In 1925, however, the Ford Motor Company bought out the Stout Aircraft Company and began construction of the all-metal Ford Trimotor, which became the first successful American airliner. With a 12-passenger capacity, the Trimotor made passenger service potentially profitable. Air service was seen as a supplement to rail service in the American transportation network.

At the same time, Juan Trippe began a crusade to create an air network that would link America to the world, and he achieved this goal through his airline, Pan American World Airways, with a fleet of flying boats that linked Los Angeles to Shanghai and Boston to London. Pan Am and Northwest Airways (which began flights to Canada in the 1920s) were the only U.S. airlines to go international before the 1940s. With the introduction of the Boeing 247 and Douglas DC-3 in the 1930s, the U.S. airline industry was generally profitable, even during the Great Depression. This trend continued until the beginning of World War II.

North-West Airways

Development Since 1945

As governments met to set the standards and scope for an emergent civil air industry toward the end of the war, it was no surprise that the U.S. took a position of maximum operating freedom. After all, U.S. airline companies were not devastated by the war, as European companies and the few Asian companies had been. This preference for "open skies" operating regimes continues, within limitations, to this day.

World War II, like World War I, brought new life to the airline industry. Many airlines in the Allied countries were flush from lease contracts to the military, and foresaw a future explosive demand for civil air transport, for both passengers and cargo. They were eager to invest in the newly emerging flagships of air travel such as the Boeing Stratocruiser, Lockheed Constellation, and Douglas DC-6. Most of these new aircraft were based on American bombers such as the B-29, which had spearheaded research into new technologies such as pressurization. Most offered increased efficiency from both added speed and greater payload.

Boeing Stratocruiser

In the 1950s, the De Havilland Comet, Boeing 707, Douglas DC-8, and Sud Aviation Caravelle became the first flagships of the Jet Age in the West, while the Soviet Union bloc countered with the Tupolev Tu-104 and Tupolev Tu-124 in the fleets of state-owned carriers such as Aeroflot and Interflug. The Vickers Viscount and Lockheed L-188 Electra inaugurated turboprop transport.

Douglas DC-8

The next big boost for the airlines would come in the 1970s, when the Boeing 747, McDonnell Douglas DC-10, and Lockheed L-1011 inaugurated wide body ("jumbo jet") service, which is still the standard in international travel. The Tupolev Tu-144 and its Western counterpart, Concorde, made supersonic travel a reality. Concorde first flew in 1969 and operated through 2003. In 1972, Airbus began producing Europe's most commercially successful line of airliners to date. The added efficiencies for these aircraft were often not in speed, but in passenger capacity, payload, and range. Airbus also features modern electronic cockpits that were common across their aircraft to enable pilots to fly multiple aircraft with minimal cross-training.

1978's U.S. airline industry deregulation lowered barriers for new airlines. In this period, new start-ups entered during downturns in the normal 8-10 year business cycle. At that time, they find aircraft, are financed, contract hangar and maintenance services, train new employees, and recruit laid off staff from other airlines.

As the business cycle returned to normalcy, major airlines dominated their routes through aggressive pricing and additional capacity offerings, often swamping new startups. Only America West Airlines (which has since merged with US Airways) remained a significant survivor from this new entrant era, as dozens, even hundreds, have gone under.

In many ways, the biggest winner in the deregulated environment was the air passenger. Indeed, the U.S. witnessed an explosive growth in demand for air travel, as many millions who had never or rarely flown before became regular fliers, even joining frequent flyer loyalty programs and receiving free flights and other benefits from their flying. New services and higher frequencies meant that business fliers could fly to another city, do business, and return the same day, for almost any point in the country. Air travel's advantages put intercity bus lines under pressure, and most have withered away.

By the 1980s, almost half of the total flying in the world took place in the U.S., and today the domestic industry operates over 10,000 daily departures nationwide.

KLM Airlines

European Airline Industry

The Imperial Airways Empire Terminal, Victoria, London. Trains ran from here to flying boats in Southampton, and to Croydon Airport. The first countries in Europe to embrace air transport were Finland, France, Germany, the Netherlands and the United Kingdom.

KLM, the oldest carrier still operating under its original name, was founded in 1919. The first flight (operated on behalf of KLM by Aircraft Transport and Travel) transported two English passengers to Schiphol, Amsterdam from London in 1920. Like other major European airlines of the time (see France and the UK below), KLM's early growth depended heavily on the needs to service links with far-flung colonial possessions (Dutch Indies). It is only after the loss of the Dutch Empirc that KLM found itself based at a small country with few potential passengers, depending heavily on transfer traffic, and was one of the first to introduce the hub-system to facilitate easy connections.

France began an air mail service to Morocco in 1919 that was bought out in 1927, renamed Aéropostale, and injected with capital to become a major international carrier. In 1933, Aéropostale went bankrupt, was nationalized and merged with several other airlines into what became Air France.

In Finland, the charter establishing Aero O/Y (now Finnair, one of the oldest still-operating airlines in the world) was signed in the city of Helsinki on September 12, 1923. Junkers F 13 D-335 became the first aircraft of the company, when Aero took delivery of it on March 14, 1924. The first flight was between Helsinki and Tallinn, capital of Estonia, and it took place on March 20, 1924, one week later.

Germany's Lufthansa began in 1926. Lufthansa, unlike most other airlines at the time, became a major investor in airlines outside of Europe, providing capital to Varig and Avianca. German airliners built by Junkers, Dornier, and Fokker were the most advanced in the world at the time. The peak of German air travel came in the mid-1930s, when Nazi propaganda ministers approved the start of commercial zeppelin service: the big airships were a symbol of industrial might, but the fact that they used flammable hydrogen gas raised safety concerns that culminated with the Hindenburg disaster of 1937. The reason they used hydrogen instead of the not-flammable helium gas was a United States military embargo on helium.

The British company Aircraft Transport and Travel commenced a London to Paris service on August 25, 1919; this was the world's first regular international flight. The United Kingdom's flag carrier during this period was Imperial Airways, which became BOAC (British Overseas Airways Co.) in 1939. Imperial Airways used huge Handley-Page biplanes for routes between London, the Middle East, and India: images of Imperial aircraft in the middle of the Rub'al Khali, being maintained by Bedouins, are among the most famous pictures from the heyday of the British Empire.

Deregulation

Deregulation of the European Union airspace in the early 1990s has had substantial effect on structure of the industry there. The shift towards 'budget' airlines on shorter routes has been significant. Airlines such as Easyjet and Ryanair have grown at the expense of the traditional national airlines.

There has also been a trend for these national airlines themselves to be privatised such as has occurred for Aer Lingus (Ireland) and British Airways. Other national airlines, including Italy's Alitalia, have suffered - particularly with the rapid increase of oil prices in early 2008.

Dubai International Airport

ASIAN AIRLINE INDUSTRY

Some of the first countries in Asia to embrace air transport were India, Hong Kong, Indonesia, Malaysia, Pakistan and the Philippines. One of the first countries in Asia to embrace air transport was the Philippines. Philippine Airlines was founded on February 26, 1941, making it Asia's oldest carrier and the oldest operating under its current name. The airline was started by a group of businessmen led by Andres Soriano, hailed as one of the Philippines' leading industrialists at the time. The airline's first flight was made on March 15, 1941 with a single Beech Model 18 NPC-54 aircraft, which started its daily services between Manila (from Nielson Field) and Baguio, later to expand with larger aircraft such as the DC-3 and Vickers Viscount. Notably Philippine Airlines leased Japan Airlines their first aircraft, a DC-3 named "Kinsei". On July 31, 1946, a chartered Philippine Airlines DC-4 ferried 40 American servicemen to Oakland, California from Nielson Airport in Makati City with stops in Guam, Wake Island, Johnston Atoll and Honolulu, Hawaii, making PAL the first Asian airline to cross the Pacific Ocean. A regular service between Manila and San Francisco was started in December. It was during this year that the airline was designated as the Philippines flag carrier.

Pakistan International Airlines Boeing 747-300. The Government of Pakistan is the majority stake-holder in Pakistan International Airlines. Another airline company to begin early operations was Air India, which had its beginning as Tata Airlines in 1932, a division of Tata Sons Ltd. (now Tata Group) by India's leading industrialist JRD Tata. On October 15, 1932, J. R. D. Tata himself flew a single engined De Havilland Puss Moth carrying air mail (postal mail of Imperial Airways) from Karachi to Bombay via Ahmedabad. The aircraft continued to Madras via Bellary piloted by Royal Air Force pilot Nevill Vincent.

With the outbreak of World War Two, the airline presence in Asia came to a relative halt, with many new flag carriers donating their aircraft for military aid and other uses.

Following the end of World War II, regular commercial service was restored in India and Tata Airlines became a public limited company on July 29, 1946 under the name Air India. After the Independence of India, 49% of the airline was acquired by the Government of India. In return, the airline was granted status to operate international services from India as the designated flag carrier under the name Air India International.

Neighbouring countries also soon embraced air transport, notably with the beginning of a new nation, Pakistan began Orient Airways Ltd (Pakistan International Airlines), Cathay Pacific founded in 1946, Singapore Airlines and Malaysian Airlines in 1947 (as Malayan Airways), Garuda Indonesia in 1949, Japan Airlines in 1951, and Korean Air in 1962.

Air India

Importance

In Inter-continental or long-distance travel, air transport has been responsible for the 'Explosion' in World tourism and in certain areas where the terrain and other conditions prevent normal development of other forms of transport, air travel is the only means of tourism. Historically, it is established that the improvements in travel facilities, especially reduced time and increased comfort, have encouraged and influenced travel movement and created an upsurge in the volume of Traffic.

Air transport is essentially international, large and above al a dynamic and developing industry. Its extensive network spans all continents, serves nearly all countries. Air transport has become the largest single item in international trade (barring oil) and its importance to tourism cannot be over-emphasised. Only air transport has brought tourism on a large industrial scale to many tourist centres, not least to developing countries, thereby contributing in an unprecedented way to their social and economic amelioration. Jets in particular have revolutionised travel and Jumbos have dramatically accelerated the revolutionary charge. By their achievements in speed, safety, comfort and economy, they have attracted great number of travellers.

The considerable increase in international tourism world is mainly due to air-transport, which has facilitated long-distance travel, particularly for passengers with higher incomes from the developed countries. The UN conference on International Travel and Tourism held in 1963 at Rome recognised the paramount importance of Public and Private Transport as an element in the growth of tourism.

LOW-COST CARRIER

A low-cost carrier (LCC) or low-cost airlines — also known as a no-frills, discount, or budget airline — is an airline that offers generally low fares by eliminating many traditional passenger services. This concept, experienced first in the United States with Pacific Southwest Airlines in the early 1950s, gave birth to one of the biggest success stories of the last twenty years in the air travel industry. Southwest Airlines, which began service in 1971, is LCC 's biggest U.S. success story. They have been a model that other low-cost carriers have emulated. The LCCs now represent over 30 percent of total air travel in the United States and 25 percent in Europe, and are making gains in Asia.

Some typical business practices of LCCs are:

- ☹ One passenger class
- ☹ One type of airplane to reduce fleet maintenance costs
- ☹ Using secondary airports
- ☹ Quick airport turnarounds
- ☹ Point-to-point service
- ☹ Unreserved seating
- ☹ Employees working in multiple roles
- ☹ Internet booking
- ☹ No frills, just low fares

Low-cost carriers are growing, threatening the major carriers and making major carrier profitability a more difficult task. Brand names like Southwest, JetBlue, Ryan air, West Jet, and easy Jet are growing and gaining ground against their larger competitors. They are also making a profit. They are being joined by new low-cost carriers in all parts of the world.

The bright spot in the global air industry is Asia and the Pacific. The dynamic economy of the region is making its own airlines profitable and helping carriers from outside the region with extensive Asia/Pacific operations. At present, the Orient is the world's number-one growth center for air travel.

The world's economy and the tourism industry need a healthy air transportation system. Without airline passengers, rental cars go unrented, hotel beds go unsold, and attractions go unvisited. The airlines have revolutionized long - haul travel and the range and speed of jet travel have greatly expanded what tourists or business travellers could once accomplish with the equivalent time and funds at their disposal. Today, for example, it is possible to fly around the globe in less time than it takes to drive across the United States. The system is also incredibly efficient. You need to make only one call to an airline or a travel agent or get on the Internet to purchase a ticket to your desired destination; then all you have to do is go to the airport and check your bags through to the final destination. The logistics that make it happen are complex, but the system works well. For example, United Airlines (including United Express and Ted) offers over

3600 fiights a day to 210 domestic and international destinations. Other airlines have similar structures and combine to make a total system that blankets the world.

Although the major advantage of air travel is speed, which results in more time for other activities, there are negative aspects for those who wish to travel by air. These include some people's fear of flying and a lack of geographic accessibility, since many communities in the country are not served by air transportation. An additional not getting to and from the airport. Frequently, this time exceeds that spent en route.

In the United States, air carriers are classified as major if they record over $1 billion in revenue annually. There are twenty: ABX, AirTran Airways, Alaska Airlines, American Airlines, American Eagle, ATA, Atlas/Polar, Comair, Continental Airlines, Delta Air Lines, ExpressJet, FedEx, JetBlue, Mesa, Northwest Airlines, SkyWest, Southwest Airlines, United Airlines, UPS Airlines, and US Airways. National carriers are those recording annual revenues of $100 million to $1 billion and include Air Transport International, Air Wisconsin Airlines, Allegiant, Aloha Airlines, Amerijet International, ASTAR Air Cargo, Atlantic Southeast, Champion Air, Continental Micronesia, Evergreen International Airlines, Executive Airlines, Florida West, Frontier Airlines, Gemini Air Cargo, Hawaiian Airlines, Horizon Air, Independence Air, Kalitta Air, Mesaba Airlines, Miami Air International, Midwest Airlines, North American Airlines, Omni Air International, Pinnacle Airlines dba Northwest Airlink, PSA Airlines, Ryan International Airlines, Spirit Airlines, Sun Country Airlines, Trans States Airlines, Transmeridian, USA 3000 Airlines, USA Jet, and World Airways. There are about thirty-one regional airlines with annual revenues under $100 million. In addition, there are fifty-five small certified commuter airlines.

FUTURE OF TOURISM AND AVIATION

The travel and tourism industry employs 72 million people worldwide. Global tourism expenditure is estimated to be nearly US$ 3 trillion. Tourism accounts directly for 3.8% of worlds GDP. Tourism is expected to maintain its growth by 2014, the World Travel and Tourism Council expects the torsion industry to employ more than 84 million people globally.

Tourism as an upcoming industry .The World Tourism Organization (UNWTO) forecasts that international tourism will continue growing at the average annual rate of 4%. By 2020 Europe will remain the most popular destination, but its share will drop from 60% in 1995 to 46 %. Long haul will grow slightly faster than intraregional travel and by 2020 its share will increase from 18% in 1995 to 24%.

With the advent of e-commerce, tourism products have become one of the most traded items on the Internet. Tourism products and services have been made available through intermediaries, although tourism providers (hotels, airlines, etc.) can sell their services directly. This has put pressure on intermediaries from both on-line and traditional shops.

It has been suggested there is a strong correlation between Tourism expenditure per capita and the degree to which countries play in the global context. Not only as a result of the important economic contribution of the tourism industry, but also as an indicator of the degree of confidence with which global citizens leverage the resources of the globe for the benefit of their local economies.

Space tourism is expected to "take off" in the first quarter of the 21st century, although compared with traditional destinations the number of tourists in orbit will remain low until technologies such as a space elevator make space travel cheap.

Technological improvement is likely to make possible air-ship hotels, based either on solar-powered airplanes or large dirigibles. Underwater hotels, such as Hydropolis, expected to open in Dubai in 2009. On the ocean tourists will be welcomed by ever larger cruise ships and perhaps floating cities.

Some futurists expect that movable hotel "pods" will be created that could be temporarily erected anywhere on the planet, where building a permanent resort would be unacceptable politically, economically or environmentally.

LET US SUM UP

A hotel is an establishment that provides paid lodging, usually on a short-term basis. The provision of basic accommodation, in times past, consisting only of a room with a bed, a cupboard, a small table and a washstand has largely been replaced by rooms with modern facilities, including en-suite bathrooms and air conditioning or climate control. Additional common features found in hotel rooms are a telephone, an alarm clock, a television, and Internet connectivity; snack foods and drinks may be supplied in a mini-bar, and facilities for making hot drinks. Larger hotels may provide a number of additional guest facilities such as a restaurant, a swimming pool or childcare, and have conference and social function services.

An airline provides air transport services for passengers or freight, generally with a recognized operating certificate or license. Airlines lease or own their aircraft with which to supply these services and may form partnerships or alliances with other airlines for mutual benefit.

Airlines vary from those with a single airplane carrying mail or cargo, through full-service international airlines operating many hundreds of airplanes. Airline services can be categorized as being intercontinental, intercontinental, or domestic and may be operated as scheduled services or charters.

The global value chain in tourism takes the shape which is similar to that of a network whose influence reaches various areas of the economy starting from the tourist industry, through international transportation, to the banking sector and financial activities. The described network of relations and links is more of a form of interconnected chains oriented both horizontally (cooperation of enterprises and corporations, mutual relations, supra links and alliances within the industry represented by a given enterprise) and vertically (activities and relations among various companies, not necessarily from the same industry but involved in the creation of a product or service). One example is partnerships of large hotels with various enterprises such as airlines, travel agents, car rentals, credit card distributors, restaurants, shopping centres, etc. The primary role in this orientation is played by the companies creating a product, intermediaries and the consumer who is the last link in the value chain.

CHECK YOUR PROGRESS

(A) True/False

(i) Accommodation constitutes a vital and fundamental part of tourism.

(ii) The United Nations conference of International Travel and Tourism held in Rome in 1990.

(iii) In old times 'Tavern' was a popular accommodation in USA.

(B) Fill in the Blanks

(i) 'Dharamsala' are found in ....

(ii) The word hotel is derived from ....

(iii) Floating hotels are located on the surface of the ....

(C) True /False

(i) Costa Rica tree house is an example of unusual hotel.

(ii) Capsule hotels are found in Japan.

(iii) Motel is synonymous to hotel

LESSON AND ACTIVITY

Scan the environment and write a note on how Indian Aviation Industry is taking shape. (Mention about the mergers of Kingfisher and Deccan, Sahara and Jet Airlines and various other challenges in terms of increased ATF prices, competition and current economic turmoil after the fall of Lehmann Brothers in 2008)

KEY WORDS

Hotel: A hotel is an establishment that provides paid lodging, usually on a short-term basis.

Airline: An airline provides air transport services for passengers or freight, generally with a recognized operating certificate or license. Airlines lease or own their aircraft with which to supply these services and may form partnerships or alliances with other airlines for mutual benefit. Airlines vary from those with a single airplane carrying mail or cargo, through full-service international airlines operating many hundreds of airplanes. Airline services can be categorized as being intercontinental, intercontinental, or domestic and may be operated as scheduled services or charters.

Value Chain in Tourism Industry: It is the network that tourism industry has with other industries like airlines, travel agents, car rentals, credit card distributors, restaurants, shopping centres etc.

QUESTIONS FOR DISCUSSION

(1) Explain the importance of Hotels in development of tourism industry.

(2) Write a small note on Indian Hotel Industry – Past, Present and Future.

(3) "Value chain is very important in Hotel Business" - Explain

(4) Write briefly about the evolution of aviation industry.

(5) Explain the importance of Aviation Industry in tourism industry.

CHECK YOUR PROGRESS: MODEL ANSWER

(A) *(i)* T *(ii)* F *(iii)* T

(B) *(i)* India *(ii)* French world 'Hote' *(iii)* Water

(C) *(i)* F *(ii)* T *(iii)* F

❑ ❑ ❑

3

Role of State in Promoting Tourism

Chapter Outline

- *Introduction*
- *Level of State Involvement*
- *WTO (Organisation, activities, member states)*
- *IMF (Organization, activities)*
- *NTO (Organization, activities)*
- *IHA (Organization, activities)*
- *IHRA (Organization, activities)*
- *IATA (Organization, activities)*

Learning Objective

At the conclusion of this lesson you should be able to understand:

- *Involvement of State in the development of Tourism*
- *The role of WTO*
- *IMF and its functions*
- *Organisation of IHA*
- *IHRA and its functions*
- *Organisation of NTO and its functions*

"Like all great travellers, I have seen more than I remember and remember more than I have seen."

– Benjamin Disraeli (1804-1881)
British politician and author.

INTRODUCTION

Governments have to play a key role in the planning development, regulation and marketing of tourism. Tourism helps every government because it provides employment to the citizens and earns foreign currency for the country. Therefore, practically every government in the world, irrespective of its size has a NTO. It may be called a Department of Tourism as in the case of India, a Tourist Promotion Board as in the case of Singapore, a Tourism Authority as in the UK and Thailand or a Tourism Ministry as in the Philippines. The NTOs are involved in planning, development, promotion and administration of tourism. While planning a beach or mountain resort, an NTO tries to make sure that there is no overcrowding, pollution and destruction of historic or archaeological landmarks as a result of the new area development for tourism. To promote tourism, an NTO opens tourist offices overseas to attract foreign tourists to their shores. They also have tourist information offices within their own countries to provide information to foreign visitors on arrival and also to domestic travellers who wish to travel within their own country.

In India, the Central Department of Tourism has eleven tourist offices in foreign countries and twenty-one within India. In large countries like India, there are several government tourist organisations. For instance, almost all the twenty-eight state governments of India and seven Union Territories have their departments of tourism and majority of them have government–owned State Tourism Development Corporation. This lesson will help you to understand about role of state in promoting tourism.

LEVEL OF STATE INVOLVEMENT

The level of involvement of government in the field of tourism of a country depends on several factors:

(i) In countries where the percentage of GDP contributed by tourist industry is larger, the greater would be the government involvement.

(ii) Centrally controlled economies would be characterized by high government involvement in all sectors of economy including tourism. In open market economies the government involvement would be minimum.

(iii) In lesser developed countries, the investment from private investors especially in the area of high capital infrastructural development may not be enough. In these countries, government intervention therefore is required in order for the industry to grow.

(iv) Countries for instance like China where the sudden growth of tourism had certain problems will have a more centralized role in organising and controlling tourism than other countries.

WTO

The World Tourism Organization Building is in Madrid.

WORLD TOURISM ORGANIZATION
ORGANISATION MONDIALE DU TOURISME
ORGANIZACIÓN MUNDIAL DEL TURISMO
ВСЕМИРНАЯ ТУРИСТСКАЯ ОРГАНИЗАЦИЯ
منظمة السياحة العالمية

The **United Nations World Tourism Organization** (**UNWTO**), headquartered in Madrid, Spain, is a United Nations agency dealing with questions relating to tourism. It compiles the World Tourism Rankings. The World Tourism Organization is a significant global body concerned with the collection and collation of statistical information on international tourism. This organization represents public sector tourism bodies from most countries in the world and the publication of its data makes possible comparisons of the flow and growth of tourism on a global scale.

Organizational aims

UNWTO plays a role in promoting the development of responsible, sustainable and universally accessible tourism, paying particular attention to the interests of developing countries .

The Organization encourages the implementation of the Global Code of Ethics for Tourism, with a view to ensuring that member countries, tourist destinations and businesses maximize the positive economic, social and cultural effects of tourism and fully reap its benefits, while minimizing its negative social and environmental impacts.

UNWTO is committed to the United Nations Millennium Development Goals, geared toward reducing poverty and fostering sustainable development.

History

The origin of the United Nation World Tourism Organization stems back to 1925 when the International Congress of Official Tourist Traffic Associations (ICOTT) was formed at The Hague. Some articles from early volumes of the Annals of Tourism Research claim that the UNWTO originated from the International Union of Official Tourist Publicity Organizations (IUOTPO), although the UNWTO states that the ICOTT became the International Union of Official Tourist Propaganda Organizations first in 1934.

Following the end of the Second World War and with international travel numbers increasing, the IUOTPO restructured itself into the International Union of Official Travel Organizations (IUOTO). A technical, non-governmental organization, the IUOTO was made up of a combination of national tourist organizations, industry and consumer groups. The goals and objectives of the IUOTO were not only to promote tourism in general but also to extract the best out of tourism as an international trade component and as an economic development strategy for developing nations.

Towards the end of the 1960s, the IUOTO realized the need for further transformation to enhance its role on an international level. The 20th IUOTO general assembly in Tokyo, 1967, declared the need for the creation of an intergovernmental body with the necessary abilities to function on an international level in cooperation with other international agencies, in particular the United Nations. Throughout the existence of the IUOTO, close ties had been established between the organization and the United Nations (UN) and initial suggestions had the IUOTO becoming part of the UN. However, following the circulation of a draft convention, consensus held that any resultant intergovernmental organization should be closely linked to the UN but preserve its "complete administrative and financial autonomy".

It was on the recommendations of the UN that the formation of the new intergovernmental tourism organization was based. Resolution 2529 of the XXIVth UN general assembly stated:

In 1970, the IUOTO general assembly voted in favor of forming the World Tourism Organization (WTO), based on statutes of the IUOTO, and after ratification by the prescribed 51 states, the WTO came into operation on November 1, 1974.

Most recently, at the fifteenth general assembly in 2003, the WTO general council and the UN agreed to establish the WTO as a specialized agency of the UN. The significance of this collaboration, WTO Secretary-General Mr. Francesco Frangialli claimed, would lie in "the increased visibility it gives the WTO, and the recognition that will be accorded to [it].Tourism will be considered on an equal footing with other major activities of human society".

As of 2007, its membership included 150 countries, seven territories and some 350 affiliate members, representing the private sector, educational institutions, tourism associations and local tourism authorities. The frequent confusion between the two WTOs – World Tourism Organization and the Geneva-based World Trade Organization – officially ended on 1 December 2005, when the General Assembly approved to add the letters UN (for United Nations) to the start of abbreviation of the leading international tourism body in English and in Russian. UNWTO abbreviation remains OMT in French and Spanish. UNWTO General Assembly concluded its work at its 16th session in Dakar, Senegal, on 2 December, 2005.

Activities

- *(i)* Constant review of tourism trends and developments and exercising vigilance over changes in world economic and social conditions affecting tourism, market fluctuations and maintenance of standards within the tourism sectors.
- *(ii)* Clearing house for all available information on international and domestic tourism including statistical data, legislation and regulations, facilities and special events.
- *(iii)* Systematic collection, analysis and dissemination of data on various aspects of tourism.
- *(iv)* Collecting legislative texts, regulations and documentation on all aspects of travel.
- *(v)* Conducting research studies covering tourism markets, plant and enterprises, physical planning and area development, promotion and marketing, economic analysis and financing techniques etc.
- *(vi)* Regular supply of studies, as well as updated information on trends in the various fields of tourism to its members.
- *(vii)* Fostering co-operation with competent specialised bodies regarding simplifying frontier formalities and removing barriers to the free movement of tourists.
- *(viii)* Organising and convening international conferences, seminars, workshops, round tables and technical meetings on all aspects of tourism.
- *(ix)* Preparation of draft international agreements on tourism.
- *(x)* Examining vocational training programmes with a view to contributing to the establishment of suitable teaching programmes tailored to specific needs, especially in the developing countries.

STRUCTURE

General Assembly

The General Assembly is the supreme organ of the Organization. Its ordinary sessions, held every two years, are attended by delegates of the Full and Associate Members, as well as representatives from the Business Council.

It is the most important meeting of senior tourism officials and high-level representatives of the private sector from all over the world.

Previous sessions:

Session	Venue	Date
I	Madrid, Spain	May 1975
II	Torremolinos, Spain	May/June 1977
III	Torremolinos, Spain	September 1979
IV	Rome, Italy	September 1981
V	New Delhi, India	October 1983
VI	Sofia, Bulgaria	September 1985
VII	Madrid, Spain	September/October 1987
VII	Paris, France	August/September 1989
IX	Buenos Aires, Argentina	September/October 1991
X	Bali, Indonesia	October 1993
XI	Cairo, Egypt	October 1995
XII	Istanbul, Turkey	October 1997
XIII	Santiago, Chile	September/October 1999
XIV	Seoul, Republic of Korea/Osaka, Japan	September 2001
XV	Beijing, China	October 2003
XVI	Dakar, Senegal	November/December 2005
XVII	Cartagena de Indias, Colombia	November 2007

Regional Commissions

Established in 1975 as subsidiary organs of the General Assembly, the six Regional Commissions normally meet once a year. They enable member States to maintain contact with one another and with the Secretariat between sessions of the General Assembly, to which they submit their proposals and convey their concerns. Each Commission elects one Chairman and its Vice-Chairmen from among its Members for a term of two years commencing from one session to the next session of the assembly.

Officers (2009-2011)

- UNWTO Commission for Africa (CAF)
  Chairman: Cameroon, Vice-Chairmen: Algeria, Burkina Faso
- UNWTO Commission for the Americas (CAM)
  Chairman: Venezuela , Vice-Chairmen: Ecuador, Paraguay
- UNWTO Commission for East Asia and the Pacific (CAP)
  Chairman: Thailand , Vice-Chairmen: Japan, Malaysia

- UNWTO Commission for South Asia (CSA)
  Chairman: Iran, Vice-Chairmen: Bangladesh, Bhutan
- UNWTO Commission for Europe (CEU)
  Chairman: Slovenia, Vice-Chairmen: France, Montenegro
- UNWTO Commission for Middle East (CME)
  Chairman: Lebanon, Vice-Chairmen: Saudi Arabia, Syrian Arab Republic

Executive Council
Officers for 2010

Chairman: Costa Rica

First Vice-Chairman: Kenya

Second Vice-Chairman: Italy

The Executive Council's task is to take all necessary measures, in consultation with the Secretary-General, for the implementation of its own decisions and recommendations of the Assembly and report thereon to the Assembly.

The Council meets at least twice a year.

The Council consists of Full Members elected by the Assembly in the proportion of one Member for every five Full Members, in accordance with the Rules of Procedure laid down by the Assembly with a view to achieving fair and equitable geographical distribution.

The term of office of Members elected to the Council is four years and elections for one-half of the Council membership are held every two years. Spain is a Permanent Member of the Executive Council.

The Council elects one Chairman and two Vice-Chairmen from among its Members.

Subsidiary Organs

Programme Committee (England, France, Spain)

Committee on Budget and Finance (England, France, Spain)

Committee on Market and Competitiveness (England, France, Spain)

Committee on Statistics and the Tourism Satellite account (England, France, Spain)

Sustainable Development of Tourism Committee (England, France, Spain)

Committee on Poverty Reduction

Committee for the Review of Applications for Affiliate Membership (England, France, Spain)

Secretariat

The Secretariat is led by Secretary-General ad interim Taleb Rifai of Jordan, who supervises about 110 full-time staff at UNWTO's Madrid Headquarters. These officials are responsible for implementing UNWTO's programme of work and serving the needs of Members. The Affiliate Members are supported by a full-time Executive Director at the

Madrid Headquarters. The Secretariat also includes a regional support office for Asia-Pacific in Osaka, Japan, financed by the Japanese Government. The official languages of UNWTO are Arabic, English, French, Russian and Spanish.

IMF

The International Monetary Fund (IMF) is an international organization that oversees the global financial system by following the macroeconomic policies of its member countries; in particular those with an impact on exchange rates and the balance of payments. It also offers financial and technical assistance to its members, making it an international lender of last resort. Its headquarters are located in Washington, D.C., USA.

The International Monetary Fund was created in 1944 , with a goal to stabilize exchange rates and supervise the reconstruction of the world's international payment system. Countries contributed to a pool which could be borrowed from, on a temporary basis, by countries with payment imbalances. (Condon, 2007).

The IMF describes itself as "an organization of 185 countries (Montenegro being the 185th, as of January 18, 2007), working to foster global monetary cooperation, secure financial stability, facilitate international trade, promote high employment and sustainable economic growth, and reduce poverty". With the exception of North Korea, Cuba, Andorra, Monaco, Liechtenstein, Tuvalu, and Nauru, all UN member states participate directly in the IMF. Most are represented by other member states on a 24-member Executive Board but all member countries belong to the IMF's Board of Governors.

History

The International Monetary Fund was formally created in July, 1944 during the United Nations Monetary and Financial Conference. The representatives of 45 governments met in the Mount Washington Hotel in the area of Bretton Woods, New Hampshire, United States of America, with the delegates to the conference agreeing on a framework for international economic cooperation. The IMF was formally organized on December 27, 1945, when the first 29 countries signed its Articles of Agreement. The statutory purposes of the IMF today are the same as when they were formulated in 1944.

Today

The IMF's influence in the global economy steadily increased as it accumulated more members. The number of IMF member countries has more than quadrupled from the 44 states involved in its establishment, reflecting in particular the attainment of political independence by many developing countries and more recently the collapse of the Soviet bloc. The expansion of the IMF's membership, together with the changes in the world economy, has required the IMF to adapt in a variety of ways to continue serving its purposes effectively.

In an apparent move to curb the sudden rise of gold prices, and to shore up the falling value of the US Dollar, the International Monetary Fund's executive board approved a broad financial overhaul plan that could lead to the eventual sale of a little over 400 tons of its substantial gold supplies. IMF Managing Director Dominique Strauss-Kahn welcomed the board's decision April 7, 2008 to propose a new framework for the fund, designed to close a projected $400 million budget deficit over the next few years. The budget proposal includes sharp spending cuts of $100 million until 2011 that will include up to 380 staff dismissals.

The international monetary system refers to the institutional arrangements to govern exchange rates. The foreign exchange market was the primary institution for determining exchange rates and the impersonal market forces of demand and supply determined the relative value of any two currencies (i.e., their exchange rate). Furthermore, we explained that the demand and supply of currencies is influenced by their respective countries' relative inflation rates and interest rate. When the foreign exchange market determines the relative value of a currency, we say that the country is adhering to a floating exchange rate regime. The world's four major trading currencies – the US Dollar, The European Union's Euro, the Japanese Yen and the British Pound – are all free to float against each other. Thus, their exchange rates are determined by market forces and fluctuate against each other on a day-to-day, if not minute-to-minute, basis. However the exchange rates of any currencies are not determined by the free play of market forces; other institutional arrangements are adopted.

Many of the world's smaller nations peg their currencies, primarily to the dollar or the euro. A pegged exchange rate means the value of the currency is fixed relative to a reference currency, such as the US dollar, and then the exchange rate between that currency and other currencies is determined by the reference currency exchange rate.

Other countries, while not adopting a formal pegged rate, try to hold the value of their currency within some range against an important reference currency such as the US dollar. This is often referred to as a dirty float. It is a float because in theory, the value of the currency is determined by market forces, but it is a dirty float (as opposed to a clean float) because the central bank of a country will intervene in the foreign exchange market to try to maintain the value of its currency if it depreciates too rapidly against an important reference currency.

Still other countries have operated with a fixed exchange rate system, in which the values of a set of currencies are fixed against each other at some mutually agreed on exchange rate. Before the introduction of the euro in 2000, several member states of the EU operated with fixed exchange rates within the context of the European Monetary System (EMS).

The IMF is another important player in the international monetary system. The IMF does not simply lend money to a country in trouble. In exchange for the loan, it requires that the government adopt policies designed to correct whatever economic problems caused the depreciation in the nation's currency.

The Role of the IMF

The IMF Articles of Agreement were heavily influenced by the worldwide financial collapse, competitive devaluations, trade wars, high unemployment, hyperinflation in Germany and elsewhere, and general economic disintegration that occurred between the two world wars. The aim of the Bretton Woods agreement, of which the IMF was the main custodian, was to try to avoid a repetition of that chaos through a combination of discipline and flexibility.

Discipline

A fixed exchange rate regime imposes discipline in two ways. First, the need to maintain a fixed exchange rate puts a brake on competitive devaluations and brings stability to the world trade environment. Second, a fixed exchange rate regime imposes monetary discipline on countries, thereby curtailing price inflation. For example, consider what would happen under a fixed exchange rate regime if Great Britain rapidly increased its money supply would lead to price inflation. Given fixed exchange rates, inflation would make British goods uncompetitive in world markets, while the prices of imports would become more attractive in Great Britain. The result would be a widening trade deficit in Great Britain, with the country importing more than it exports. To correct this trade imbalance under a fixed exchange rate regime, Great Britain would be required to restrict the rate of growth in its money supply to bring price inflation back under control. Thus, fixed exchange rates are seen as a mechanism for controlling inflation and imposing economic discipline on countries.

Flexibility

Although monetary discipline was a central objective of the Brctton Woods agreement, it was recognized that a rigid policy of fixed exchange rates would be too inflexible. It would probably break down just as the gold standard had. In some cases, a country's attempts to reduce its money supply growth and correct a persistent balance of payment deficit could force the country into recession and create high unemployment. The architects of the Bretton Woods agreement wanted to avoid high unemployment, so they build limited flexibility into the system. Two major features of the IMF Articles of Agreement fostered this flexibility: IMF lending facilities and adjustable parities.

The IMF stood ready to lend foreign currencies to members to tide them over during short periods of balance of payments deficits, when a rapid tightening of monetary or fiscal policy would hurt domestic employment. A pool of gold and currencies contributed by IMF members provided the resources for these lending operations. A persistent balance of payments deficit can lead to a depletion of a country's reserves of foreign currency, forcing it to devalue its currency. By providing deficit–laden countries with short-term foreign currency loans, IMF funds would buy time for countries to bring down their inflation rates and reduce their balance of payments deficits. The belief was that such loans would reduce pressures for devaluation and allow for a more orderly and less painful adjustment.

Countries were to be allowed to borrow a limited amount from the IMF without adhering to any specific agreements. However, extensive drawings from IMF funds would require a country to agree to increasingly stringent IMF supervision of its macroeconomics policies. Heavy borrowers from the IMF must agree to monetary and fiscal conditions set down by the IMF, which typically included IMF mandated targets on domestic money supply growth, exchange rate policy, tax policy, government spending, and so on.

NATIONAL TOURIST ORGANISATION

The NTO is the body responsible for the formulation and implementation of national tourist policy. It is the proper agency and instrument for the execution of the national government's responsibilities for the control, direction and promotion of tourism. All countries which are engaged in tourism have a national tourist organisation which plays a leading role in both the formulation and which plays a leading role in both the formulation and the implementation of the Government's tourism programme. This organization is also responsible for coordinating the different activities of all the bodies interested in tourism development. The national tourist organisation may be a full fledged ministry, a directorate general, a department, corporation or a board.

There is, however, no set formula as to what constitutes the most satisfactory constitutional arrangement for the national tourism body. Tourism ranks as a full ministry in some countries with Minister enjoying a cabinet rank. Another arrangement in many countries is for tourism to share a Minister with information or with arts, sports and culture. Yet other possibilities include attaching the tourism office to the presidency of the council, putting it in the charge of an official of the rank of a Deputy Secretary with an occasional voice in the council of Ministers. In others it has semi-autonomous status of a Corporation and functions not as an organ of the Government but rather as a professional body outside it.

Functions

At the Estoril Seminar in 1966 in (England) it was agreed that the NTO would normally undertake the following functions.

- Research,
- Information and promotion within the country,
- Regularization of standards of lodging and restaurants,
- Control of activities of private travel agencies,
- Publicity overseas,
- Technical and judicial problems,
- International relations,
- Development of selected areas, and
- Overall tourism policy and promotion.

Research is a basic function of a national tourist organisation. A concomitant of institutional promotion is research into the tourism potential of the principal markets and investigation into the marketability of the country's tourist product. This is an important direct responsibility of NTO. Information and promotion within the country helps not only the actual international tourist but also the domestic tourist.

Control of activities of private travel agencies is another important supervisory role of the NTO. More and more tourists are utilizing the services of private travel agencies. It is essential that the tourists should get good and efficient service and protection.

Technical and judicial problems are those which are related with the administration of law. This is very crucial as on it will depend the quality of various services provided by various sectors. NTOs have to be very cautious while administering law. Technical problems on the other hand are concerned with the development and maintenance of various services. Continuous detailed assessment has to be made of the extent to which the infrastructure, superstructure and organisation planned are likely to meet future tourism demand.

International relations are very important part of tourism. International contacts resulting from tourism have always been among the most important ways of spreading ideas about other cultures. Tourism can be a vehicle for international understanding by way of bringing diverse people face to face. It has been cited as a major contributor to international goodwill and as a prime means of developing social and cultural understanding among all people of the world.

Development of selected areas to attract tourists is necessary. In every country there are hundreds of areas of tourist potential. However due to various constraints, it is not possible to develop all these areas. It is important to identify and select certain areas which have the maximum potential for tourism development.

Overall tourism policy and promotion is very essential as it helps in the optimum utilisation of resources. In calculating returns from investments in tourism, national tourist policy cannot restrict itself to limited considerations of immediate financial and economic profitability. It has to consider the beneficial effects of tourism of general national development where considerations of non-economic character may be equally or even more important, than purely economic returns, *viz.*, cultural considerations, social considerations, political considerations, etc.

The organisation and work of NTO

The administration

It will be concerned with the personnel of the organisation with the part to be played by tourism in the overall national developmental plan – with tradition, culture, effective liaison with concerned government departments like finance, home, planning, health, transport, communications, education, culture, public works, labour, etc.

The Production

It will be concerned with all those elements and activities which make up the tourism product. Production will include the inventory and assessment of the country's natural attractions and the development and protection of these assets–the listing, assessing and forecasting the country's tourism plans, the requirements in infrastructure where tourist development is planned, the drawing up of plans for regional or area development, the establishment of close relations with the hotel, catering and transport sectors of tourism, the requirements in infrastructure where tourist development is planned, the drawing up of plans for regional or area development, the establishment of close relations with the hotel, catering and transport sectors of tourism etc.

The Marketing

It will be concerned with research into the principal and potential tourist markets, their size, socio-economic characteristics, preferences of tourists for food and accommodation, spending power and the like, with sales promotion, public relations, advertising, maintenance of overseas offices, etc.

The Finance

It will involve investment in financing of tourism in the country like providing financial assistance for approved tourist projects; approve loans or grants for hotels, the provision of amenities, etc.

IHA (International Hotel Association)

Founded on 18th March, 1946 in London on the initiative of Societe Suisse des Hoteliers, the International Hotel Association (IHA) replaced the International Hotel Mens Associations set up in June, 1869 and International Hotel Alliance set up in April, 1925. The main aim of the new association was to bring together members who could be of mutual benefit to each other. The IHA was registered by a French Ministerial Decree on 23 September, 1949 having its headquarters in Paris.

The priority objectives of IHA include the protection and coordination of hotel interests in their relations with travel agencies who often play an important intermediary role between hotels and clients. Through the IHA/UFTAA Convention, there is a formal codification and confirmation of international practice governing relations between hoteliers and travel agencies. It informs hoteliers on their rights concerning payment, commission, cancellation, late arrival or no-show and relevant compensations.

Membership

IHA has a membership spanning 160 countries, comprising hotel and restaurants whether chains, both national or international, or individual establishments, who wish to participate directly in the Association's activities, even whilst being represented by their National Associations.

In addition, there are hotels and tourist personalities as individual members. Affiliates like hotel schools, training centres, tourist organisations, suppliers and services companies etc., also participate in IHA activities. The Association today represents more than 700,000 hotels and restaurants throughout 160 countries and more than seven million hotel industry wage earners.

Aims:

- To federate National Hotel Association of all countries;
- To study problems affecting the international hotel industry and international tourist traffic including re-establishment of free traffic, economic policy for hotels and restaurants, hotel guides, international currency exchanges, hotel insurances and conditions of work and personnel;
- To create an international employment service for qualified hotel personnel;
- To inform members of international problems concerning hotels; and
- To give commercial information concerning travel agencies.

Services provided

- Annual IHA international meetings
- International Hotel Guidebook
- Hotels & Restaurants International
- International Bibliography
- The World Directory of Travel Agents.

IHRA (International Hotel and Restaurants Association)

At international level, the interests of hotels and restaurants are represented by the International Hotel and Restaurants Association (IHRA). Founded in 1947 and representing Hotel Associations of some one hundred and fifty countries, IHRA is based in Paris. It interacts with other international organisations relating to travel and tourism like WTO, ILO, UNO, IATA, UFTAA etc. To train the hotel personnel, the IHRA has a training cell-with a special focus on the training of personnel from developing countries. It has two regional offices one in Asia Pacific and the other in Latin America.

ACTIVITIES

(1) Monitor issues that are raised by major international organizations involved in tourism.

(2) Represent the collective industry interests before policy makers.

(3) Lobby for better recognition of the hospitality industry worldwide.

(4) Lobby against damaging or costly attempts to regulate the industry.

(5) Create Global Councils around industry issues to debate positions & create s solutions.

(6) Listen to its members to ensure that all issues are addressed.

(7) Create Programs to serve the industry (i.e., International Worker Exchange, Youth Councils, Youth at Risk...)

(8) Provides a website platform for members to secure relevant information on the industry worldwide.

(9) Plan a series of informative Council and Board meetings and an annual Congress.

(10) Provide support where requested to lend weight to local and regional issues.

ACHIEVEMENTS

Protecting Your Bottom Line

- Ensured Flexibility of Working Conditions.
- Opposed Redundant & Costly Standards & Regulations.
- Protected Members' Interest on "International Hotel Classification".
- Fought Increased Copyright Licensing Fees.
- Battled Trademark Violations.

Spearheading Other Initiatives

- Sustainable Development of Tourism via the IH&RA Annual Environmental Award with UNEP and publications and training packs like "Sowing the Seeds of Change".
- Co-Created World Heritage Site Hotel Programme (Memories of the Future Restoration Project with UNESCO).
- Founding Co-drafter of "ECPAT Code" of Conduct for the Protection of Children from Sexual Exploitation in Travel & Tourism.
- Safety in the Workplace – HIV/AIDS in the Workplace, published with UN/AIDS.

Recognised Experts in Our Field

- Contributed to Hospitality Statistics & Rescarch.
- Published the joint IH&RA/WTO Report on Hotel Classification, the only comparative analysis and inventory of worldwide hotel classification schemes.

- Served as Expert Advisor to Countries on Hotel Classification Systems (Jordan, Syria).

IH&RA WORKING STYLE

Being a membership-driven not-for-profit organisation, IH&RA works through a series of Councils focusing the expertise of its members on issues considered of vital importance to membership and to the industry generally. These councils identify issues, set priorities and propose future action.

They are:

- NACE – National Association Chief Executives – Council
- Chains Council
- Global Councils

These Councils make recommendations to the **Board of Directors**, the main executive organ of the IH&RA. The Board provides strategic direction to the Association deliberates on recommendations for action from the Councils and reviews IH&RA activities and management. The Board meets three times a year, once in conjunction with the Annual Congress and twice in stand-alone meetings.

The Board of Directors makes recommendations to the **General Assembly**, the supervisory organ of the Association. The General Assembly meets annually to review the activities and management of the Association, elect its President, Vice-Presidents and officers forming the Board of Directors. The General Assembly approves the accounts of the previous year and the budget for the coming year as well as membership fees. It also approves new members, resignation and dismissal of members.

IATA

Mission: To represent, lead and serve the airline industry.

Leadership

- Chairman of IATA Board of Governors (2009-2010), Tony Tyler, CEO, Cathay Pacific Airways
- IATA Director General and CEO, Giovanni Bisignani

Membership

- IATA membership: some 230 airlines, 125 countries.
- Flights by IATA members represent 93% of world's international scheduled traffic (Available Seat Kilometres)
- IATA members total freight – 42.4 million tonnes in 2008, of which 28.2 million tonnes were international
- IATA members total passengers 2008 (scheduled) – 1.6 billion of which 709 million were international

History

IATA was founded in Havana, Cuba, in April 1945

IATA Offices

- IATA has 74 offices in 68 countries covering 148 nations
- Head Office: Montreal, Canada
- Executive Office: Geneva, Switzerland
- Regional Offices in Amman, Beijing, Johannesburg, Miami, Moscow, Singapore, Washington

IATA Annual General Meeting & World Air Transport Summit

- Formalizes industry positions on industry and public policy issues and provides a focus for emerging industry issues
- Attended by representatives from IATA member airlines, industry partners, international and regional associations, manufacturers and suppliers and government
- The first AGM was held in Montreal, Canada in October 1945
- The 2009 AGM is being held in Kuala Lumpur, Malaysia on 7-9 June 2009
- The last time that this event was hosted in Malaysia was in 1995.
- The 66th AGM will be held in Berlin, Germany on 6-8 June 2010

IATA Financial Services

- In 2008 IATA handled some US$350 billion
- IATA Clearing House—US$50 billion
- IATA Currency Clearance Service — US$30.5 billion
- Billing and Settlement Plan (BSP) — US$240 billion
- Cargo Account Settlement Systems (CASS) — US$28 billion
- Other – US$1.5 billion

2009 Priorities

Safety

- Conduct 80 ISAGO audits, improving safety while reducing redundant audits and ramp injuries and damage.
- Launch Global Safety Information Centre by:
- Expanding IATA's incident data programme, to include IOSA, ISAGO and other data sources
- Developing and distributing Runway Safety Toolkit.

Environment

- Achieve a reduction of at least 10 million tonnes of CO_2 from operations and infrastructure.
- 15 airlines participating in industry carbon offset programme and travel agency sales captured through at least one GDS.
- Secure the support of ICAO/GIACC for the IATA four-pillar strategy and opposition to environmental taxation.

Simplifying the Business

Fast Travel Program:

- 10 airlines offer "bags ready-to-go" (2 shared environment locations);
- 10 airlines offer self-boarding (1 with international passenger identity checks);
- 10 airlines offer self-service bag recovery (2 shared environments); and
- 75 CUSS sites offering document scanning.

BCBP

- 60% airport passenger capability.

BIP

- Complete diagnosis visits to 20 of the top 80 mishandling airports.

IATA e-freight

- Expand to 23 new locations, 44 new airports and 3 more documents.

Financial

- Achieve savings/cost avoidance of USD 1.5 billion in industry taxes, charges & fuel fees, including at least USD 1 billion in real reductions.
- Achieve a 10% reduction in BSP and 15% reduction in CASS unit charge

Our mission at the Air Transport Industry's side

Air transport is one of the most dynamic industries in the world. The International Air Transport Association (IATA) is its global trade organization.

Over 60 years, IATA has developed the commercial standards that built a global industry. Today, IATA's mission is to represent, lead and serve the airline industry. Its members comprise *some 230 airlines* - the world's leading passenger and cargo airlines among them - representing 93 percent of scheduled international air traffic.

Representing...

IATA seeks to improve understanding of the industry among decision makers and increase awareness of the benefits that aviation brings to national and global economies. It fights for the interests of airlines across the globe, challenging unreasonable rules and charges, holding regulators and governments to account, and striving for sensible regulation.

Leading...

IATA's aim is to help airlines help themselves by simplifying processes and increasing passenger convenience while reducing costs and improving efficiency. The groundbreaking Simplifying the Business initiative is crucial in this area. Moreover, safety is IATA's number one priority, and IATA's goal is to continually improve safety standards, notably through IATA's Operational Safety Audit (IOSA). Another main concern is to minimize the impact of air transport on environment.

Serving...

IATA ensures that people and goods can move around the global airline network as easily as if they were on a single airline in a single country. In addition, it provides essential professional support to all industry stakeholders with a wide range of products and expert services, such as publications, training and consulting. IATA's financial systems also help carriers and the travel industry maximize revenues.

... For the benefit for all parties involved:

- For consumers, IATA simplifies the travel and shipping processes, while keeping costs down. Passengers can make one telephone call to reserve a ticket, pay in one currency and then use the ticket on several airlines in several countries.
- IATA allows airlines to operate safely, securely, efficiently and economically under clearly defined rules.
- IATA serves as an intermediary between airlines and passenger as well as cargo agents via neutrally applied agency service standards and centralized financial systems.
- A large network of industry suppliers and service providers gathered by IATA provides solid expertise to airlines in a variety of industry solutions.
- For governments, IATA seeks to ensure they are well informed about the complexities of the aviation industry to ensure better, long-term decisions.

WTTC

WORLD
TRAVEL &
TOURISM
COUNCIL

From the initial discussions between industry CEOs in the late 1980s to the Council as it is today, WTTC has achieved many things and developed enormously, but its core mission remains the same – to raise the awareness of the full economic and social impact and potential of the Travel & Tourism industry.

WTTC – the early years

James Robinson III, then of American Express, and a group of CEOs came to the realization in the 1980s that although Travel & Tourism was the largest industry in the world and the biggest provider of jobs, nobody knew it. There was no consolidated data or voice for the industry to convey this message to the elected officials and policy makers.

The industry was considered frivolous or "non-essential". This realization lead to an initial meeting in Paris in 1989 where Henry Kissinger sent out a powerful message to the CEOs gathered, saying that they represented the world's biggest industry but that it was not recognized as the industry was too fragmented.

WTTC was therefore established in 1990 with James Robinson III as Chairman and Geoffrey Lipman as President.

At the time of the first AGM in Washington in 1991, 32 Members made up the Council and the atmosphere was one of nervousness in the aftermath of the Gulf War. At the meeting, objectives were established and issues were addressed. The three main issues that came out of the early meetings were:

- promoting recognition of the travel industry's economic contribution
- expanding markets in harmony with the environment
- reducing barriers to growth

WTTC – Development through the 1990s

By the time Bob Burns took over as Chairman in 1993, there were 68 Members and WTTC was focusing on developing its economic research with its partner WEFA. The Tourism Satellite Account (TSA) offers WTTC and its Members the possibility to substantiate their message with concrete figures, which have become widely recognized as a credible resource. In 1999, the TSA was finally recognized by the United Nations at the World Conference on the Measurement of the Economic Impact of Tourism.

WTTC, with its partner Oxford Economic Forecasting, now produces annual forecasts for 174 countries and carries out in-depth studies for a growing number of countries or regions each year.

The Council expanded its activities during the 1990s to include air transport liberalization, education and training, taxation and sustainable development. In this regard, WTTC set up the World Travel & Tourism Human Resources Centre in Vancouver and the World Travel & Tourism Taxation Policy Centre in the USA.

WTTC launched the GREEN GLOBE environmental awareness programme, providing a practical, cost-efficient means for all Travel & Tourism companies to make environmental improvements. GREEN GLOBE is still going strong today, operating as an autonomous organization.

Agenda 21 for Travel & Tourism was a public/private sector effort that WTTC was involved in with the World Tourism Organization (WTO) and the Earth Council. Its aim was to ensure that as Travel & Tourism grows globally, its impact at local level does not have an unnecessarily adverse effect on the environment.

By 1997, membership had reached the target 100 and it was estimated that more than 100 million jobs would be created in the next decade. The Council's first ever Summit, focused on jobs, and took place in Vilamoura, Portugal. The outcome of the event took the form of the 'Vilamoura Declaration', which called on all policy makers to factor Travel & Tourism into their employment policies.

Whilst WTTC continued to concentrate on global issues, it began to turn its attention to particular regions of the world that were deemed in need of special focus on raising awareness of the potential impact of the industry among governments.

Latin America was the first region taken for such an initiative. The WTTC Latin America Programme was run from January 1999 – December 2001. During this period WTTC worked with key players from the region to raise awareness of the economic importance of Travel & Tourism in Argentina, Brazil, Ecuador and Peru. Whilst WTTC no longer has an active initiative in Latin America, we continue to recognize the importance of Travel & Tourism in this region.

The most successful regional initiative was the India Initiative. WTTC Executive Committee Member PRS Oberoi agreed to be the patron of the programme and its Members, with the support of WTTC, have been successful in influencing tourism policy in the country. WTTC was credited with inspiring the Prime Minister to speak of the importance of the tourism industry in 2002. The India Initiative now operates autonomously from the WTTC headquarters.

WTTC in the 21st Century

The new millennium saw the Council's first ever change of President. After ten years at the helm, Geoffrey Lipman stepped down and Jean-Claude Baumgarten was taken on to take the organization forward. With 25 years of experience in the airline industry, mainly in senior management at Air France, he was the ideal choice.

The millennium began positively for the industry, and WTTC, who convened its 2nd World Travel & Tourism Summit in Vilamoura with the President and Prime Minister of Portugal in attendance.

On September 11, 2001, WTTC management were in New York City to sign a new partnership agreement with the Travel Business Roundtable (TBR), a US-based lobbying organization for the travel and transportation industries. However, the terrorist attacks that took place in the US that day shocked the world and had a devastating effect on the Travel & Tourism industry.

WTTC's Members suffered greatly as a result of the attacks and consequently some withdrew their membership from the Council. However, WTTC took positive steps to regain the public's confidence in the industry and to encourage the world to begin travelling again. Internally, staff held daily crisis meetings and externally, WTTC gathered together its friends and partner organizations to form a global coalition of industry bodies.

The coalition's statement called upon governments to work together in partnership to ensure that measures to strengthen security were effective, harmonized internationally and applied globally. The aim was to help to restore consumer confidence in Travel & Tourism, the economic health of the industry and the livelihood of all those who worked in it.

WTTC also ran an advertising campaign, "Go out and meet your neighbours", which appeared in the global print media, including Time and Newsweek. For the first time ever, the annual TSA research for that year was revised to take into account the potential loss on the industry as a result of the attacks.

By 2003, a number of global events had affected the world to such an extent that the industry was a very different place. The war in Iraq, the SARS crisis and increased terrorism meant that WTTC had to continue and extend its campaign to rebuild confidence among travellers.

The Summit in 2003 was the first one to be opened up to the global press and media and the theme – Building New Tourism – came out of the atmosphere in the industry at that time. WTTC released data on the impact of the SARS crisis on the industry in China, Hong Kong, Singapore and Vietnam and attracted a great deal of media attention.

The outcomes of the Summit were deemed so rich that they shaped the future of the Council's vision and the Blueprint for New Tourism, the Council's mission publication, was launched later that year.

The following two Summits, Driving Change in Doha, Qatar and Realizing the Potential in New Delhi, India, developed and grew and the event has become the major event in the industry's calendar. The revolutionary 'in the round' format, conceived by WTTC, uses media representatives as moderators and facilitates genuine, lively discussion.

WTTC Today

The World Travel & Tourism Council of 2007 is an organization that has hugely developed since its inception, yet it still holds the same core values and purpose. The three main messages that form the framework for the Blueprint for New Tourism are in keeping with the vision of the CEOs who founded the Council in 1990:

(1) Governments recognizing Travel & Tourism as a top priority

(2) Business balancing economics with people, culture and environment

(3) A shared pursuit of long-term growth and prosperity

The Global Travel & Tourism Summit, which will take place in Washington, DC, in 2006 now attracts bids each year from destinations who are keen to host the Summit.

The annual TSA research now covers 174 countries and in-depth country reports are being requested by more and more countries, with Brunei, Romania, Greece, Namibia and an update of the China report currently in the pipeline. There are also plans to carry out TSA reports for individual cities.

WTTC has developed a Crisis Impact Forecasting Model, to assess the potential impact of a crisis on the industry within 48 hours. It has been put into place following the crises of the London and Egypt bombings in 2005.

Regional initiatives are underway in China and the EU, encouraging discourse between the public and private sectors.

The Council now attracts an unprecedented amount of regional interest. In July 2005, following the release of the research to show the potential impact of the London bombings on the UK economy, the number of articles written about WTTC was 5.5 times more than the same period the previous year. WTTC's Members remain the driving force behind its activities and policies. The industry has changed such that the membership now includes the entire spectrum of the Travel & Tourism industry, from airlines, to tour operators, online distribution, cruise lines, investment companies, hotels, car transport, and the gaming industry.

International Civil Aviation Organization

The International Civil Aviation Organization (ICAO), a UN specialized agency, is the global forum for civil aviation. The organization was established in 1944. ICAO works to achieve its vision of safe, secure, and sustainable development of civil aviation through cooperation of its member states. To implement this vision, the organization has established six strategic objectives for the period 2005 to 2010:

(1) Enhance global civil aviation safety,

(2) Enhance global civil aviation security,

(3) Minimize the adverse effect of global civil aviation on the environment,

(4) Enhance the efficiency of aviation operations,

(5) maintain the continuity of aviation operations, and

(6) Strengthen law governing international civil aviation. Visit the ICAO Web site at http://www.icao.int

DEVELOPMENTAL ORGANIZATIONS (INTERNATIONAL AND NATIONAL)

Financing is always a major problem in tourism development. Large financial organizations are willing to make developmental loans. Examples include the World Bank (United States), International Finance Corporation (United States), the OPEC Fund for International Development (Austria), African Development Bank, East African Development Bank (Uganda), Inter-American Development Bank (United States), Caribbean Development Bank (Barbados), Asian Development Bank (Philippines), European Investment Bank (Luxembourg), European Regional Development Fund (Belgium), European Bank for Reconstruction and Development (United Kingdom), Islamic Development Bank (Saudi Arabia), and the Arab Fund for Economic and Social Development (Kuwait). Examples of national organizations are FONATUR (Mexico) and Embratur (Brazil). Further sources include governments of countries that want additional hotel development or other supply components and are willing to make low-interest loans or grants or offer other financial inducements for such types of development.

Organization for Economic Cooperation and Development

The Organization for Economic Cooperation and Development (OECD) was set up under a convention, signed in Paris on December 14, 1960, that provides that the OECD shall promote policies designed to (1) achieve the highest sustainable economic growth and employment and a rising standard of living in member countries while maintaining financial stability, and thus to contribute to the development of the world economy; (2) contribute to sound economic expansion in member as well as non-member countries in the process of economic development; and (3) contribute to the expansion of world trade on a multilateral, nondiscriminatory basis in accordance with international obligations.

Members of OECD are Australia, Austria, Belgium, Canada, Czech Republic, Denmark, Finland, France, Germany, Greece, Hungary, Iceland, Ireland, Italy, Japan, Korea, Luxembourg, Mexico, Netherlands, New Zealand, Norway, Poland, Portugal, Slovak Republic, Spain, Sweden, Switzerland, Turkey, the United Kingdom, and the United States. OECD's Tourism Committee acts as a forum of exchange for monitoring policies and structural changes affecting the development of international tourism. It encourages further liberalization of tourism activities, both within and outside the OECD area, and has undertaken the development of innovative statistics to improve the understanding of the role of tourism in the economy. Visit the OECD Web site at http://www.oecd.org.

REGIONAL INTERNATIONAL ORGANIZATIONS

Pacific Asia Travel Association

Founded in Hawaii in 1951 to develop, promote, and facilitate travel to and among the destination areas in and bordering the Pacific Ocean, the Pacific Asia Travel Association

(PATA) brings together governments, airline and steamship companies, hoteliers, tour operators, travel agents, and a wide range of other tourism-related organizations. Today, PATA is the global leader in Pacific Asian tourism. Members exchange ideas, seek solutions to problems, and participate in shaping the future of travel in Asia and the Pacific area. Membership totals over two thousand organizations world-wide. Since its founding, the association has become an important source of accurate, up to date information for its members in the fields of marketing, development, information, education, sustainability, and other travel-related activities. PATA's activities and long-range plans are examined and adjusted each year at the association's annual conference.

The future of the tourism industry depends on protecting the region's environmental, heritage, and cultural resources. PATA develops industry-wide initiatives and sponsors conservation conferences to ensure sustainable growth. The association also honors significant accomplishments in this arena under its Gold Awards program.

The work of the official PATA organization is greatly augmented by thousands of travel professionals who belong to a global network of PATA chapters. PATA's operational headquarters is in Bangkok, Thailand; the association's administrative head-quarters is located in Oakland, California. Other offices are located in Sydney, Beijing, Dubai, and Frankfurt. Visit the association's Web site at http://www.pata.org.

European Travel Commission

The European Travel Commission (ETC) is the strategic alliance that provides for the collaboration between national tourism organizations (NTOs) of thirty-six member countries. Founded in 1948, the ETC has a unique role in functioning as a "National Tourism Office of Europe". Its goal is to attract millions of potential and existing overseas customers from the major overseas markets to come to Europe. This is done through promotional campaigns and industry trade shows. The headquarters of the ETC is located in Brussels, Belgium. Visit their Web site at: http://www.visiteurope.com.

LET US SUM UP

In India we have one association called IHA named Indian Hotel Association similar to the line of IHA – International Hotel Association. Find out from various sources (website, book, journal etc) about the functions of IHA and mention its contributions in development of the Indian Hotel Industry.

The ***United Nations World Tourism Organization (UNWTO)****, headquartered in Madrid, Spain, is a United Nations agency dealing with questions relating to tourism. It compiles the World Tourism Rankings. The World Tourism Organization is a significant global body concerned with the collection and collation of statistical information on international tourism. This organization represents public sector tourism bodies from most countries in the world and the publication of its data makes possible comparisons of the flow and growth of tourism on a global scale.*

The International Monetary Fund (IMF) is an international organization that oversees the global financial system by following the macroeconomic policies of its member countries; in particular those with an impact on exchange rates and the balance of payments. It also offers financial and technical assistance to its members, making it an international lender of last resort. Its headquarters are located in Washington, D.C., USA.

The International Monetary Fund was created in 1944 , with a goal to stabilize exchange rates and supervise the reconstruction of the world's international payment system. Countries contributed to a pool which could be borrowed from, on a temporary basis, by countries with payment imbalances. (Condon, 2007)

The NTO is the body responsible for the formulation and implementation of national tourist policy. It is the proper agency and instrument for the execution of the national government's responsibilities for the control, direction and promotion of tourism. All countries which are engaged in tourism have a national tourist organisation which plays a leading role in both the formulation and which plays a leading role in both the formulation and the implementation of the Government's tourism programme. This organization is also responsible for coordinating the different activities of all the bodies interested in tourism development. The national tourist organisation ma be a full fledged ministry, a directorate general, a department, corporation or a board.

Founded on 18th March, 1946 in London on the initiative of Societe Suisse des Hoteliers, the International Hotel Association (IHA) replaced. The International Hotel Mens Associations set up in June 1869 and International Hotel Alliance set up in April 1925. The main aim of the new association was to bring together members who could be of mutual benefit to each other. The IHA was registered by a French Ministerial Decree of 23 September, 1949 having its headquarters in Paris.

The priority objectives of IHA include the protection and coordination of hotel interests in their relations with travel agencies who often play an important intermediary role between hotels and clients. Through the IHA/UFTAA Convention, there is a formal codification and confirmation of international practice governing relations between hoteliers and travel agencies. It informs hoteliers on their rights concerning payment, commission, cancellation, late arrival or no-show and relevant compensations.

At international level, the interests of hotels and restaurants are represented by the international Hotel and Restaurants Association (IHRA). Founded in 1947 and representing Hotel Associations of some one hundred and fifty countries, IHRA is based in Paris. It interacts with other international organisations relating to travel and tourism like WOT, ILO, UNO, IATA, and UFTAA etc. To train the hotel personnel, the IHRA has a training cell- with a special focus on the training of personnel from developing countries. It has two regional offices one in Asia Pacific and the other in Latin America.

Governments have to play a key role in the planning development, regulation and marketing of tourism. Tourism helps every government because it provides employment to the citizens and earns foreign currency for the country. Therefore, practically every government in the world, irrespective of its size has a NTO.

CHECK YOUR PROGRESS

(A) Fill in the blanks

(i) IMF stands for................................

(ii) NTO stands for..............................

(iii) IHA stands for ....

(B) True/ False

(i) WTO building is in Madrid.

(ii) IMF look for the global financial system.

(iii) NTO is responsible for formulation and implementation of National Tourist Policy.

(C) Fill in the Blanks

(i) IHA was founded in the year ....

(ii) The two IHRA regional offices are located; one in .... and the other office in ....

(iii) IHA has a membership spanning ....Countries.

LESSON AND ACTIVITY

Explain the role of Indian Government in the Development of Tourism Industry in North –East India.

KEY WORDS

IMF (International Monetary Fund): The International Monetary Fund (IMF) is an international organization that oversees the global financial system by following the macroeconomic policies of its member countries.

IHRA (International Hotel and Restaurant Association): It interacts with other international organisations relating to travel and tourism like WOT, ILO, UNO, IATA, UFTAA

IHA (International Hotel Association): It mainly emphasize on the protection and coordination of hotel interests in their relations with travel agencies.

WTO (World Tourism Organisation): The World Tourism Organization is a significant global body concerned with the collection and collation of statistical information on international tourism.

QUESTIONS FOR DISCUSSION

(1) Explain the involvement of state in the development of tourism industry.

(2) Write a brief note on World Tourism Organisation.

(3) Explain the functions of WTO.

(4) Explain the role of IMF in world economy.

(5) Explain the organisation of NTO and its contributions in the development of tourist industry.

(6) Describe the activities of NTO.

(7) Explain the role of IHA and IHRA.

CHECK YOUR PROGRESS: MODEL ANSWER

(A) *(i)* International Monetary Fund

(ii) National Tourism Organisation

(iii) International Hotel Association

(B) *(i)* T *(ii)* T *(iii)* T

(C) *(i)* 1916 *(ii)* Asia Pacific, Latin America *(iii)* 160 countries.

❑ ❑ ❑

4

Travel Barriers, Travel Advisories, Crisis Management

Chapter Outline

- *Introduction*
- *Barriers to Travels*
- *Risk Management*
- *Crisis Management*
- *Political Stability & Political Risk*
- *Influence of Govt. on Travel Advisories*

Learning Objective

At the conclusion of this lesson you should be able to understand:

- *Different barriers to travels.*
- *Risk management in tourism industry*
- *Crisis management in tourism industry.*
- *Impact of political instability on tourism industry.*
- *Government's role as travel advisories.*

"The use of travelling is to regulate imagination by reality, and instead of thinking how things may be, to see them as they are."

— Samuel Johnson (1709-1784)
British author.

INTRODUCTION

Even the tourism industry is growing at a rocket speed but there are some barriers to travel may be imposed by the state government or else artificially created. Risk management is an importance aspect along with the crisis management.

BARRIERS TO TRAVELS

Obviously immigration laws and visa requirements, language barriers, currency exchange rates and infrastructure (roads, power, etc., in less developed nations). And not least customs and cultures, think of women in Islamic countries.

Wealthy countries obviously want tourism but have to consider the fact that some tourists could be immigrants in disguise. That's why most countries require a certain amount of currency to enter the country. And also why they have time limitations on visas that vary depending on the "risk" of the country of origin.

Language barriers can be overcome for airports, hotels and conferences but not for the entire country. Foreign languages are one thing, but unfamiliar alphabets often put travellers at a disadvantage (Latin, Russian, Chinese, Japanese, Thai, Hebrew etc.).

Currency exchange rates can vary wildly and expose hotels and travellers alike to sudden changes in costs. Wealthy tourists will always be able to afford it, but the masses might not be that lucky.

Without adequate infrastructure there is little hope of mass tourism. Some African countries have a lot to offer but also need to be able to effectively handle both travellers and their needs (food, services and equipment). Infrastructure is very costly to create and maintain, but if there's a return on their investment it can be done.

Some of the barriers are as listed below:

- Passports, entry and exit visas
- Exchange controls, currency restrictions, travel allowances
- Travel insurance
- Exit taxes
- Customs regulations, duties
- Equity requirements
- Domestic policy bias
- Transparency
- Foreign remittances
- Import restrictions, domestic content laws, tariffs
- Domestic personnel requirements
- Inefficient telecommunications systems

- Language
- Extensive documentation

TYPES OF TOURISM BARRIERS

- **Non-tariff barriers:** travel allowance restrictions (TAR's), e.g., currency controls, duty-free limits, compulsory bank deposits, documentation, quotas
- **Tariff barriers:** e.g., departure taxes.
- **Subsidies:** e.g., preferential exchange rates, price concessions.
- **Restrictions on Firms:** e.g., licenses, labour laws, investment laws.

RISK MANAGEMENT

What is a Risk?

A risk is the chance of something adverse happening. Risk arises out of uncertainty. It is measured in terms of the likelihood of it happening and the consequences if it does happen.

Fig. 4.1. Destinations can be vulnerable

What is Risk Management?

It is as much about identifying opportunities as it is about avoiding losses.

Why do you need to manage risks?

Ignoring the risks that apply to your business activities or the events you have planned could impact on:

- the health and safety of employees, customers, volunteers and participants
- your reputation, credibility and status
- public and customer confidence in your organisation
- your financial position; and
- equipment and the environment
- Adopting effective risk management techniques can help you to improve safety and business performance in your organisation.

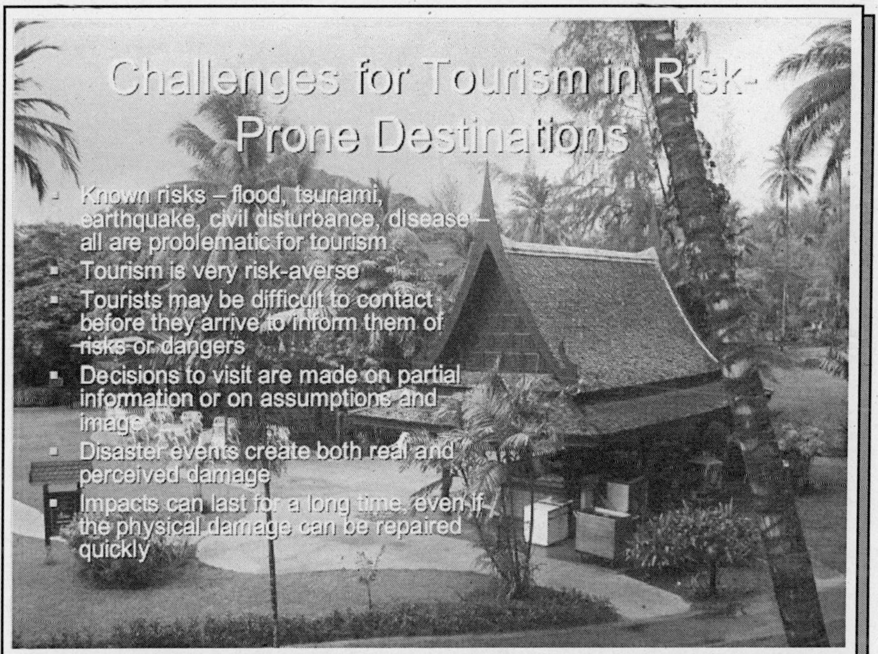

Fig. 4.2. Risk prone destination – Challenges

Benefits of Risk Management

There are many benefits in implementing risk management procedures. Some of these include:

- more effective strategic planning;
- better cost control;
- enhancing shareholder value by minimizing losses and maximising opportunities;
- increased knowledge and understanding of exposure to risk a systematic, well-informed and thorough method of decision making;
- minimized disruptions;
- better utilisation of resources;
- strengthening culture for continued improvement; and
- creating a best practice and quality organisation.

Why is risk management important to the tourism industry?

Risk management and risk assessment has become, and will remain, a vital component of the way all businesses operate within the tourism industry. Across the tourism industry, there is a multitude of opportunities for 'risks' to turn into 'disaster' or an upheaval event.

Tourism is particularly prone to external shocks, which by their nature are unpredictable and need to be addressed through effective crisis management processes. Tourism operators must ensure a detailed crisis management plan is in place to respond to the chance of an unforeseen event occurring.

Fig. 4.3. Tsunami Case

Security concerns, natural disasters and outbreaks of infectious diseases have a tremendous impact on the tourism industry. Contributions from industry and government to address traditional concerns for tourism, such as crime, as well as the very modern and relevant threats posed by terrorism and natural disasters such as Cyclone Larry, have all made the tourism industry very conscious of the need to protect its customers.

CRISIS MANAGEMENT

Undoubtedly, the tourism industry is one of the most susceptible and vulnerable industries to crises. Recent major events that had devastating impacts on the industry ranges from natural disasters to epidemics, and from mismanagement to terrorist attacks. These kinds of episodes are not confined to any geographical region, as crises respect no political or cultural boundaries. Two major recent events illustrate this point: the BSE crisis in the UK in the 1990s, which was followed by the foot and mouth disease in 2000 and 2001, crippled the industry in several regions of England. Most recently, the events of September 11th in New York and Washington changed the way the industry operates forever. Crises are not new to the tourism industry.

Definition of Crisis Management

Crisis situation is an event that has a fundamental impact on any organization's reputation, image, its future liabilities and its ability to operate. Yet to avoid a crisis becoming a catastrophe, many people need to be aware of their roles and responsibilities. Furthermore, the employees also need to be familiar with the problems that they are likely to encounter after an incident (Taylor, 1999). Crises inevitably receive media attention and consequently attract public interest, particularly from potential tourists. Hence, corporate image, reputation and financial outcomes may be seriously undermined by crises. Businesses that is inadequately prepared as well as destinations where consumer safety is compromised risk losing customers. Examples of widely cited costs of past crisis situations are Pan Am Lockerbie ($652 million) and P&O Zeebrugge sinking ($70 million) (**Regester and Larkin,** 2002).

Crisis management relates to managing a critical event that may have major repercussions on the viability of business. According to **Regster and Larkin,** (2002, p. 122), the core of crisis management lies in the 'finding, cultivating and harvesting' of the success that could potentially stem from a crisis. The basic outline of a crisis management operation is to recognise that a crisis is occurring, to take appropriate action and to make that action public, i.e., to be seen to be dealing with and attempting to rectify the situation. An effective crisis management strategy allows an organisation to reduce the potential risk to its reputation presented by the crises or disaster situation. This is vital since poorly handled crisis and the resulting bad publicity can affect the public's perception of a company for a much longer time period than the duration of the crisis itself.

Importance of Managing Crisis in the Tourism (and Hospitality) Industry

Crises within tourism and hospitality must be handled with particular care for a number of reasons: firstly, the majority of the industry relies on discressionary expenditure by the consumer. This means that tourism and hospitality organisations are particularly sensitive to ill-will, since the purchase of the product or service is not fundamentally important to the consumers and they can (relatively) easily go without. The marketing of tourism products and services depends largely on the perception the tourist holds about the destination and the degree of risk he/she is willing to bear. The higher the perceived risk, insecurity and uncertainty regarding a tourist destination, the lower the demand for it.

Therefore, any element that contributes to an increase in the perceived risk in using a tourism product or service will negatively affect the consumer's purchasing behavior. This consequence also applies to generic business crises (Gondlez-Hmero and Pratt, 1998).

Theories and Methods Employed in Managing Crisis. The crisis situations typically evolve in cycles of pre-crisis, crisis and post-crisis. The company (and its environment) start from a normal situation and eventually return back to it. It is the events between these stages of normality that are of interest in this paper. A number of principles have been developed in the area of crisis management, with most theories of best practice stemming from experience.

The key issue in crisis management is preparation in advance: there are several important decisions that should be made before the actual crisis event. These are crisis management training; planned prevention and immediate response. In order for crisis management to be effective, it should be practiced pro-actively with the aim to defend and protect the interests of the company. In essence, crisis management is part of the strategic planning required from an organisation.

The best method of crisis management is preparation before a crisis occurs — first implementing effort to prevent the crisis from occurring at all, and then developing the ability to react immediately and effectively should an outbreak or incident arise. This means a disaster (crisis) plan must be developed.

Good crisis management requires policies to deal with each stage of a crisis situation if a destination is to prevent or minimize a crisis. First, one needs detection policies. This requires a monitoring system of the macro-environment to make sure one is detecting problems and anticipating tomorrow rather than reacting to yesterday. The second requirement is for prevention or minimization policies. This involves such areas as legislation, law enforcement, security devices, and safety and security training for employees.

The third need is for readiness policies that require leadership for crisis coordination, emergency response, and assistance for families, internal and external communications, information dissemination, and media relations. Fourth, response policies, which include effective emergency response and answering the public call for information, should be put in place. Telling the truth is a vital crisis management policy. Finally, recovery policies to enable a return to normalcy are a high priority. These include the rebuilding process, information dissemination, publicity, public relations, and marketing.

The concern of the United Nations World Tourism Organization (UNWTO) about crises resulted in their creating the UNWTO Recovery Committee. This committee has published Crisis Guidelines for the Tourism Industry, which offers a one – step reference document suggesting specific actions to take before, during, and immediately after a crisis to get tourists returning to a destination as quickly as possible.

Methodology: A Case Study

Interviews with key members from the Greek passenger shipping industry are used to assess the industry sector's preparedness to handle potential crisis issues today.

A qualitative approach and in particular the in-depth interview method was adopted in order to gather primary information (**Sekaran,** 2003). Due to the sensitivity of the research topic complete anonymity of responding individuals was assured. The sample for the interviews consisted of twelve executives related to the Greek passenger shipping industry (four interviews per segment): managers of different passenger shipping companies; consultants and academics of crises management including media relations agencies in Greece; the regulatory and governmental agencies. The interviews took place during the Summer Months of 2003 and the interview language was Greek to ensure that the finer 'nuances' of verbal communication was captured. Back translation technique was used in question wording.

Findings and Discussion

In order for a company to be ready to respond to a crisis, the management needs to get prepared ahead of time. The most common problems to a shipping company are: wreckages, collisions, fire, economical crisis, labor accidents and other issues caused by external factors. The companies interviewed classified each situation according to its severity and responded accordingly. For instance, if loss of life is involved in the incident, then this is considered of primary importance and is handled as such by the teams. In a similar way, a mechanical problem that is faced on a regular basis may not require the same mobilization.

The industry has adopted a pro-active approach to their media handling by fostering good relations with local/national media through direct, regular and friendly communication. Press releases, press conferences as well as special edition publications (magazines and newsletters) are used to work together with the media and individual journalists. Such 'direct' lines of communication are valuable in crisis situations when the organization and the journalists can work together to ensure the accuracy of any news reports.

POLITICAL STABILITY & POLITICAL RISK

Political instability is described as a condition of a country where a government has been toppled, or is controlled by factions following a coup, or where basic functional pre-requisites for social-order control and maintenance are unstable and periodically disrupted" (**Cook,** 1990).

- Multifaceted and complex character
- Impact in various countries worldwide is multilevel and multidimensional.

The political aspects of tourism are interwoven with its economic consequences... tourism is not only a "continuation of politics" but an integral part of the world's political economy. In short, tourism is, or can be, a tool used not only for economic but for political means" (**Edgell,** 1990).

- Unwillingness on the part of many decision makers both in government and in the private sector to acknowledge the political nature of tourism.
- Lack of official interest in conducting research into the politics of tourism.
- Tourism not regarded as a serious scholarly subject.

Effects of Political violence

China – Tiananmen Square, June 4 1989

Prime time news coverage showed army tanks threatening the civilian population. After the Tiananmen Square incident Hotel occupancy rates in Beijing dipped below 30 per cent. Tourism earnings declined by $430 million in 1989 alone.

Effects of Military Coups

Fiji – 1987: As a result of a mainly non-Fijian government being elected. Two military coups occurred within four months. Qantas imposed a two-month ban on flights to Fiji, following the hijacking attempt of an Air New Zealand Boeing 747. Travel Insurance cover was withdrawn after negative Australian government travel advice.

Effects of Revolutions

Ejtrcito Zapatista de Liberacion National (EZLN) initiated an armed rebellion against the Mexican government. The revolution resulted in 145 to 500 deaths (figures vary depending on the source). 1994 visitation to Mexico dropped by 70 per cent.

Effects of Civil War

Yugoslavia – 1991, Army attacks Slovenia

Conflict continued for 10 days before moving to Croatia in 1991, and Bosnia-Herzegovina in1992 .Tour operators for Yugoslavia lost over one million bookings in 1991. Two years after the war, figures for Slovenian tourism are still far behind pre-war figures.

THE INFLUENCE OF GOVERNMENT TRAVEL ADVISORIES

- Governments issue regular travel advisories for their citizens warning them of risks in travelling to certain destinations.
- Governments can and do exert political pressure through tourism and use it as a promotional vehicle to convey a positive image or as a sanction against unfriendly countries.
- The tourist may take into account the perceived risk of travelling to destinations that receive government warnings, and therefore choose not to travel or may alter the travel destination.

Crisis Management Becomes Integral to Travel and Tourism

The announcement of Schedules for Terrorism Awareness Training Courses, developed by the Department of Homeland Security, directed toward stadiums and arenas, is but one more clear indication that terrorism — and the need to counter it — has become an integral part of our daily lives.

As discussed earlier, nowhere is the significance of the reality of terrorism more important than in tourism. Because we, in the tourism industry, are encouraging the members of any population to travel on a discretionary basis, we have a special obligation to do all we can to take every step possible to provide travellers with security.

Why do terrorists attack tourism centers? According to the Futurist, terrorists seek out tourist destinations for four primary reasons:

- An attack on a tourism center is an attack on a nation's entire economy — a fact that further emphasizes the economic significance of tourism.
- Tourism is highly media - oriented — terrorism seeks publicity, and tourist attractions like sporting events and festivals are likely to have media already at the site.
- Tourist attractions such as museums, historic sites, and beautiful scenery represent the spirit and essence of a nation.
- Tourist spots provide terrorists with relative anonymity. Police and security professionals rarely know the identities or motivations of visitors at sites and events.

As a consequence of the foregoing, increasing security will be a must for airlines, hotels, restaurants, and other tourism services. Furthermore, security experts in the travel industry must address the possibility of a "suicide disease carrier" seeking to infect an entire population.

The tourism industry must, however, go beyond mere security management and put in place a crisis management system that is capable of dealing with a wide range of catastrophes. Examples of recent tourism-related crises include:

- Britain: foot-and-mouth disease in cattle
- Cuba, Haiti, and Florida: the advent of successive major hurricanes
- China: SARS
- Bali: nightclub bombing

- Egypt: Luxor killings of tourists
- Thailand: avian (bird) flu and the threat of its spreading to humans
- Asia: tsunami

Terrorism affecting tourism has become so serious that costly efforts to develop missile warning systems and expendable decoys to protect commercial aircraft against shoulder fired missile attacks are now taking place.

LET US SUM UP

There are some barriers to travel like passports, entry and exit visas, exchange controls, currency restrictions, travel allowances, travel insurance, exit taxes, customs regulations, duties, equity requirements, domestic policy bias, transparency, foreign remittances, import restrictions, domestic content laws, tariffs, domestic personnel requirements, inefficient telecommunications systems.

Risk management and risk assessment has become, and will remain, a vital component of the way all businesses operate within the tourism industry. Across the tourism industry, there is a multitude of opportunities for 'risks' to turn into 'disaster' or an upheaval event.

Tourism is particularly prone to external shocks, which by their nature are unpredictable and need to be addressed through effective crisis management processes. Tourism operators must ensure a detailed crisis management plan is in place to respond to the chance of an unforeseen event occurring.

Undoubtedly, the tourism industry is one of the most susceptible and vulnerable industries to crises. Recent major events that had devastating impacts on the industry ranges from natural disasters to epidemics, and from mismanagement to terrorist attacks. These kinds of episodes are not confined to any geographical region, as crises respect no political or cultural boundaries. Two major recent events illustrate this point: the BSE crisis in the UK in the 1990s, which was followed by the foot and mouth disease in 2000 and 2001, crippled the industry in several regions of England. Most recently, the events of September 11th in New York and Washington changed the way the industry operates forever. Crises are not new to the tourism industry.

Government plays vital role as travel advisory like Governments issue regular travel advisories for their citizens warning them of risks in travelling to certain destinations. Governments can and do exert political pressure through tourism and use it as a promotional vehicle to convey a positive image or as a sanction against unfriendly countries.

CHECK YOUR PROGRESS

(A) Fill in the Blanks

(i) Tiananmen Square is in ....

(ii) Fiji military coup occurred in ....

(iii) Yugoslavia Civil war stated in the year..............

(B) True/False

(i) Government plays important role as travel advisory.

(ii) Tourism is not only a continuation of politics but an integral part of world's political economy.

(iii) Political instability does not affect tourism.

(C) True/False

(i) In-depth interview is a tourism research technique.

(ii) The key issue in crisis management is preparation in advance.

(iii) Crisis management relates to managing a critical event that may have major repercussions on the viability of business.

LESSON & ACTIVITY

How ULFA militancy in Assam and other militant outfits across North-East India has harmed the prospect of highly potential tourism industry? Also mention few tourism places and its point of attractions in NE.

KEY WORDS

Risk: A risk is the chance of something adverse happening. Risk arises out of uncertainty. It is measured in terms of the likelihood of it happening and the consequences if it does happen.

Risk Management: It is as much about identifying opportunities as it is about avoiding losses.

Crisis: Crisis situation is an event that has a fundamental impact on any organization's reputation, image, its future liabilities and its ability to operate.

QUESTIONS FOR DISCUSSION

(1) Explain the barriers to travel industry.

(2) What do you understand by risk management? Explain how risk can be minimized in tourism industry?

(3) How effectively crisis can be managed in tourism industry?

(4) How political stability can affect the tourism industry?

(5) Explain the government's role as travel advisory.

(6) Give some example of political instability across the world which impacted tourism industry negatively.

CHECK YOUR PROGRESS: MODEL ANSWER

(A) *(i)* China *(ii)* 1987 *(iii)* 1991

(B) *(i)* T *(ii)* T *(iii)* F

(C) *(i)* T *(ii)* T *(iii)* T

❑ ❑ ❑

5

INTERNATIONAL HOTELS

Chapter Outline

- *Introduction*
- *Hotels Operating in a Multinational Environment*
- *Examples of International Hotel*
- *Importance of International Hotel Chain*
- *International Rules and Regulations*

Learning Objective

At the conclusion of this lesson you should be able to understand:

- *Operation of hotels in international environment.*
- *Names of few international hotel chains.*
- *Importance of international hotel chains.*
- *Rules and regulations pertaining to international hotels.*

"Your true traveller finds boredom rather agreeable than painful. It is the symbol of his liberty — his excessive freedom. He accepts his boredom, when it comes, not merely philosophically, but almost with pleasure."

— Aldous Huxley (1894-1963)
British author.

INTRODUCTION

Intense competition and the augmentation of business opportunities are two distinct characteristics of the globalizations of worldwide markets and economies. These trends are valid across many industries but are particularly applicable to the global tourism industry, and more specifically, to the international hotel sector. In its endeavour to exploit the benefits of globalization, international hotel chains need to adopt a more sophisticated approach to strategic marketing and planning. This chapter will help you to understand the hotel chains operation across the world, challenges and importance of hotel value chain.

HOTELS OPERATING IN A MULTINATIONAL ENVIRONMENT

The role of the multinational companies is significant with their increasing contribution to the Economy. Basically Services are intangible deeds, processes and performances that cannot be touched, seen or felt but can be experienced. The Service sector is characterized by its diversity. Global opportunities are growing due to accelerated growth of the service economy.

In the hospitality industry, Average room rate (ARR) and occupancy are the two most critical factors that determine the profitability, since most of the marginal revenue gets added to the bottom-line. ARR in turn depends upon location, brand image, star rating, quality of facilities, pricing of value added services, complementary services offered and the seasonal factor. The hotels to manage and invest their fund in India adopt many business strategies to establish their place of business and create innovative service packages to their custom. In a long-term perspective, these measures bring significant financial returns.

CURRENT SCENARIO – An Indian Perspective: The hotel industry in India has a latent potential for growth. This is because India is an ideal destination for tourists as it is the only country with the most diverse topography and relative political stability. At present India attracts approximately 2.5 Million tourists every year, which is just 0.4% of the world tourist arrivals.

Normally the multi national hotels operated In India can be owned, leased or acquired under management contract basis. Hotel operators want the leverage on their management expertise and brand equity without making enormous capital investment. In management contract agreements a fee calculated as a percentage of revenue and/or operating profit is charged. Typically, the management fee is to the tune of 3% of the total revenue and 7% of gross operating profits.

Most players, with the exemption of IHCL and EIH, have entered into a marketing tie-ups with major international hotel chains. Thus, we have Hyatt Regency a renowned international hotel chain having tied up with AHL, Leela having tied up with Kempinski and ITCH having a franchisee agreement with ITT Sheraton to use the latter's brand name.

The American Hotel has returned to its fomer glory of the mid 19th century and offers welcoming rooms, fine dining and a friendly staff, attentive to all of its guests.

For the Indian hotel owners and the international hotel chains the benefit is mutual, tie-up with an international hotel chain puts the hotel on the global map with access to chain's reservation network worldwide. For the international hotel chain they can ride on the boom of the industry without making enormous capital investments on infrastructure and facilities. Associations with international brand also play a major role in image building and attracting foreign tourists. However the value of the international brand gets diluted if a foreign entity enters an agreement with several Indian companies.

SOME FINANCIAL ISSUES: Luxury hotels operate under single tariff structure whereby the foreign tourists are charged in dollar terms whereas the domestic guest is charged the equivalent amount in rupees. The luxury hotels earn about two-thirds of their revenue from foreign tourists. Leisure travellers constitute approximately 76.5% of the total tourist arrivals whereas business travellers constitute 23% of the total arrivals. The remainder is accounted by students. The hotel industry is the second largest foreign exchange earner.

Hotels benefit from rupee depreciation as over 60% of revenues in the luxury hotel segment are in foreign currencies. Thus, any depreciation of the rupee goes directly to the bottom line (FOREX income is also fully tax exempt), as none of the costs are directly linked to the exchange rate.

The hotel debt environment is also improving. While many countries are hampered by a still sluggish economy, those with a low interest rate environment with relatively stable-banking conditions will provide opportunities for hotel investors to raise capital. For hotel lenders, from a risk/return basis, there has never been a better time to provide new capital to this industry in India.

Currently, guest retention and repeat clientele is the name of the game. Hotels those are able to provide guests a product where the service is consistent and of a level required by the target market, will only survive. The Hotel industry, always ready with innovative ambitious business plans and the spirited management plotting the right strategies, is contributing its might to improve the position of the Economy. So the role of multinational chains/groups of Hotels in the Indian hospitality industry and their contribution to the Indian Economy is significant. There have not been many exploratory researches in this area. But there is every need to work on the economics for a proper planned growth at a macro level. Also the WORLD definitely looks better and happy with ALL the hospitality it can muster.

EXAMPLES OF INTERNATIONAL HOTELS

Tourism – Hotel Chains

Accor Group, A.H.M.I. Hotels, Akzent Hotels, All Suites International, Alp'Azur Hotels, Alpine Classics Private Hotels, Althoff Hotels, Amari Hotels, Armor Passion, Ashley, House, Astron Hotels, Ata Hotels, Atlas Hotels, Austrotel, Bally's, Barcelo Hotels, Best Western International, Bonaparte Hotel Group, Boscolo Group, Bristol Hotels and Resorts, Camino Real Hotels & Resorts, Campanile, Canadian Pacific Hotels, Caesar Resort Hotels, Caesars Chase Suite Hotels, Choice Hotels International, City & Country Line Hotels, Clarion Hotels, Club Med, Coastal Inns, Coast and Country Hotels, Coast Hotels and Resorts, Comfort Inns, Concorde Hotels, Concorde Hotels and Resorts, Dan Hotels, Delta, Derby Hotels, Dynasty Suites Hotels, Embassy Suites, Executive Inns & Suites, Fairfield Inns, Felix Hotels & Resorts, Fountainhead Hotels, Four Points Hotels by Sheraton, Four Seasons, Friendship Inns, Golden Leaf Hotels & Residences, Golden Tulip, Grand Heritage, Grantham Resorts, Great Southern Hotels, Hampton Inn & Suites, Hankyu Group, Heritage Hotels (India), Hilton Hotels, Hilton International Hotels, Holiday Inn, Homewood Suites, Howard Johnson, H30 Hotels, Hyatt, Knights Inn, La Quinta, Leading Hotels of the World, Lee Hotels, Le Meridien Hotels, Manhattan East Suite Hotels, Marriott Hotels, Oberoi Hotels, Quality Inns, Radisson, Sheraton, Taj Group of Hotels, Taylor Hotel Group, Wyndham Hotels and Resorts.

IMPORTANCE OF INTERNATIONAL HOTEL CHAINS

Intense competition and the augmentation of business opportunities are two distinct characteristics of the globalisation of worldwide markets and economies. These trends are valid across many industries but are particularly applicable to the global tourism industry, and more specifically, to the international hotel sector in its endeavour to exploit the benefits of globalisation, international hotel chains need to adopt a more sophisticated approach to strategic marketing and planning. One approach currently finding favour is that of collaboration. In response to this growing trend among international hotel chains, this paper focuses on horizontal forms of collaboration in the international hotel chain sector. The collaborative strategies enable international hotel chains to compete and develop successfully in worldwide markets. However, given the lack of sophistication in areas determining success in collaborative strategies of the international hotel chain industry, the paper also debates key issues that affect the effectiveness of these practices.

Over recent decades the world economy has undergone considerable transformation. Influenced by advances in technology and the spread of global capitalism, the shrinkage of geographical and cultural distances has allowed companies to widen substantially their geographical markets and sources of supply. This in turn has served as the catalytic focus for the creation of new business opportunities, yet at the same time creating an enormously more complex marketing environment for businesses to operate in. Across virtually all sectors of the global economy, collaboration—frequently in the form of alliances—is reshaping the interactions of companies and transforming traditional business rivalry (**Gomes-Casseres,** 1996; **Spekman, Isabella, & MacAvoy,** 2000). As businesses continue to search for the most effective means to strengthen their positioning in this new competitive arena, increasing numbers consider the development of long-term, mutually beneficial collaborative relationships as the solution (**Axelrod,** 1984; **Best,** 1990; **Cateora & Ghauri,** 2000; **Dunning,** 1997; **Hunt,** 1997).

The above is of particular relevance to the international hotel industry, where the drift towards consolidation has already produced large-scale international companies and a plethora of collaborative strategies—most frequently marketing alliances, partnerships and consortia (**Witt & Moutinho,** 1995). A typical example of such relationships is that of The Leading Hotels of the World with the Small Luxury Hotels of the World. Other major hotel chains that have been participating in collaborative partnerships include Accor, Marriott, Bvlgari Hotels and Resorts, and Six Continents Hotels. Hotel chains that participate in collaborative partnerships gain a plethora of advantages. For example, previously heavily dependent on tour operators and other intermediaries, international hotels are now able to achieve economies of scale through cost effective collaborative practices, and gain easier access to worldwide markets; which is in many cases achieved by the use of common reservation systems and customer databases. Marketing strategies of international hotels and hotel chains, therefore, now need to acquire an even greater international perspective and adjust to the new requirements of global competition. To remain profitable they need to understand the changing characteristics of both the marketplace and the consumers, and the need to gain a durable competitive advantage. Even the largest international hotel chains, instead of competing in the global marketplace on their own, are now seeking to build extensive global business networks by creating strategic collaborative forms with foreign organisations to extend their global reach. However, with the migration towards collaborative marketing strategies, international hotel chains are now aiming to protect and complement their core competitive advantages, and, in situations where they outsource activities previously undertaken internally, treat these as an integral part of their value-adding activities.

The unprecedented rate of alliance formation has been characterized by increasing diversity of these partnerships in terms of partners' nationalities, motives and goals pursued by participating organisations, and formal structures employed to organize them. As a result of the numerous choices in structuring these relationships, numerous forms of collaboration exist (**Gulati & Singh,** 1998; **DePamphilis,** 2003). For example, "alliances" are observed to be voluntary agreements (**Gulati,** 1998), as well as obligatory—unintentional or inevitable—in the sense that their purpose is to overcome regulatory barriers (**Evans,** 2003). From a strategic standpoint, they could be primarily defensive against dominant organisations in the market or offensive and intended to secure a stronger position within the industry and/or reduce opportunities for new entrants (**Child & Faulkner,** 1998). (**Bleeke and Ernst,** 1993, p. 300) found that alliances generally fall into six categories, which they name based on their potential outcomes: "collisions between competitors, alliances of the weak, disguised sales, bootstrap alliance, evolutions to a sale, and alliances of complementary equals". Another classification of the forms of collaborative partnerships considers the number of companies that participate. While the majority of scholars focus the discussion regarding strategic alliances between two companies, there is an increasing trend in the global competitive arena towards multi-company alliances (**Elmuti & Kathawala,** 2003).

INTERNATIONAL RULES & REGULATIONS

The United Nations Conference on International Travel and Tourism held in Rome in the year 1963 also emphasised the need for some sort of regulation of accommodation with a view to safeguard the interests of the users. Considering that special attention should be given to relations between the public authorities and the operators of tourist accommodation facilities, the conference observed that many states classify tourist hotels or are considering doing so. Acting upon the recommendations put forward by the International Chamber of Commerce, the conference advocated the standardization of methods of classification and in particular the sub-division of hotels into five categories, each identified by a conventional sign (stars) in conformity with the sets of standards appropriate to different climatic conditions. The conference also considered the question of classifying supplementary means of accommodation such as tourist bungalows and camps.

Registration

The aim of registration is to provide a complete list or register of tourist accommodation within a particular definition. A registration scheme results in an inventory of accommodation which can be kept up-to-date. In order to be comprehensive, it normally has to have statutory legal authority and it administered by a government authority or statutory body. Because of the wider range of accommodation used by the tourists, scheme of registration should normally cover all forms of accommodation used by them.

Gradation

Grading separates accommodation into different categories or grades, on the basis of judgments such as standards of amenities and service. A grading scheme provides qualitative judgments on the amenities, and facilities of a particular accommodation unit in a form which enables the user to choose the quality of accommodation he requires. This may refer to the physical facilities, food and other services of the establishments, various amenities provided, etc. The establishments are graded individually or collectively by way of giving those numbers, letters or symbols.

Classification

The Main aim of classification is to maintain standardization of services and security for tourists. By establishing uniform standards of classification, it is easier for all concerned with tourism (tour operators, travel agents, tourist enterprise and tourists themselves) to know exactly what standard of services is offered by each hotel (according to the number of stars) thus leading to more effective uniformity both in statistics and in regulatory and control standards. The adopted scheme envisages that hotel establishments are to be divided into five categories, symbolized by stars, and based on objective standards. The categories are assigned on the basis of two types of requirements:

- Minimum requirements common total categories, as stated in the classification scheme, concerning health, sanitary, material and staff standards.
- Minimum requirements for each category, expressed as specific conditions for the hotel (as a building), the rooms, additional accommodation, facilities and guest service.

LET US SUM UP

Intense competition and the augmentation of business opportunities are two distinct characteristics of the globalizations of worldwide markets and economies. These trends are valid across many industries but are particularly applicable to the global tourism industry, and more specifically, to the international hotel sector. in its endeavour to exploit the benefits of globalization, international hotel chains need to adopt a more sophisticated approach to strategic marketing and planning.

Intense competition and the augmentation of business opportunities are two distinct characteristics of the globalisation of worldwide markets and economies. These trends are valid across many industries but are particularly applicable to the global tourism industry, and more specifically, to the international hotel sector in its endeavour to exploit the benefits of globalisation, international hotel chains need to adopt a more sophisticated approach to strategic marketing and planning.

The United Nations Conference on International Travel and Tourism held in Rome in the year 1963 also emphasised the need for some sort of regulation of accommodation with a view to safeguard the interests of the users. Considering that special attention should be given to relations between the public authorities and the operators of tourist accommodation facilities, the conference observed that many states classify tourist hotels or are considering doing so. Acting upon the recommendations put forward by the International Chamber of Commerce, the conference advocated the standardization of methods of classification and in particular the sub-division of hotels into five categories, each identified by a conventional sign (stars) in conformity with the sets of standards appropriate to different climatic conditions. The conference also considered the question of classifying supplementary means of accommodation such as tourist bungalows and camps.

CHECK YOUR PROGRESS

(A) True/False

(i) Luxury hotels operate under single tariff structure.

(ii) Leisure travel constitutes major percentage of the total tourist arrivals across the world.

(iii) Multinational hotel be owned, leased or acquired under management contract basis.

LESSON & ACTIVITY

Name an Indian MNC hotel chain and its contributions towards growth of Indian Tourism Industry.

KEY WORDS

Topography: Climatic condition.

Multinational environment: Perfect competitive market without any kind of restrictions, rules and regulations.

Horizontal cooperation: Two or more companies join together for business.

QUESTIONS FOR DISCUSSION

(1) Explain how a hotel operates in a multinational environment.

(2) Name few international hotel chains.

(3) Define strategic marketing plan.

(4) Explain the importance of international hotel chain.

(5) Briefly explain the various rules and regulations governing international hotel chains.

CHECK YOUR PROGRESS: MODEL ANSWER

(A) True/False

(i) True *(ii)* True *(iii)* True

❑ ❑ ❑

6

HR AND TOURISM INDUSTRY

Chapter Outline

- *Introduction*
- *HR in Tourism Industry*
- *Cultural Diversity and Tourism Industry*
- *Social and Cultural Impacts of Tourism*

Learning Objective

At the conclusion of this lesson you should be able to understand:

- *Importance of human resources in tourism industry*
- *Cultural diversity and tourism industry*
- *Cultural and social impact of tourism industry*

"I am not much an advocate for travelling, and I observe that men run away to other countries because they are not good in their own, and run back to their own because they pass for nothing in the new places. For the most part, only the light characters travel. Who are you that have no task to keep you at home?"

- Ralph Waldo Emerson (1803-1882)
U.S. poet, essayist and lecturer

INTRODUCTION

It is obvious that the labor force is essential to tourism. We give the example of the guide: hundreds of people from various places where the tourist travels can work very hard give their best effort, yet the guide, who has the microphone in his hand and the tourists' time, can ruin everything, or, on the contrary, may create a timeless memory. Many times, the phrase "wolf in sheep's clothing" is true in tourism. A small negligence, especially now, in this age of tourism, deletes the effort of all those involved. But tourism is an activity with a pronounced seasonal character, and, as we all know, poorly paid.

Problems need to be solved ever since the personnel are prepared. Here is the needed human resource and the forming offer on professional categories in Brazil, a similar situation with all developing countries:

Demand		*Offer*	
Professional categories according to number	%	Classes offered on professional categories	%
Execution personnel	63	Entrepreneurs	86
Administrative personnel	8	Personnel with medium or high studies	57
Medium and superior personnel by qualification	7	Specialized personnel	43
Maintenance personnel	6	Execution personnel	29
Specialized technical personnel	5	Maintenance personnel	14
Level of studies required		*Required level of studies*	
Secondary	12	Superior	8
Primary	50	Secondary	68
Elementary	25	Primary	24
No studies required	27		
(travel agency: secondary)	70		

Source : *Instituto de Hospitalidade: Demanda por capacicao professional no sector de turismo-Salvador 2000*

Tourism personnel must accept labour flexibility, basically, in more and smaller size hotels the same people are receptionists as well as waiters and they also do other connected activities. Multi-qualification is essential to overcome seasonal periods, seasonal meaning is the fact that some jobs are less required from time to time. Usually, employees must be familiarized with all modern methods of management, with equipment and software which is employed: many times, a diploma is not the deciding factor, rather the certificate which makes him able to use certain technologies.

Tourism jobs bring several advantages which are not negligible: a pleasant environment, meals are usually assured, protective clothing, continuous perfection. This is why the concept of career organizing was achieved. New technologies brought forth new professions, but moreover grouped them under the same roof: hotel chains opened tourism agencies, car rentals, casinos, stock sales, health services, etc., all of the above using information technology. Economic knowledge, although integrated in system software, remain a means for promotion, allowing for an optimization of the decision. Continuous preparation is required, as well as learning new skills. Theory says that large hotel chains have a tendency to invest in the careers of their employees. Classes are compulsory in order to understand, but also to better impregnate the philosophy of a respective group. This is why a brand changing basically means a new qualification. Perhaps the most important requirement of modern tourism is linguistic polyvalence. A receptionist, a guide, basically an employee in contact with tourism must know around 4-5 languages to be employed. Even a housekeeping lady must have minimum knowledge in several languages. Formation is thus a reality, for those who want to resist.

The educational system in developed countries has completely changed in the last 10-15 years. If, in Europe (the USA has a different system, according to its quality standards) there were 2-3 acknowledged tourism faculties, which provided required management and 4-5 superior schools which were assuring the required middle management positions (hotel manager, restaurant manager, fun park manager, etc.) the rest of the personnel was formed in professional schools.

Now we are witnessing an educational integration. More and more formation institutes have a larger and larger number of students at professional studies (usually after completing compulsory education) – apprenticing basically disappeared – from where students are being recruited for middle management or top management for the latter, another stage being compulsory: croupier, oenologist, diet specialist, IT specialist, ticketing agent, etc., to obtain the required authorization certificate in order to practice. This is also the place where from most of the students for advanced studies are being recruited. It is remarkable that the number of tourism faculties is on the decrease, and that their graduates are forced to specialize in certain fields: hospitality, leisure, tourist destination management, park organization, event management, etc.

Moreover, distance education is widespread, for jobs that allow this. One must underline the fact that there are jobs which require a big investment (like chef), where the cost of raw materials, practice time, etc., or maitre d hotel, etc. Anyway, the practical exam is the *sine qua non* requisite. Free labour travelling (in the limits of established contingents) means not only recognition of diplomas but also their equivalence. Educational programs begin to be uniform. The same thing cannot be said about developing countries, where, as is the case of Romania, large funds are being allocated, as compared to their economic force for preparing a capable labour force, which is usually incompatible with international requirements, graduates often accepting inferior jobs which are lower paid. Furthermore, there is a major lack in equilibrium between formation and market demand, high costs, usually supported for the fashion and pride of attending certain studies, without informing themselves of real perspectives. Precisely to use this reserve, international structures have introduced distance education in order to obtain authorization certificates, which are organized and paid for separately, through long distance classes guaranteed by their issuers.

Today we are used to meet personnel from all over the world in tourism agencies. But in great hotel chains, national identity vanishes instead values promoted are those of chain philosophy. Standards and rules regarding necessary knowledge of personnel are imposed by the great enterprises which also use most of the personnel, as we have seen in the case of hotels, restaurants and coffee shops in Europe.

In an era of increasing emphasis on quality in the delivery of tourism services, service quality and the human support such service demands can be looked upon as a competitive opportunities as well as strategic issue. Consideration of the role of human resources in creating quality and its efficient management has widely been recognised as one of the most important methods to improve quality and competitiveness. At the same time, the tourism industry, worldwide, is characterised by ambiguous attitudes to investment in human capital, inflexible employment practices and an unsustainable approach to its development (**Jithendran & Baum,** 2000). Often perceived purely in operational terms (**Baum,** 1993), the management and development of human resources in tourism is readily described as an example of *ad hocism* in that formal planning of a long-term and strategic nature rarely takes place within the sector. It is also an area of activity that has repercussions far beyond the operational domain in organisations and clearly impacts on the marketing and financial effectiveness of tourism businesses.

This generic analysis with respect to the role of human resources in tourism is of direct relevance in the context of tourism services and experiences which are located in what co-authors to this volume describe as extreme tourism destinations, whether extremity is this context relates to remote location, insularity or climate or, indeed, a combination of all three. Indeed, this chapter will endeavour to demonstrate that the challenges faced by organisations operating within extreme tourism destinations with respect to: (1) labour market features; (2) sourcing and recruitment of staff to work in the sector; (3) employee retention; (4) training and development; and (5) career progression, are different in both kind and extent from the issues faced by destinations located in more 'normal' tourism environments. This lesson will help you to understand the role of HR and challenges in Tourism Industry.

HR IN TOURISM INDUSTRY

There can be no denying the success of the tourism industry in the last three decades. This success bears a large part of the responsibility for the widespread practice of simply extrapolating figures to show that demand will continue to rise in the future. The same reasoning would have it that tourism input is a linear function, and that the curves depicting its progress will raise steadily and evenly over the next few years.

Tourism businesses, resorts and regions, and the public authorities responsible for the sector can all therefore look tomorrow straight in the eye, switch on the automatic cruise control and sit back, leaving events to run their calculated course. Education and the training of human resources for the tourism industry will occupy their usual place in this orderly system and teaching establishments need do no more than seek out sufficient funding to accomplish their task in the light of the growing demand for employment. Nothing could be further from the truth. Never, since the age of mass tourism began, shortly after the Second World War, has the tourism industry been subject to such far-reaching and rapid changes.

The professionalization and extreme segmentation of demand, the extensive application of new technologies, environmental considerations and, in general, deep-rooted worldwide socio-political upheavals which are still only in their infancy, all entail an irreversible change in Ford's business paradigm when applied to the tourism sector. The rules of the game of mass tourism are losing their validity. The familiar path has come to an end and the terra incognita we can just make out ahead will require business practices and the public management of tourism to be completely reinvented.

In this context, we cannot help but notice the extent to which tourism training fails to match up to the needs of the sector. Whilst it is true that certain companies and authorities have embarked on strategies designed to achieve a new kind of competitiveness, this is extremely rare in the case of the training of human resources for tourism. Tourism education is the final frontier. It is the final frontier in the sense that educational establishments and the training initiatives taken by businesses and public authorities are still guided more by intuition and inertia than by the pressure of circumstances and the needs of the sector, both real and predictable. The Total Quality methodology — which has been around in the secondary sector for decades, and is already well established in large areas of the service industries, including tourism— is still no more than an exotic curio in the world of tourism education. Indeed, the beginning of the industrial era may, in many cases, be the most fitting comparison for the state of affairs in the teaching of tourism where the attitude is: "The main thing is to produce (in this case education), the customer (education recipients and employers) will buy anyway".

The customer's actual needs matter little at this stage: "You can buy any vehicle you choose, provided it is a Ford, a T model and always black". And yet it is becoming increasingly obvious that the future of the tourism industry will depend more on humanology than on technology. In a world where knowledge is perhaps the only genuine value added of the productive process, we need to determine not only how much, but also what, when, where and how we need to know

CULTURAL DIVERSITY AND TOURISM

At the broadest level, the natural and cultural heritage belongs to all people. We each have a right and responsibility to understand, appreciate and conserve its universal values.

Heritage is a broad concept and includes the natural as well as the cultural environment. It encompasses landscapes, historic places, sites and built environments, as well as biodiversity, collections, past and continuing cultural practices, knowledge and living experiences. It records and expresses the long processes of historic development, forming the essence of diverse national, regional, indigenous and local identities and is an integral part of modern life. It is a dynamic reference point and positive instrument for growth and change. The particular heritage and collective memory of each locality or community is irreplaceable and an important foundation for development, both now and into the future.

At a time of increasing globalisation, the protection, conservation, interpretation and presentation of the heritage and cultural diversity of any particular place or region is an important challenge for people everywhere. However, management of that heritage, within a framework of internationally recognised and appropriately applied standards, is usually the responsibility of the particular community or custodian group.

A primary objective for managing heritage is to communicate its significance and need for its conservation to its host community and to visitors. Reasonable and well managed physical, intellectual and/or emotive access to heritage and cultural development is both a right and a privilege. It brings with it a duty of respect for the heritage values, interests and equity of the present-day host community, indigenous custodians or owners of historic property and for the landscapes and cultures from which that heritage evolved.

The Dynamic Interaction between Tourism and Cultural Heritage

Domestic and international tourism continues to be among the foremost vehicles for cultural exchange, providing a personal experience, not only of that which has survived from the past, but of the contemporary life and society of others. It is increasingly appreciated as a positive force for natural and cultural conservation. Tourism can capture the economic characteristics of the heritage and harness these for conservation by generating funding, educating the community and influencing policy. It is an essential part of many national and regional economies and can be an important factor in development, when managed successfully.

Tourism itself has become an increasingly complex phenomenon, with political, economic, social, cultural, educational, bio-physical, ecological and aesthetic dimensions. The achievement of a beneficial inter-action between the potentially conflicting expectations and aspirations of visitors and host or local communities, presents many challenges and opportunities.

The natural and cultural heritage, diversities and living cultures are major tourism attractions. Excessive or poorly-managed tourism and tourism related development can threaten their physical nature, integrity and significant characteristics. The ecological setting, culture and lifestyles of host communities may also be degraded, along with the visitor's experience of the place.

Tourism should bring benefits to host communities and provide an important means and motivation for them to care for and maintain their heritage and cultural practices. The involvement and co-operation of local and/or indigenous community representatives, conservationists, tourism operators, property owners, policy makers, those preparing national development plans and site managers is necessary to achieve a sustainable tourism industry and enhance the protection of heritage resources for future generations.

ICOMOS, the International Council on Monuments and Sites, as the author of this Charter, other international organisations and the tourism industry, are dedicated to this challenge.

SOCIAL AND CULTURAL IMPACTS OF TOURISM

Tourism is a fast growing industry and a valuable sector, contributing significantly to the economy. Tourism affects the economy and lives of communities and has proven to be a lifesaver for many destinations. There are real and perceived fears that are sometimes attributed to tourism and largely related to poorly managed or mass tourism ventures. As with any economic activity, tourism can have negative impacts on communities. These must be minimized and measured against the benefits that tourism brings.

There is some concern that tourism development may lead to destinations losing their cultural identity by catering for the perceived needs of tourists – particularly from international markets. This is based on the observations of other "destinations" having compromised their sense of identity. However, research shows that most tourists travel, not to visit home away from home, but because they want to experience the personality and true character of Australian towns, communities and attractions. The tourism experience is different to what they can see or do at home and this includes experiencing the real life and lifestyle of the destinations they visit.

Sustainable tourism is thoughtful tourism. It is "derived," not "contrived." A community involved in the planning and implementation of tourism has a more positive attitude, is more supportive and has better chance of making a profit than a population passively ruled – or overrun – by tourism. One of the core elements of sustainable tourism development is community development. This is giving the community the process and capacity to make decisions that consider the long-term economy, ecology and equity of all communities.

Services such as tourism act as an economic "shock absorber" helping to support communities, particularly in rural areas, through economic drought, as services are more recession-proof than goods. The tourism industry is "decentralized" meaning that there is little dependence on urban centres and imports to sustain tourism activity. Sustainable/ community based tourism relies on small, locally operated business, local features and products and thrives on entrepreneurial activity from individuals.

Tourism provides opportunities for regional development particularly for regional areas undergoing structural change. Being a labour intensive industry, with the right encouragement tourism can deliver great employment and training opportunities particularly for young people. Development of tourism product does not necessarily require building "tourist things." Tourism is often structured around existing points of interest, be it natural, heritage, cultural experiences or economic activities. Communities need to overcome the perception that they must "build things" to become a tourist destination. Instead, they must focus on what they do best rather than trying to replicate other "tourist" attractions.

Tourism development that "leverages" existing attributes often brings a range of benefits to host communities. Improved infrastructure (power, water, and telecommunications), access, services (banks, transport) and new investments, all serve to enhance the lifestyles of communities. Community support will follow developments that service the community and provide ongoing benefits.

Tourism can help foster a sense of community pride as visitors choose to visit a location for a reason. However, community pride is generally related to economic prosperity with affluent communities more likely to take pride in their district. Well-presented towns and well-maintained facilities help visitors to feel welcome and can contribute to community pride.

Tourism is an interface for cultural exchange, facilitating the interaction between communities and visitors (domestic and international). Economic benefits aside, outside contact draws attention to the host community. People want to interact with other cultures, learn about traditions and even confront themselves with new perspectives on life and society. It has been said that travel is a means to "discover those things unknown or forgotten within ourselves." Tourism is largely an experience driven industry, and local culture is a unique experience – more so local personality, hospitality and food than "built attractions." The more one knows and learns about a destination, the more fulfilling the experience will be.

Tourism can be used as a tool for raising awareness. Branding of local product and achievements creates regional identity both nationally and internationally. Tourism can also raise awareness of local issues and needs.

There is a global trend towards investment in interpretation of natural and cultural resources.

Attraction to natural and heritage icons often helps fund conservation efforts and provides opportunities for effective management of sensitive and significant areas. However, cultural attractions are not the sole draw card for visitation but provide one of many experiences.

A growing number of cultural celebrations are emerging highlighting important events and paying homage to ancestry. Cultural events assert cultural identity and help preserve local traditions in younger generations while influencing visitors firsthand. Australia's primary urban areas are multicultural and have developed their own unique cultures, however many regional areas are still heavily influenced by the food and culture of their founders. Tourism allows for local crafts, foods and personalities to be kept alive while raising funds for the community.

Tourism can boost the preservation and transmission of cultural and historical traditions. This often contributes to the conservation and sustainable management of natural resources, the protection of local heritage, and a revival of indigenous cultures, cultural arts and crafts.

Negative Impacts of Tourism

Many of the fears surrounding tourism are closely associated with uncontrolled, unsustainable and massed tourism growth. Tourism is an industry and is dominated by private enterprise with a purpose of making money by selling experiences. Market led planning can fail to achieve the objectives of sustainable tourism and has a tendency to forget environmental, social and cultural impacts. Like all industries, impacts do occur, but the extent to which impacts are negative can be minimized.

In the extremes, tourism has contributed to a wide range of issues – many of which seem insignificant but detract from the quality of life of local residents. Intrusion on daily life, loss of privacy, and a sense of crowding contribute to ill feelings towards tourism development.

Tourism infrastructure is often accused of taking the "best sites" and local secrets seen as being spectacle and losing their destination appeal. Planning authorities should ensure that only sites that are tourism ready should be selected for tourism development, if necessary.

Tourism is often seen as "the solution" to economic hardship rather than a diversification of the local economy. It is easy for small communities to become reliant on tourism drawing labour away from staple industries such as agriculture and manufacture.

Tourism is a service and experience based industry. Tourists often have their own set images about destinations before they arrive. Communities should concentrate on what they do best and must be careful not to manufacture the tourism experience to meet the preconceived touristy ideals. It is up to tourism agencies and retailers to ensure that travellers receive accurate information about destinations.

Many impacts are socio-cultural and an outcome of lack of information, false impressions, misinformation, poor communication and poor knowledge. Negative perceptions and attitudes towards visitors and tourism can also affect tourism/ communities. Ill feelings towards tourism, delays/obstructions to tourism product development and lack of council/authority support can prevent tourism from flourishing; perhaps these communities are not ready for tourism. It is easy to blame tourism for any economic, social and environmental problems. Open communication channels, proper consultation, transparency and involvement at the community level at all stages of the planning process can aid in communities taking ownership of their tourism product.

To many people the label tourist has become a negative term; in fact many travellers do not consider themselves tourists. There is a noticeable shift in attitude in both communities and travellers to the concept of "visitor." The visitor concept reinforces the fact that travellers are guests within a community, and that their stay is a privilege and not a right.

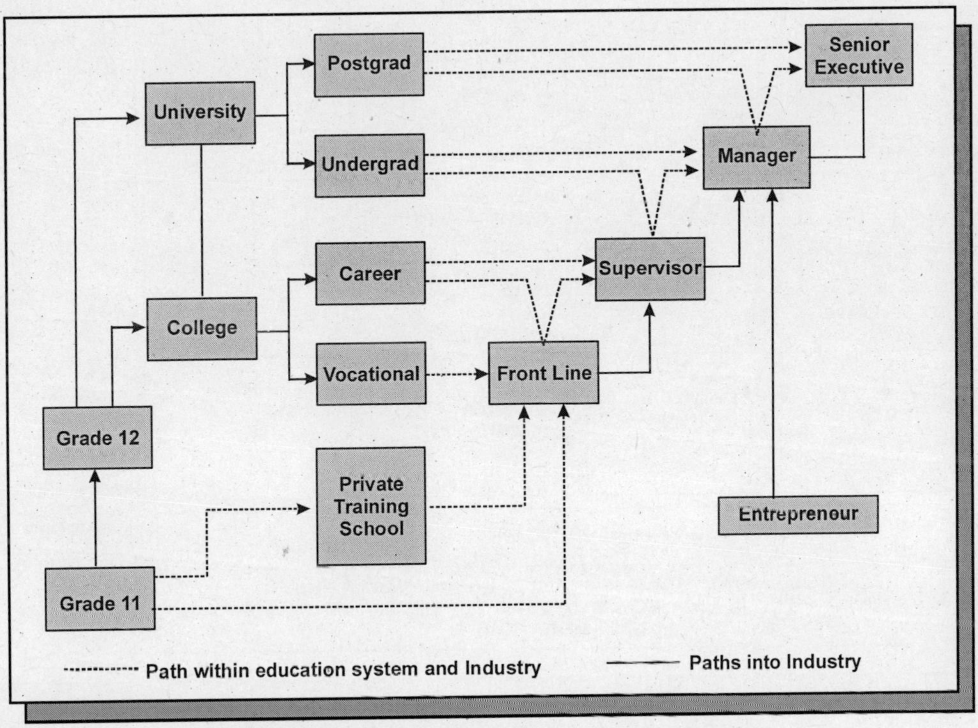

Fig. 6.1. Career paths within the tourism industry

	Food & Beverage	Accommodations	Tour & Travel	Attractions
ENTREPRENEUR	**FOOD & BEVERAGE RESTAURANT OWNER** ● Independence ● Flexible Work Hours ● Financial & Personal Business ● Control ● Novelty/Change	**ACCOMODATIONS HOTEL OWNER** ● Independence ● Regular Work Hours ● Control ● Money ● People ● Novelty/Change ● Business	**TOUR & TRAVEL TOUR BUS LINE OWNER** ● Quality ● Commitment ● Work Ethics ● Optimism ● People/Employees ● Challenge ● Growth ● Humor ● Flexibility ● Organization ● Working with Numbers	**ALTRACTIONS AMUSEMENT PARK GENERAL MANAGER** ● Quality ● Toursm and Tours ● Organization ● Attention to Detail ● Flexibility/Diversity ● People ● Creativity ● Business ● Irragular Work Hours
MANAGER	**RESTAURANT MANAGER** ● Quality ● People ● Leadership ● Novelty/Change ● Nutrition	**HOTEL MANAGER** ● Intersing People ● Novelty/Change ● Curiosity ● Compattion ● People ● Problem Solving ● Status	**TOUR BUS LINE MANAGER** ● Quality ● Commiment ● Work ● People ● Challenge ● Flexibility ● Growth ● Humor ● Organization ● Innovation ● Working with Numbers	**DIRECTOR OF SPECIAL ATTRACTIONS** ● Young People ● Professonallsm ● Work Ethic ● Obseivity ● Imagular Work Hours ● Variable Work Environment ● Challange ● Econemic Value ● Celsure/Fun ● Analysis
SUPERVISOR	**MAITRE D'** ● People ● Quality ● Challenge ● Food Industry	**ASSISTANT EXECUTIVE HOUSEKEEPER** ● People ● Quality ● Cook Effectiveness ● Team Efficency ● Problem Solving ● Challenge	**SUPERINTENDENT OF BUS MAINTENANCE** ● People and Their Safety ● Quality ● Vareity/Novelty ● Machinery ● Problems ● Organization	**AMUSEMENT PARK SUPERVISOR** ● People ● Quality ● Machinery ● Challenge ● Efficiency
	BARTENDER ● People ● Quality ● Creativity ● Flexible Work Hours	**OPERATIONS CHAMBERMAID** ● People ● Neatness ● Fun ● Variety ● Cleanring	**TOUR BUS DRIVER** ● People ● Power Control ● Being Buddy ● Routine	**OPERATION RIDE OPERATOR** ● People ● Intiative ● Work ● Teamwork ● Being Buddy
ENTRY LEVEL	**FOOD & BEVERAGE SERVER** ● People ● Flexibility ● Work Condtor	**ENTRY CHAMBERMAID** ● People ● Cleaniness ● Cutural Variety	**TICKET AGENT** ● People ● Help/Lines ● Challenge ● Clerical Tasts ● Man ● Travel ● Novelty/Variety	**ENTRY RIDE OPERATOR** ● People ● Fun
PRE-EMPLOMENT	Personal Worth Work			

PREDOMINANT VALUES AND INTERESTS (Entrepreneur, Manager and Supervisor levels):

PEOPLE
QUALITY
CHALLENGE
FLEXIBILITY
NOVELTY/CHANGE

(Operations and Entry levels): PEOPLE

*NOTE
The values and interests issued here are samples.
A small sample of was used in data collection.

*Created for the INDUSTRY ANALYSIS AND TRANING INFORMATION BRANCH DEPARTMENT OF CAREER DEVELOPMENT AND EMPOLYMENT, GOVERNMENT OF ALBERTA BY CAREER DEVELOPMENT INSTITUTE

Fig.6.2. Various levels of jobs in tourism industry

LET US SUM UP

Tourism businesses, resorts and regions, and the public authorities responsible for the sector can all therefore look tomorrow straight in the eye, switch on the automatic cruise control and sit back, leaving events to run their calculated course. Education and the training of human resources for the tourism industry will occupy their usual place in this orderly system and teaching establishments need do no more than seek out sufficient funding to accomplish their task in the light of the growing demand for employment. Nothing could be further from the truth. Never, since the age of mass tourism began, shortly after the Second World War, has the tourism industry been subject to such far-reaching and rapid changes.

At a time of increasing globalisation, the protection, conservation, interpretation and presentation of the heritage and cultural diversity of any particular place or region is an important challenge for people everywhere. However, management of that heritage, within a framework of internationally recognised and appropriately applied standards, is usually the responsibility of the particular community or custodian group.

Tourism is a fast growing industry and a valuable sector, contributing significantly to the economy. Tourism affects the economy and lives of communities and has proven to be a lifesaver for many destinations. There are real and perceived fears that are sometimes attributed to tourism and largely related to poorly managed or mass tourism ventures. As with any economic activity, tourism can have negative impacts on communities. These must be minimized and measured against the benefits that tourism brings.

CHECK YOUR PROGRESS

(A) True/False

(i) Tourist evaluation is the final frontier for the growth of tourism industry.

(ii) Heritage includes natural as well as cultural environment.

(iii) Tourism is a simple phenomenon.

(B) Fill in the Blanks

(i) ICOMOS stands for...

(ii) One of the core elements of sustainable tourism development is ....

(iii) At the broadest level , the natural and cultural heritage belongs to all.........

(C) True/False

(i) Tourism is a capital intensive industry.

(ii) Tourism is an interface for cultural exchange

(iii) Tourism is largely an experience driven industry.

LESSON & ACTIVITY

"Tourism industry requires professionally qualified smart people" – Comments and cite one example from real life.

KEY WORDS

Heritage: It is a broad concept and includes the natural as well as the cultural environment. It encompasses landscapes, historic places, sites and built environments, as well as biodiversity, collections, past and continuing cultural practices, knowledge and living experiences.

Culture: Lifestyle, social norms and values of a community.

Sustainable development: Long lasting development without harming environment, spoiling culture.

QUESTIONS FOR DISCUSSION

(1) Explain the importance of HR in tourism industry.

(2) Explain how cultural diversity helps in the growth of tourism industry.

(3) Explain the social and cultural impact of tourism.

(4) Explain the negative impacts of tourism.

CHECK YOUR PROGRESS: MODEL ANSWER

(A) *(i)* T *(ii)* T *(iii)* F

(B) *(i)* International Council on Monument and Sites.

(ii) Community Development

(iii) People

(C) *(i)* F *(ii)* T *(iii)* T

❑ ❑ ❑

7

International Tourism Sales and Marketing

Chapter Outline

- Introduction
- Marketing Concept
- Marketing Philosophies
- Tourism Marketing
- Characteristics of Tourism Marketing
- Importance of Tourism Marketing
- Implications of Marketing Concept in Tourism
- The Purpose of Marketing Planning in Tourism
- Marketing Mix

Learning Objective

At the conclusion of this lesson you should be able to understand:

- The concept of marketing management.
- Different orientation to marketing
- Marketing Mix
- Tourism marketing
- Characteristics of tourism marketing and its importance
- The importance of marketing planning in tourism
- How successfully marketing concept can be applied in tourism industry

"Journeys end in lovers meeting."

— William Shakespeare (1564-1616)
British poet and playwright

INTRODUCTION

Tourism Marketing is a very complex industry because of its multi-faceted activities which together produces the tourism 'product' and various rule-sectors that are by themselves complete industries like lodging industry and transport industry. The tourism marketing industry's complexities grows further more as its promotion is directed at a large number of people in various lands of different socio-economic structures having different needs, tastes, attitudes, expectations and behaviour patterns. Efficient marketing is that which understands that people are different in the same market and helping in penetrating their different tastes and preferences. This whole system of business activity is customer-oriented and is directed to the creation and satisfaction of customers. It also envisages a dynamic process of a total system of interaction. It incorporates an idea of dealt with a maximum of effectiveness and a minimum of cost. It also establishes a healthy relationship between production and consumption and seeks to prevent a decreased level of economic activity. Sometimes to develop tourism marketing in the world nations which is subject to various internal and external economic forces needs plenty of courage, revolutionary zeal and farsightedness. This chapter will help you understand the implications of marketing strategies in tourism industry.

MARKETING CONCEPT

There are numerous alternative definitions of marketing. Frequently, the particular form reflects the preoccupations of individual authors. Most have certain basic features in common, especially the notion of looking at the firm from the point of view of the customer or striving to ensure mutual profitability from the marketing exchange. Other definitions place their emphasis on the essentially managerial nature of marketing. This can be seen in the definition put forward by the **Institute of Marketing (UK):**

Marketing is the management process, which identifies, anticipates and supplies customer requirements efficiently and profitably.

A complementary but more directive approach is adopted by **Stapleton**:

[It is] fundamental policy-forming activity devoted to selecting and developing suitable products for sale—promoting and distributing these products in a manner providing the optimal return on capital employed.

Recently, increasing numbers of writers have emphasised *this process* perspective on marketing, i.e., defining it in terms of the process of moving goods from concept to consumption in the most effective way (from both the customer's and the supplier's point of view). **Runyon** captured this nicely with his description of it as:

The performance of business activities that direct the flow of goods and services from producers to consumers.

Even this falls short of the all-encompassing approach, increasingly used to bring out the wider applicability of marketing. **Kotler** provides one of the widest definitions:

Marketing is human activity directed at satisfying needs and wants through exchange processes.

This extends the approach to include many forms of non-commercial transaction, including education, community activities and most social and political processes. It is a perspective, which has generated considerable controversy, not least because it has challenged many traditional assumptions about roles and responsibilities in a variety of exchange-based situations.

American Marketing Association – "It is the process of planning & executing the conception, pricing, promotion & distribution of ideas, goods & services to create exchange that satisfy individual & organisational goals"

MARKETING PHILOSOPHY

Production Concept:

This Concept holds that consumers favour those products that are widely available and inexpensive.

(a) *Organizational Goals:* Managers of production oriented businesses concentrate on achieving high production efficiency, Low-costs and mass distribution.

(b) Assumption about consumer:

- The managers assume that consumers are primarily interested in product availability and low prices.
- The consumers have full knowledge about the competing brands.
- They do not attach importance to non-price factors within a product class.
- In developing countries the consumers are more interested in obtaining a product.

(c) Consequences:

- This concept usually leads to an impersonal and poor quality of service to customers.

(d) Suitability:

- It is useful in developing countries where demand exceeds supply.
- It is useful when the company wants to expand its market.

(e) Examples:

- Ford's T-model car was built with no regard to customer taste. The focus was on mass production and low pricing.
- Intel aggressively invested in research and production till the mid 1990s in making microprocessor chips.

Product Concept:

A management orientation that presumes consumer's favour those products, which offer most quality, performance or innovative features.

(a) Organizational Goals:

- The managers' focus on making superior products with improved quality and features.
- Trusted engineer are made to build products and the do not depend on customer opinion or competitor analysis.

(b) Assumptions about customer:

- They assume that buyer's can evaluate quality and performance.

(c) Consequences:

- It usually leads to the "better mouse-trap" fallacy or marketing myopia.

(d) Suitability:

- It is useful in those industries where product innovation is important.

(e) Examples:

- Coca-Cola focused on soft drinks market ignoring competition from coffee bars and fruit juices.
- McDonald's focused on hamburgers alone, they did not give much importance to sandwiches, pizzas and fast foods.
- Web-TV formed with partnership of Sony and Philips failed to impress couch potatoes because of their wrong marketing pitch. Later Microsoft acquired web-TV and introduced it with right marketing and called it Ultimate TV.

Selling Concept:

This concept holds that management orientation that presumes consumers will not buy enough of organizations product unless there is aggressive selling and promotional efforts.

(a) Organizational Goals:

- The managers believe in creating a strong sales department in order to hard sell.
- The key to earn profits is aggressive selling.

(b) Assumptions about customer:

- Customers typically show buying inertia and must be coaxed into buying.
- The company has a whole battery of effective selling and promotional tools to stimulate buying.

(c) Consequences:

- The consumers have full knowledge about the competing brands.
- Post-purchase dissatisfaction.

- The customers tend to bad mouth the product and this is faster through the Internet.

(d) Suitability:

- It is suitable when a firm has over capacity in production.
- It is useful for unsought goods like insurance, encyclopedias, funeral plots, fund-raising etc.

(e) Examples:

- Coca-Cola's former Vice-president Sergio Zyman said, "The purpose of marketing is to sell more stuff to more people, more often, for more money to make more profit".
- Political parties sell their candidates to voters.

Marketing Concept:

It holds that the key to achieving its organizational goals consists of the company being more effective than competitor in creating, delivering and communicating customer value to its chosen target markets.

It has been expressed colorfully as:

- "Meeting needs Profitability"
- "Find wants and fill them"
- "Love the customer not the product"
- "You're the boss" (United Airlines)
- "Partners for Profit" (Milliken and company)

This concept rests on 4 pillars, namely

(1) Target Market

(2) Customer needs

(3) Integrated marketing

(4) Profitability.

The marketing concept can be better understood when the concepts in it are defined. Companies choose their target market and carefully prepare tailored marketing programs. Este'e Lauder targeted African Americans with special product lines designed for darker skin tones.

Customer Needs

A human need is a state of self-deprivation in a person. Needs are complex and plentiful. Wants are an expression of human needs shaped by a person's culture and individual development. Individuals are shaped by culture. Marketers cannot create needs but can create wants. However, a pre-existing need is essential. There are different types of needs:

(1) Stated Needs – which are expressed by the customer?

(2) Real Needs - The customer wants a car whose operating cost, not initial price, is low.

(3) Unstated needs – The customer expects good service from the client.

(4) Delight needs – The customer would like the dealer to include an onboard navigation system.

(5) Secret needs – The customer wants to be seen by friends as a savvy consumer.

Societal Marketing:

The Organizations task is to determine needs, wants and interest of target markets and deliver the desired satisfaction more effectively and efficiently than competitors in a way that preserves or enhances the consumer and society's well being.

(a) Organizational goals:

- Build ethical and social consideration into marketing practices.
- Balancing conflicting criteria of company profits, consumer wants and satisfaction and public interest.

(b) Assumptions about customer:

- Customers may not know their long-term interest but the organization has to consider them.
- Cause related marketing will increase customer loyalty and build sales.

(c) Consequences:

- It raises brand awareness and corporate reputation.
- It creates awareness about societal issues and business responsibility.

(d) Suitability:

- In industries where ecological damage is an issue, societal marketing is seen as desirable.

(e) Examples:

- Patagonia is practicing societal concept called as cause-related marketing.
- McDonald has replaced its plastic ware with paper.
- Dexter Corporation assigned a task force to produce a special paper to make tea bags without creating hazardous wastes in the process.
- Body shop, Ben & Jerry.

Customer Concept:

In the modern world companies practicing the marketing concept work at the level of customer segments. A growing number of today's companies are now shaping offers, services and messages to individual customers. These companies collect information on each customer's past transactions, demographics, media and distribution preferences.

TOURISM MARKETING

Accommodation sector
Hotels/motels
Guest houses/bed & breakfast
Farmhouses
Apartments/villas/flats/cottages
Condominiums/time share resorts
Vacation villages/holidy centres
Conference/exhibition centres
Static and touring caravan/camping sites
Marinas

Attraction sector
Theme parks
Museums & galleries
National parks
Wildlife parks
Gardens
Heritage sites & centres
Sports/activity centres
Themed retail/leisure/entertainment centres
Festival and events

Transport sector
Airlines
Shipping lines/ferries
Railways
Bus/coach operators
Car rental operators

Travel organizers' sector
Tour operators
Tour wholesalers/brokers
Retail travel agents
Conference organizers
Booking agencies (e.g., accommodation)
Incentive travel organizers

Destination organization sector
National tourist offices (NTOs)
Destination marketing organizations (DMOs)
Regional/state tourist offices
Local tourist offices
Tourist assocations

Fig. 7.1. The five main components of travel and tourism industry

Tourism marketing is defined in a number of ways. It could be defined as the 'systematic and coordinated efforts exerted by the National Tourist Organisations and/or the tourist enterprises at international, national and local levels to optimize the satisfaction of tourists, groups and individuals, in view of the sustained tourism growth'.

According to **Krippendorf, J.,** Marketing in tourism means 'Systematic and coordinated execution of business policy by tourist undertaking and coordinated execution of business policy by tourist undertaking whether private or state owned at local, regional, national or international level to achieve the optimal satisfaction of the needs to identifiable consumer groups, and in doing so to achieve an appropriate return'.

Comparing marketing in travel and tourism to other forms of marketing Students of travel and tourism often find it difficult to be clear about the way marketing in travel and tourism differs from other forms of consumer marketing practice. Standard texts on marketing principles are not much help. Generally speaking, however, it is common ground that the principles of the body of knowledge about marketing and its main theoretical elements hold good for all types of product. In other words the basic or core principles of marketing are relevant to all products, whether they are based on services or manufactured goods. Marketing managers at senior levels of responsibility can, and frequently do, switch between industries with little difficulty. This is only possible because of the integrity of the body of knowledge. In travel and tourism in particular, many marketing managers have been brought in from manufacturing and other service industries to bring their expertise to bear as firms grow faster than the level of expertise available from within their own sector of business.

Against this evidence of common ground, however, experience convinces many in the industry, including the authors of this book, that there are some special characteristics of travel and tourism services that are so dominant in their implications that standard marketing principles must be considerably adapted to ensure success in an operational context.

This is clearly a very important consideration and it is based on the belief that marketing in travel and tourism reflects five aspects of demand and supply in the industry, which individually and combined give marketing practice its special approach and style.

- The characteristics of demand
- The characteristics of supply
- Products and prices, which match the supply to the demand (see
- Characteristics of promotion used to influence demand
- Characteristics of distribution used to facilitate purchase

CHARACTERISTICS OF TOURISM MARKETING

(1) Tourism is an Intangible Non-Material Product: No tangible product is bought or sold. Services, facilities, installations are given for a specified time in exchange for money. A room in a hotel, a house boat, skiing services, sight-seeing tours is carried out to customer or advice or information offered to him by the local tourist authorities.

(2) Production and Consumption are Inter-related: Production can only take place when the customer is really present. Most services can only be personal and to no other person can it be exchanged or transferred. The tourist service can be very unreliable and risky as the customer cannot see, inspect, compare or try out tourist services before deciding to use them.

(3) A Wide Range of Services Constitute the Tourism Marketing Product: This cannot be provided by a single enterprise. Each component of the tourist service requires a high degree of excellence, perfection and specialization and its total is a part of the final product. Naturally the need for cooperation and coordination is of paramount importance in Tourism Marketing.

(4) Highly Unstable Nature of the Tourism Demand: Different factors – seasonal, economic, political, etc., influence tourist demand. Seasonal places puts strain on the transport system and hotel divisions. So not only is employment affected but also return from investments. In these days of escalating violence, political unrest cause fluctuation in tourism growth and even damages it for longer period.

(5) Dominant role of Intermediaries: As in most industries where manufacturers control distribution, promotion and pricing, in tourism the manufacturers are sales intermediaries like tour operators, travel agents, airline operators, hotel brokers who play the most important role and enjoy superior marketing strength. Different pricing to suit different levels of tourists for different services, package deals pricing policies and promotion strategies to be adopted by tourist enterprises is decided primarily by travel sales intermediaries.

(6) Diverse Motivation: Prompt people to take diverse destinations and there is simply no concrete reason for certain decisions. The subjective and objective reasons, expectations and desires influence tourist's choice for holiday destination type of accommodations and vacation activities which are heterogeneous.

IMPORTANCE OF TOURISM MARKETING

(1) Marketing helps to create new customers by offering to satisfy their needs and aims primarily at customer satisfaction. His second task is to motivate potential customers to purchase their services. Their crucial role is in promoting distinct destination prints citing cultural, social scenically important, historical and entertainment–oriented places. Tourism marketing begins by a detailed assessment of the actual and potential demand and on this assessment developing facilities and services for use of these customers.

(2) Customer needs in tourism are more than particular products: What the traveller needs on his travel is a hygienic and a good place to sleep, safe, clean place to eat moderately priced good food and a comfortable mode of travel be it by train, bus or plane. Such basic needs can be a effectively given by the hots. Hospitality should become a way of life and personal prejudices as sexist, religious and racist should be effectively controlled.

(3) Merchandising becomes more effective under tourism marketing management because management view their tasks as that of supplying want satisfaction rather than creating demand for its products among the customers. The physical product is only a part of the satisfaction rather than creating demand for its products among the customers. The physical product is only a part of the satisfactions sought by the buyer because he wants in addition convenience, service and certain other symbolic values.

(4) The managements are able to create more harmony between their own interests and those of the society because the market orientation under this concept means that the management build, their future products from satisfying human needs better.

Marketing in tourism duet to the various factors mentioned above needs a somewhat different approach unlike the normal consumer product or service.

IMPLICATIONS OF MARKETING CONCEPT IN TOURISM

Before we can consider how marketing policy and strategy might be incorporated in a destination's overall tourism development approach, we need to consider those basic characteristics of tourism that have implications for the marketing function.

Fragmentation of Supply

The tourist product is a composite one, a combination of attractions, transport, accommodation, entertainment and other services. In most countries, there are many separate suppliers of these various components – airlines, hotel companies, tour excursion organizers etc. It is an important feature of tourism that, though an individual supplier of tourist services may serve more than one market, rarely, if ever, does a single supplier provide the entire range of products/services required by a tourist on a visit to a destination. Whether sold as a package or assembled by the tourist himself or by a travel agent, the tourist product is in practice a composite one. It is apparent, then, that given the fragmented nature of supply on one hand, and the demand for a combined set of products on the other, a fundamental challenge for a destination is to achieve coordination and integration of all components across all sub-sectors of the tourism industry - that is, of supply.

Interdependence and Complementarity of Tourist Services

It follows from the fact that tourism demand is for a composite product that the various tourist products and services are interdependent and complementary. The supply of one (for example international air transport to/from a destination) depends on the supply of another (such as hotel accommodation) and they complement each other. A destination's reputation can be set by the weakest link in the tourist product chain. This leads to the marketing policies and actions of one enterprise directly influencing other enterprises. A country with a liberal charter policy and/or an airline with an aggressive pricing policy may result in the attraction of low budget tourists, something that could damage the high quality image central to the marketing of a five-star hotel chain in the destination. There is again then the need for coordination and cooperation in order to enhance the effectiveness of individual marketing and promotional efforts of the various tourism suppliers.

Rigidity of Supply

Much tourism demand cannot be easily and quickly be adjusted in the short term to variation in demand. A hotel, for example, cannot add or remove rooms in line with demand. This relative lack of flexibility has obvious operational and economic implications. When demand falls below capacity, waste of resources occurs; when it exceeds capacity, the tourism industry fails to maximise its revenue. This "short term" can extend to years if the rigidity is caused by lack of airport or hotel capacity, given the extensive lead-time to construct a new airport or hotel.

Fixed in Time and Space

The composite tourism product cannot be stored – it is perishable – so a hotel room on a particular night or a seat on a given flight is available only once, and if not utilised, the sales opportunity is lost. Similarly, it cannot be transported. The need is to bring the consumer to the tourist product. The importance of ensuring, through marketing, as high a level of utilisation as possible is particularly marked because of the high fixed costs of many tourist operations. A hotel has to meet its fixed costs whether it has 5 guests or 200. The non-transportability of tourism products means there is no physical distribution in the strict sense in tourism marketing. Similarly, there are limited opportunities for merchandising activities, in consequence of the fact that the tourist product, unlike consumer goods, cannot be displayed at points of sale other than via proxy representations.

Intangible – "expectation - experience - memory"

Tourist products, except items like souvenirs, are services rather than goods. As such they are intangible. The tourism product is subjectively perceived – each destination or individual tourist operation is a mental concept for each individual prospective tourist encompassing both physical characteristics and other abstract attributes. The subjective nature of perception involves an emotional and also an irrational element. In consequence, the tourist has to be offered psychological benefits. Clearly, this has important implications for advertising and promotion in tourism and generally on how a tourist product is presented to consumer groups.

In consequence of the intangibility of tourist products, when a supplier of a tourist services considers the potential market, the essential thought process should be: expectations – experiences – memories. This is the same whether the supplier is a destination promotion authority seeking to attract tourists to a specific country or location within that country, or the operator of a fixed-site facility like a hotel, restaurant or attraction, or a provider of tour excursion.

Each tourist is a set of expectations. The tourism product cannot be test driven or known about with certainty in advance of being consumed. The tourist therefore builds mental images of the destination and of the facilities and other components of the tourism product of that destination. He/she has a set of expectations about the place to be visited.

Experiences because the intangibility of tourism products means that the tourist engages in a series of activities – typically, for example, riding on transport, visiting attractions, staying in some form of accommodation, eating, drinking, recreating, interacting with other people – none of which produce a final physical product to take home. Each tourist trip, therefore, is a combination of various experiences.

At then end of the trip the tourist is left with nothing more than memories – the derivation of the word souvenirs – and proxies of the trip – such as photos or videos.

The key for the marketer is that the expectations created achieve the fine balance between attracting the tourist while not promising more than can be delivered. The experiences are assessed by the tourist against his/her pre-trip expectations. A major determinant of success is how well the experiences match or exceed these expectations. This assessment has relative as well absolute dimensions. A destination may have a perception in the marketplace of being expensive or offering poor service, something which will limit its drawing power. If the tourist finds it is not so costly or that service is better than expected, his/her level of satisfaction will be higher. Of course, the reverse can also be the case with more damaging consequences for the destination.

The intangibility of the tourist product and the consequent need for the marketer to address the potential market's perceptions of the tourist product has two dimensions: first, the need to offer psychological benefits to the prospective tourist; and, second, to recognise that the perception is the reality - with each tourist having sovereign power over his/her destination decision making – and that marketing activities should be designed to alter the market's prevailing images in line with the marketer's desired position.

Price Elasticity of Demand

Most forms of tourism demand involve the use of what economists call personal discretionary disposable income and free time. Holidaymakers or vacation travellers need both money and time to engage in tourism. They have freedom of choice as to how to use their money and time for tourism purposes, affecting decisions such as how much to spend, how long to go for, where to go, when to go etc. As a result, tourists are highly sensitive to price, and generally their demand for tourist services exhibits a significant degree of price elasticity.

The marketing implication of these demand characteristics is that the travelling public is susceptible to price inducements and to other marketing efforts in respect of choices relating to destination, place and type of accommodation, and timing of the trip. The price elasticity factor is growing in significance because of two interlinked factors, namely increased pressure on free time and greater ease of international travel ie more frequent services to more destinations at fares rising below prevailing rates of inflation. This will increasingly lead to a pattern of shorter but more frequent holidays.

Seasonality

It is a characteristic of most tourism markets that demand fluctuates over the course of the year. The principal determinant is climatic – either in the destination or the tourist generating markets. Residents of northern parts of the European and North American continents tend mostly to take domestic or intra-regional holidays in the summer months of June – September whereas they take long haul, inter-regional holidays more in the winter when the climate at home is generally cold and wet. As a result, tourist operators have periods when demand is near capacity and others when the level of utilisation can be 30 per cent or even less, with the remaining months – the shoulder season – falling in between these two extremes.

These demand variations are all the more acute because of the fact that any tourism product cannot be stored – the perishability factor – and the concern of marketers is to generate as much demand in the trough periods as possible since the fixed cost element of any tourism operation do not change between seasons. The marketing response to seasonality can range from the reduction of prices in order to induce people to travel in periods other than would be their normal preference to targeting geographic markets with different seasonal patterns of travel so that the demand for the destination from one group complements that of the other group.

Other Tourists as Part of the Tourism Product

It follows from the fact that the production and consumption of tourism products and services are simultaneous – and that they cannot be made in advance and stored – that the producers/distributors of such products and services are part of the tourist experience – hence, the importance of vocational training programmes. It is also the fact that other tourists in the vicinity of the tourist when he/she is receiving tourist products/services constitute part of the experience. In tourism the customer is part of the product. This applies not only to hotels and restaurants, and tourist attractions or excursions, but to the whole destination. The type, quality, volume and other characteristics of restaurant customers, hotel guests or visitors to a destination influence the overall perception of that restaurant, hotel or destination by other potential customers, guests or visitors – that is, the market. Therefore, in marketing it is vitally important to identify and target the most appropriate market mix and ensure compatibility of the different target market segments. It would be unwise for a hotel to accept block bookings from two tour operators that specialise in older generation tourists and young tourists because the interests of these two groups are likely to be quite different and the behaviour of one an irritant to the other.

Importance of Intermediaries

A distinguishing characteristic of tourism is the relatively dominant role played by travel intermediaries. Tour operators or wholesalers and travel agents are all traditionally important in product design, pricing, distribution and promotion. In international tourism marketing the influence of travel intermediaries has its origin both in historical factors and in the physical distance between the generating tourist source markets and the destinations (or tourist receiving countries). This latter factor leads to the necessity for a special distribution channel.

At the same time, the fragmentation of supply creates the need for the coordinating and facilitating role of the travel intermediary. Further, the relative lack of marketing expertise and capital resources on the part of individual destination-based suppliers of tourism products or services makes them dependent on travel intermediaries for the distribution and sale of their individual offerings. This often gives rise to the need for destination tourism operators to promote and supply at two levels through tour operators and travel agents (intermediaries) and direct to the ultimate consumer/tourist. The advent of sophisticated electronic technology has changed the balance of power, making it easier for destination operators – even relatively small ones – to communicate direct and at low cost with consumer. Nonetheless, the travel intermediary remains a major player in tourism distribution.

THE MARKETING RESPONSE

The distinctive characteristics of all service industries - identified by Middleton and Clarke (2001) as inseparability and intangibility, perishability based on fixed capacity in the short run and inability to create stocks, seasonality, high fixed costs and interdependence - coupled with those other aspects detailed above specifically related to travel and tourism strongly influence the attitudes and decisions of management in all sectors of the travel and tourism industry as they seek to respond to, and influence, prospective customers' demand for their products and services – the marketing response.

The role of marketing in the travel and tourism industry is to manage or manipulate sales – customer purchasing behaviour – on an orderly, continuous, regular basis, in order to utilise the maximum level of available, inseparable capacity, and to generate extra or marginal sales that contributes revenue at minimal additional cost.

While the principles of the body of knowledge about marketing, and its main theoretical elements, can be applied in all industries, the special characteristics of travel and tourism are so dominant in their implications, that standard marketing principles must be considerably adapted to be successfully utilisation in travel and tourism applications.

Middleton and Clarke (2001) identify three propositions about marketing in travel and tourism that are relevant to all the forms it takes:

- In the context of opportunities and constraints arising from the business environment of a major global market, products in tourism are designed, adapted and promoted to meet the long-run needs, expectations and interests of prospective customers. This is the common ground with all forms of consumer marketing, and the cornerstone of all marketing theory;
- Service products generally have particular characteristics of inseparability and perishability, which call for a different application of the traditional marketing mix variables. This is the common ground with the developing theory of services marketing as distinct from marketing goods; and
- Marketing in travel and tourism is shaped and determined by the nature of the demand for tourism and the operating characteristics of supplying industries. The forms of promotion and distribution used for travel and tourism products have their own particular characteristics, which distinguish their use in comparison with other industries. These characteristics form the common ground on which marketing for travel and tourism is based.

USERS OF TOURISM SERVICES

The users of tourism services can be categorized in a number of ways. One such way of classifying the users is by dividing them into categories such as General, Sex, Region, Education, etc.

(1) General: Domestic, Foreign Kids, Teens, Youths, Seniors, Students, Executives, Artists, Politicians, Movie stars

(2) Sex: Men, Women

(3) Region: Rural, Urban

(4) Education: Literate, Illiterate

(5) Status: Rich, Poor

(6) Profession: Executives, Academics, Sportsmen, Artists

(7) Occupation: White collar, Blue collar

Another method of classifying users of tourism services is on the basis of the frequency of usage of services.

(1) Non-users: They lack the willingness, desire and ability (income & leisure time)

(2) Potential Users: They have the willingness but the marketing resources have not been used optimally to influence their impulse

(3) Actual Users: They are already using the services generated by the tourist organizations

(4) Occasional Users: They have not formed the habit of travelling

(5) Habitual Travellers: They have formed a habit and avail of the services regularly.

Need For Segmentation

Consumer behavior can be defined in psychological terms as the whole range of the generation of wants and their transformation into buying or using decisions. Users have values, perceptions, preferences and expectations which are the result of environmental influences. There are a number of factors that influence the behavioral profile of consumers.

In recent years, the users have become more discriminating in their using habits and therefore their needs for different services, products and brands change constantly. This makes it essential that the marketers analyze their behavioral profile and undertake segmentation so that they know the level of expectations.

In a nutshell, tourist organizations need to undertake segmentation in order to simplify their task of creating and stimulating demand. In this way they can identify the potential tourists, transform them into actual tourists and further into habitual tourists.

SEGMENTATION

Though there are a number of bases for segmentation of tourists, one of the most important is lifestyle. Travelling decisions are fantastically influenced by changing lifestyles. They are also affected by other factors such as level of income, availability of leisure time, etc.

Base of Segmentation	**Categories**
Holiday	Mass Market
	Popular Market
	Individual Market
Demand	Primary
	Secondary
	Opportunity
Geography	International
	On the basis of regions, cities, etc.
Psychography	Lifestyle
	Personality motive
	Knowledge
Demography	Age
	Sex
	Religion
Socio-economic	Rich, Poor
	Rural, Urban
	Literate, Illiterate
Purpose	Business Travel
	Cultural Tourism
	Common Interest Convention
Age	Teens
	Youth
	Seniors

Fig. 7.2. Bases for tourism market segmentation

Such segmentation is useful when deciding the offerings to target a particular segment. For example:

'...The mass market consists of vacationists that travel in large groups and prefer all-inclusive tours. They are generally conservative.

'...The popular market consists of smaller groups going on inclusive or semi-inclusive tours. This group includes pensioners and retired people.

'...The individual market consists of chairmen, senior executives, etc.

'...As the lifestyle changes, consumption of services might change. For example, a newly married couple might prefer romantic holidays, but once they have children they would prefer family vacations where there are plenty of activities to entertain kids.

'...Teens and youth might prefer adventure holidays whereas senior citizens would probably prefer more relaxing vacations.

THE PRODUCT MIX:

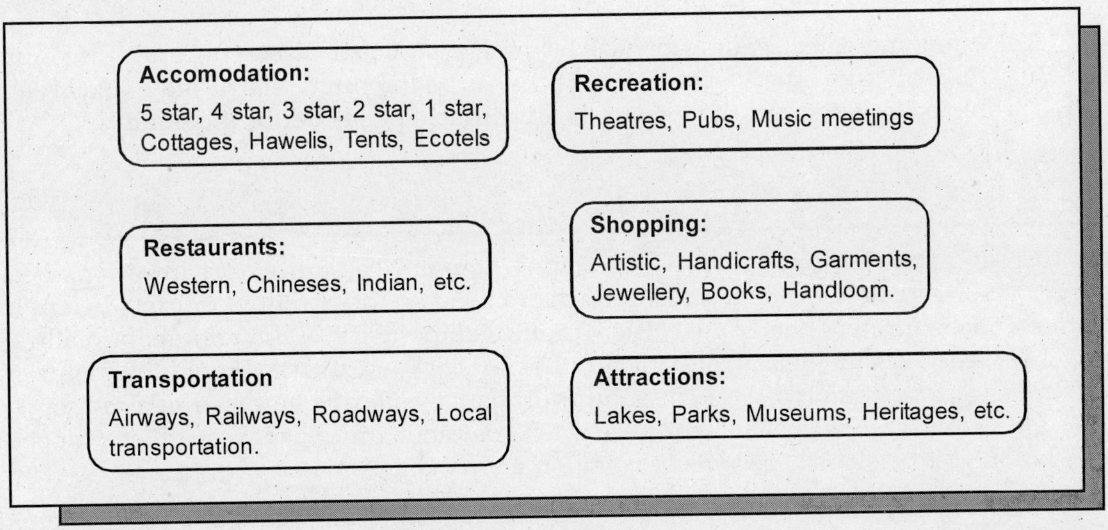

Fig. 7.3. Product Mix

The tourism product is essentially an intangible thing. Also, because tourism is a multi-segment industry, the task of formulating a product mix becomes more difficult & challenging.

Selling a holiday is 'selling dreams'. The way to win the customer's heart is through the peripheral services provided along with the core product. Thus, a tourism product is quite a complex one, including the destination, airline seat, hotel room, occasional tangible products such as souvenirs, a free bag or bottle of whisky, etc.

Innovation in the tourism industry helps to raise the sensitivity in this regard. There is nothing fixed or fundamental about the tourism product. The content factor is within the jurisdiction of the government that undertakes the maintenance, development and conservation of tourist attractions such as parks, museums, beaches, historical treasures, etc. Unless these factors are developed in the right fashion, the marketing professionals would never be successful in making the marketing resources productive.

Thus, the direct or indirect patronage of the government is essential to get a positive response. The government and private tourist organizations work together to undertake activities such as developing infrastructural facilities such as transportation, water, banking, Medicare facilities, etc., and also developing and maintain hotels, cottages, havelis, lodges, etc.

THE PRICE MIX

In pricing decisions, the product or the service mix of the tourist organization is important. They have to set prices in line with the quality of services to be made available to the customers. Pricing decisions are influenced by internal and external factors. The tourism professionals are supposed to watch the emerging trends in both the markets. They are required to think in favour of discounting price.

These may include discounts for cash payments, seasonal discounts, trade discounts etc. But while offering the discounts, it is not to be forgotten that it may also create image problem since some of the value sensitive tourists may doubt the quality.

THE PROMOTION MIX

Creation of awareness has a far reaching impact. The tourist organizations bear the responsibility of informing, persuading and sensing the potential tourists in a right fashion. The marketers need to use the various components of promotion optimally so that they succeed in increasing the number of habitual users. Promotion helps in maximizing the duration of stay, frequency of visit by offering new tourist products in the same country to areas which hitherto have remained untapped or partially tapped. The various dimensions of tourism promotion are as follows:

Advertising: Advertisement helps in furnishing important information to the actual and potential tourists. Its coverage is wide. Advertising is aimed at the public to create awareness of the travel offers available on a resort and its attractions to influence their business decisions.

Intangibility can be compensated with the help of visual exposure of scenes and events. We can project hotel bedrooms, well arranged restaurants and cafeterias, swimming pools etc.

Publicity: It focuses attention on strengthening the public relations measures by developing a rapport with media people and getting their personalized support in publicizing the business. It helps in projecting the positive image of tourists organizations since the prospects trust on the news items publicized by the media people. Eg. Kumarakom in Kerala after Prime Minister a B Vajpayee's visit. The publicity programme include regular publicity stories and photographs to the newspapers, travel editors, contact with magazines on stories etc.

There are different groups in publicity, such as advertising publicity, projected publicity, structural publicity and personal publicity.

Sales promotions: Sales promotion measures are the short term activities seeking to boost sales at peak demand periods to ensure that the firms obtain its market share and are used to help launch a new product or support an ailing or modified one. The tool of sales promotions is designed to appeal particularly to those customers who are price-sensitive. There are a number of techniques to promote sale and the tourist professional need to use them in the face of their requirements vis-à-vis the emerging trends in the business. Eg., in the tourism industry, a travel company offers give-aways to their clients, such as flight bags, wallets for tickets and forex and covers of passport.

The hotels offer a number of facilities like shoe shine, clothes, first aid, sewing kits, shower caps and shampoo. Further, the VIP clients also get fruits and flowers in their rooms.

Thomas Cook offered 3 tier sales promotion based on price and one more novel technique as detailed below:

- Cook agreed to match the price of any holiday they sold which was known as price promise.
- Money back guarantee to the clients who purchase the product or any tour operator known as trading charter.
- Matching of customers' need with a particular holiday known as formal guarantee.
- A business travel challenge in which the details of expenditure on staff business travel booked through other agents over a 3 months period were submitted by companies to Cook, specially to calculate expected savings, provided the bookings are made through them.

Word-of-mouth Promotion: Most communication about tourism takes place by word-of-mouth information which in a true sense is word-of-recommendation. In the tourism industry it is found that the word-of-mouth promoters play the role of a hidden sales-force, who instrumentalize the process of selling. The high magnitude of effectiveness of this tool of promotion is due to high credibility of the channel, specially in the eyes of the potential tourists. The sensitivity of this tool makes it clear that tourist organizations need to concentrate on the quality of services they promise and offer. The marketers or the tourist organizations need to keep their eyes open, identify the vocal persons or the opinion leaders and take a special care of them so that they keep on moving the process of stimulating and creating demand.

Personal Selling: Personal Selling is based on the personal skill of an individual. The oral representation in conversation bears the efficacy of transforming the motivation into persuasion. The travel and hotel business depend considerably on the personal selling. The development of travel and tourism has been possible due to well educated and trained sales personnel. The development of tourism business has been influenced by the services rendered by the travel agents and travel guides since they work as information carriers.

Personal selling is the personal presentation of a tangible product or intangible services or ideas to the personal customers. It is important to mention that in the tourism industry, the personnel who attend tourists form an essential ingredient of the product, such as sales personnel are found responsible for dealing with customers behind the counter, the resort representatives cater to the need of tourists when they reach the destination, etc., all of them play a vital role in ensuring that the tourism products satisfy the tourists. The phrase – the customer is always right applies specifically to the tourism industry. No reduction in price would compensate for impolite and indecent travel guide, a solvent waiter and a surly or a haughty coach driver. These facts are testimony to the proposition that the travel business is linked with the performance and behaviour of sales personnel or travel staff.

Telemarketing: it is a method of selling in which a professionally sound telemarketer expands the business. The quality of technology and the communicative ability of the telemarketers determine the magnitude of success of this component. In tourism, the travel agents, offices of airways, receptionist, secretaries cannot work efficiently if the telephonic services are not up to the mark. This makes a strong advocacy in favour of recruiting a person considered to be professionally sound, personally-committed sales personnel having an in-built creativity, innovation and imagination.

Place

Place or distribution management is concerned with two things – availability and accessibility. Researchers in tourism must determine how and where potential customers prefer to buy tourism products and services.

Most tour operators sell their services through travel agents, however some deal directly with the consumers and eliminate middlemen. Other companies may also utilize more than one method of distribution. Airlines, for example, sell tickets through travel agents, and sell seats on flights to tour operators, and also offer travellers to book seats themselves through their own booking offices.

There exist, however, a number of intermediaries in the tourism marketing channel. It depends largely on the channel type. The intangibility feature in the service sector prevents intermediaries from taking possession or ownership of goods. Tourism, however, proves an exception where cuisine and souvenirs are goods and ownership is possible for the intermediaries.

Transport also plays a major role in the tourism industry. It makes the destinations accessible to people from around the world. Also, in the case of tangible products in tourism such as souvenirs and cuisine, transportation becomes a major logistical component.

People

We cannot deny the fact that sophisticated technologies have been successful in accelerating the pace of development. We also agree with this view that new generation of information technologies have simplified the task of decision makers. At the same time we also have to accept the fact that the sophisticated technologies can't deliver goods to the development process if the employees operating and maintaining these technologies are not of world class. Technologies need due support of human resources who invent, innovate and develop technologies.

Like other industries, the tourism industry depends substantially on management of human resources. The tourism industry is an amalgam of the services of a lot of people and hence this industry cannot work efficiently if the travel agents, tour operators and travel guides lack world class professional excellence. Of course the offices of travel agents depend on the new technology but after all employees and the other staff contribute significantly to the process. The travel guides need professional excellence since the projection of a positive image regarding a destination in particular requires their due cooperation, failing which even the world class services offered by the travel agents are found meaningless. The tour operators also need to manage human resources efficiently.

In the management of people, the related organizations are required to think in favour of developing an ongoing training program so that we find a close relation between the development of technologies and the quality of personnel who are supposed to operate and maintain the same. They need a lot of credentials to fulfill the expectations of the customers. The organization has to make the environmental conditions conducive and focus has to be laid on the incentives to the employees for energizing the process of performance orientation. Employee orientation requires due weightage to efficiency generation, value-orientation and perfection.

In the tourism industry the travel agents and the travel guides are the two most important people who speak a lot about the industry. Hence it is imperative that they have to be at their best at all times. Travel guides especially, are expected to have a lot of patience, good sense of humour, tact to transform the occasional tourists into habitual ones, thorough knowledge of the places, linguistic skills etc.

THE PROCESS OF MARKETING PLANNING IN TOURISM

A marketing plan is essentially the means by which an organisation – whether a commercial company, a not-for-profit organisation or a government agency or authority – realises its goals in respect of its "market". It is a navigational chart and as such a tool for implementation, guiding the specific activities designed to influence the behaviour of the market and enabling the effectiveness of such activities to be assessed. The development of a marketing plan may not require intensive scholarly work; it is an attitude that will govern and influence the directions an organisation intends to go.

Drawing on **Gartrell** (1994), marketing plans typically include the following sections:

Executive Summary: the objective is to give a clear understanding of what the marketing plan is about without going into detail. Though presented at the beginning it is usually completed after the whole plan has been prepared. Length – 2 to 3 pages.

Situation Analysis (or what **Kotler** *et. al.*, 2002 term "place audit"): This assessment explores the structure, characteristics and performance of the sector, the community, the travel product, the economic environment, and the present and potential market. For tourism place marketing, some of the following questions should be examined:

PRODUCT	HOTEL	SCHEDULED AIRLINE	MUSEUM
Designed characterisation/ packaging	Location houlding size/grounds/design/ room size/ facilities in hotel furnishings/decor/ ambience/lighting/ catering styles	Routes/service frequency Aircraft types/size Seat size/space Decor, meals, style	Building size/ Design of collections Types of collection Size of collection Interier display/ interpretation
Service component	Staff numbers/ unforms/attitudes/ customer responsiveness	Staff numbers/ unforms/attitudes/ customer responsiveness	Staff numbers/ unforms/attitudes/ customer responsiveness
Branding	eg. Holiday Inn. Marriott, Meridien	eg. American Arilines, Britiesh Airways, Virgin Asiantic	eg. Tate Gallery (London) Metropolten Museum (New York)
Image/reputation/ position	eg. unpmarket, downmarket	eg. reliable, exectic food, badily managed	eg. dull, exciting, modern
Price Normal or regular price Promotional price (for each product offered)	**Rack rates** Corporate rates Privileged user rates Tour operator rate	First class/ business hourist fares APEX/bulk purchase fares Standby charter Consolidated fares	(assuming charge made) Adult rate, serior citizen rate Group/party rates Children rate Friends of the museum rate
Promotion (solo and collaborative) Advertising (television/radio/ press/web sites) Sales promotion/ merchanding Public relation Brochure production and distribution Sales force	Examples not provided since these are generally self-evident and specific to individual organizations (See Parts Four and Five)		
Place Challans of distribution including reservation systems, third party retailers and web sites	Computerized reservation systems (CRS) Other hotels in group Internet Travel agents Tour operators Airlines free telephone lines	Computerized reservation systems (CRS) Internet City offices Airport desks Travel agents Other arilines 800 telephone lines	Other museums Internet Tourist Information attioes Hotel desks Schools/colleges

Fig. 7.4. The marketing mix

- What is present demand for tourism attractions and activities in your area?
- What resources and facilities do you have to market to visitors?
- What is your community known for? What kind of image does it have among outsiders? And to local residents?

- What are your strengths and weaknesses, and how do they impact your tourism markets?
- What changes do you anticipate over the next five years – taking account of market and competitor trends – and how will they impact your ability to attract visitors to your destination?
- What other developments and trends might impact your community/destination?
- How responsive is your community to having visitors?
- Developing a situation analysis is fundamental to better understand the capabilities, potential and interest that may exist for visitors within a destination.

Objectives and Goals: it is important in developing a marketing plan to establish measurable goals. This requires careful consideration of the demand and supply potential of visitors to the destination. Questions that address this issue are:

- What kind of goals should be established? ie short or long term? Is there a sound baseline against which such goals can be set?
- What kinds of tourism markets should be targeted, and what goals should be set for each target segment?
- How will the organisation assess the attainment of these goals?
- Are the goals realistic in terms of the organisation's resources, timetables and travel products?

Market Segments: The third essential element in a marketing plan is that of identifying and selecting the target markets – market segmentation, a topic that is dealt with in a later session. No organisation has the financial resources to cover the whole of the market: it is necessary to identify and select those sub-groups with most interest in the products being offered. There are many means of segmenting the market.

Marketing Strategies: once the segments to be targeted are identified, the marketing strategies likely to produce the maximum penetration and benefit to the organisation are defined and specified. In selecting the most appropriate marketing approaches and deciding on the product's positioning, the organisation will need to ask itself the following questions:

- Which selected marketing strategies will be the most effective for an identified market segment?
- What are the strengths and weaknesses of a strategy?
- Who is affected by a selected strategy?
- What combination of strategies might be most productive in reaching a selected market segment?

Marketing Mix: how the product will be marketed to the targeted segments?

Arriving at the most appropriate marketing mix will be determined by answering the four key questions:

- How will the product be offered to prospective tourist customers?
- What should be the pricing structure for the product?

- How should the product's positioning and image be communicated to its target market segments?
- How will the product be distributed – made available - to tourists?

Resources: an organisation needs to allocate its resources adequately to support the programmes outlined for attaining the desired goals. Without funding and personnel, programmes will not be productive. The following questions need to be addressed:

- To what extent will personnel and money be dedicated for a specific programme?
- Will the allocation be sufficient to reach the desired programme goal?
- Does the organisation have other community resources that might be employed towards a specific programme to ensure its success?
- This section should also have a clear and transparent marketing budget.

Implementation: scheduling and timing are key determinants of the success of a marketing plan. These affect the placement of advertising and its impact on the targeted market segment. Questions that might direct the implementation of a plan include:

- When is the best time to launch a specific marketing strategy for a specific market segment?
- What kind of lead times applicable to various market segments would impact goal achievement?
- In what sequence should various marketing elements be implemented? Does one strategy need to follow another to maximise impact?
- Who is doing what? When? How? And with whom? In implementing a programme, is it coordinated for maximum efficiency?

Assessment: being able to evaluate a marketing effort is imperative. The questions to be posed include:

- What kinds of results are being sought in a specific marketing effort? Are the results quantified?
- What kinds of criteria have been established against which to assess a marketing programme?
- What kinds of contingencies have been developed for a programme that may prove less effective than intended?

Terms of Reference (ToR) for tourism marketing strategic plans vary in detail. The marketing plan is often prepared as part of an overall tourism strategic development plans; while at the other end of the scale a plan may be called for to address a particular marketing-related issue (e.g., brand image development) within an already-established marketing strategy. A number of examples of ToRs relating to typical tourism destination marketing policy and planning studies are included in the resource disk. As a general rule, these are drafted on the understanding that those undertaking the planning exercise will already be aware of the research and other tasks necessary to produce an appropriate plan. Emphasis tends to be on the liaison and reporting procedures so that the "client" organisation is kept fully informed about and is integrated within the planning process

MARKETING MIX

The marketing mix is the way in which the chosen marketing strategy is implemented. It is commonly represented in marketing text books as a combination of a set of Ps – normally four (product, promotion, place – or means of distributing the product, and price) though **Middleton and Clarke** (2001) add people, process of delivery, and physical evidence arguing they are particularly useful in travel and tourism, which is typically a high contact service (the people component), an extended and complex service (the process component) and a service that can only be evaluated by the consumer as they experience the delivery (which incorporate the physical evidence component). The production-orientation of the four Ps can be converted into consumer orientation through converting these to Cs, i.e., product = customer value, price = cost, place = convenience of access and promotion = communications. An analogy for the marketing mix is driving a car insofar as the individual elements – i.e., clutch, steering wheel, accelerator and brake in the case of the car – cannot be deployed with effect, independent of each other.

LET US SUM UP

Tourism marketing is defined in a number of ways. It could be defined as the 'systematic and coordinated efforts exerted by the National Tourist Organisations and/or the tourist enterprises at international, national and local levels to optimize the satisfaction of tourists, groups and individuals, in view of the sustained tourism growth'. The main characteristics of tourism industry are it is an intangible, non-material product, production and consumption are interrelated, a wide range of services constitute the tourism marketing product, highly unstable nature of the tourism demand etc.

Tourism Marketing helps in different ways:

- *Marketing helps to create new customers by offering to satisfy their needs and aims primarily at customer satisfaction.*
- *The second task is to motivate potential customers to purchase their services.*
- *Customer needs in tourism are more than particular products.*
- *Merchandising becomes more effective under tourism marketing management because management view their tasks as that of supplying want satisfaction rather than creating demand for its products among the customers.*
- *The managements are able to create more harmony between their own interests and those of the society because the market orientation under this concept means that the management build, their future products from satisfying human needs better.*

- *Marketing in tourism duet to the various factors mentioned above needs a somewhat different approach unlike the normal consumer product or service.*

The marketing mix is the way in which the chosen marketing strategy is implemented. It is commonly represented in marketing text books as a combination of a set of Ps – normally four (product, promotion, place – or means of distributing the product, and price) though ***Middleton and Clarke*** *(2001) add people, process of delivery, and physical evidence arguing they are particularly useful in travel and tourism, which is typically a high contact service (the people component), an extended and complex service (the process component) and a service that can only be evaluated by the consumer as they experience the delivery (which incorporate the physical evidence component).*

CHECK YOUR PROGRESS

(A) True/False

(i) Marketing is human activity deals with satisfaction of people's needs.

(ii) Tourism is non-material product.

(iii) Tourism is highly stable.

(B) True/False

(i) Merchandising becomes more effective under tourism marketing management.

(ii) Tourist product is a composite one.

(iii) Tourist product is not perishable.

(C) True/False

(i) Travel industry is a part of tourism industry.

(ii) Each tourist is a set of attractions.

(iii) Much tourism demand can not be easily and quickly be adjusted in the short time.

LESSON & ACTIVITY

Develop a Tourism Marketing plan for a neighborhood tourist spot and prepare a proper Marketing Mix strategy.

KEY WORDS

Marketing: "It is the process of planning & executing the conception, pricing, promotion & distribution of ideas, goods & services to create exchange that satisfy individual & organisational goals"

Tourism marketing: It could be defined as the 'systematic and coordinated efforts exerted by the National Tourist Organisations and/or the tourist enterprises at international, national and local levels to optimize the satisfaction of tourists, groups and individuals, in view of the sustained tourism growth'.

Marketing Mix: 4Ps- Product, Price, Place & Promotion.

QUESTIONS FOR DISCUSSION

(1) What do you understand by 'Marketing'? Explain in your own words.

(2) Explain the different orientation (philosophy) to marketing.

(3) Define tourism marketing.

(4) Explain how marketing concept can be applied in tourism?

(5) Briefly explain the characteristics of Tourism Marketing.

(6) What is the importance of Tourism Marketing? Explain

(7) Explain the importance of marketing planning in tourism.

(8) What is Marketing Mix? Explain.

(9) Explain the various bases for tourism market segmentation.

(10) Write short notes on *(i)* price mix *(ii)* product mix *(iii)* promotion mix *(iv)* place.

CHECK YOUR PROGRESS: MODEL ANSWER

(A) *(i)* T *(ii)* T *(iii)* F

(B) *(i)* T *(ii)* T *(iii)* F

(C) *(i)* T *(ii)* T *(iii)* T

❑ ❑ ❑

8

Marketing Research, Positioning & Travel Distribution System

Chapter Outline

- *Introduction*
- *Definition & Objective Research Technique*
- *International Marketing Strategy*
- *Market Positioning*
- *Travel Distribution System*
- *Global Distribution System*

Learning Objective

At the conclusion of this lesson you should be able to understand:

- *The Concept of research in tourism management*
- *Different research techniques*
- *International marketing strategy*
- *Market positioning*
- *Travel distribution system.*

"As the Spanish proverb says, "He, who would bring home the wealth of the Indies, must carry the wealth of the Indies with him.'' So it is in travelling; a man must carry knowledge with him, if he would bring home knowledge."

— Samuel Johnson (1709-1784)
British author

INTRODUCTION

Marketing research is a formalized means of acquiring information to assist in the making of marketing decisions. The American Marketing Association (AMA) defines marketing research as the function that links the consumer, customer, and public to the marketer through information—information used to identify and define marketing opportunities and problems; generate, refine, and evaluate marketing actions; monitor marketing performance; and improve understanding of marketing as a process. Marketing research specifies the information required to address these issues, designs the method for collecting information, manages and implements the data collection process, analyzes the results, and communicates the findings and their implications.

Organizations develop and maintain products through a continuous process of market research, follow-up with previous customers and interaction with current customers. Marketers utilize research to improve product value to current customers and to find new customers. For example, marketers receive feedback from customers through purchase behavior that is tracked in a database as well as through survey responses, product registration, warranty cards, etc. Thus, market research completes a communication "loop" between the seller and the market. Understanding how buyers relate to products can help organizations make better products and promote them better across the world.

DEFINITION & OBJECTIVE

A systematic design, collection, analysis and reporting of data and findings relevant to a specific marketing situation facing the company.

Objectives

- To define present market situation together with the long range trends which have led up to it
- To discover what major and underlying factors dominate that situation and how these factors can be influenced or controlled.
- To set up a plan for keeping in touch with the behaviour of these domination factors and for measuring the results of any efforts made to influence or control them.

RESEARCH TECHNIQUES

Market research is a continuous process. Among the variety of methods used, some seem to the widely resorted to because of their advantages over others. Research techniques can be grouped as:

- Desk Research
- Field Research
- Sample Surveys
- Motivation Research

Desk Research

It includes the collection and analysis of all available data, statistics and published information on tourist trends and markets. In tourism much of the basic information about tourist trends and markets is available from existing sources. There are a number of international organisations like UN, WTO, ED, OECD, IATA, ICAO etc which publish certain statistical information. Other data and statistics may be obtained from national tourist organisation, trade associations, carriers, hotel companies, etc. this information proves very useful in helping national tourist organisations to identify their markets and determine the objectives. This published information is of particular use to those countries which do not possess resources enough to undertake independent market research.

Field Research

Here, research work carried out in the tourist-generating market itself. The special investigations in the field are to be carried out with a view to know more details of the market situation. Field research includes many methods among which the most common are the sample surveys and the motivation research.

Sample survey

It could be defined as the study of a given population through only a part or a fraction thereof. Much marketing information is obtained through the use of samples. In this method the population of 'universe' for which information is required is defined, for example all households in a country might be the universe of population under investigation. Then, a statistically valid sample of the population is drawn and information is obtained from the sample. Sampling techniques consist of personal interviews of tourists, travel agents, carriers and hotel managers, etc, by way of personal interviews with the help of prepared, questionnaires, by mailing questionnaires or through telephone contacts.

The survey investigation can be classified by reference to the kind of information they seek to provide. There are surveys of market behaviour which record the holiday habits of the populations, cross analysed by socio-economic and other characteristics. The trends in holiday-making over many years may be seen and inferences made about the motives of holiday makers. Furthermore, surveys may be undertaken to monitor the conduct of marketing campaign.

Motivation Research

It attempts to describe and forecast the motives of the population under investigation, by use of techniques originally used in psychology. Assuming that every individual knows what he wants motivation research is oriented to discover the needs of potential tourists in order to adopt the tourist supply accordingly and thus be able to satisfy them. In other words motivation research is the investigation into the motives behind travel. It concerns itself to answering the 'shy' of human behaviour in contrast to answering the 'how' which is subject to sampling survey. It analyses rather than describes the attitudes of both actual and potential tourists to travelling in general and to the tourist product offered in particular. Motivation research provides answers to very important questions. Research in the past has shown that people from some countries, are traditional good travelers , while others have become a nation of travellers only recently.

POTENTIAL USERS

They have the willingness but the marketing resources have not been used optimally to influence their impulse.

1. Actual Users: They are already using the services generated by the tourist organizations

2. Occasional Users: They have not formed the habit of traveling

3. Habitual Travellers: They have formed a habit and avail of the services regularly.

Ten kinds of marketing research commonly used in travel and tourism. Because marketing research has become a large and complex sector of economic activity in its own right, it has inevitably produced its own technical vocabulary. This chapter makes no attempt to cover the full range of technical terms but ten commonly used in practice to denote different research methods will be found helpful and are discussed below.

They are:

- Continuous and *ad hoc*.
- Quantitative and qualitative.
- Primary and secondary.
- Omnibus and syndicated.
- Retail audit and consumer audit.

Commercial organizations find it increasingly necessary to measure certain key trend data on a regular or 'continuous' basis. 'Continuous' in this context typically means daily, weekly or monthly, although the growing use of Internet distribution permits literally continuous data review. Data covering enquiries, sales, booking types and patterns, market shares, customer satisfaction and seat or hotel bed occupancy, are typical examples of 'continuous' marketing-research measures in travel and tourism.

There are also many specific problems in marketing that require research relevant to a particular circumstance. For example, could a redesigned guidebook for a visitor attraction, with a print life of say three years, produce extra sales revenue? Would the introduction of a buffet- style instead of full service breakfast reduce customer satisfaction or increase it? Does the market potential warrant investment in a new hotel and, if it does, what size of hotel and what level of service would be justified? To inform such management decisions a specific or ad hoc investigation would be needed.

Most marketing research programmes are a mixture of continuous research involving ongoing investment in the monitoring of trends, and *ad hoc* surveys when the cost of research is justified to illuminate specific problems or opportunities as they occur.

Quantitative and Qualitative

Traditionally, most consumer research studies are based on questions identified in marketing decision making to be asked of random samples of existing or potential customers. For example, a coach tour operator may be aware from national surveys that some 60 per cent of adults take a holiday in a given year, of whom a third travelled abroad, stayed an average of ten nights away from home and spent £400 per person. The operator would need to find out what proportion used coaches and cars, how that proportion varied year by year and by month, the profile of coach clients, their preferred destinations and so on. With due allowance for statistical variation all these are quantifiable dimensions that can be projected into percentages and volume estimates for the coach tour market. Hence quantitative research, meaning studies to which numerical estimates can be attached. Quantitative research is always based on 'structured' questionnaires in which every respondent is asked the same questions. Mostly, because the range of possible answers is also printed on questionnaires drawing on previous experience, variations to suit individual respondents are not possible.

Quantitative methods are often used to give some basic indications of motivations. But generally, research companies cannot predict the ways in which people think about different products and such methods are unsuitable for exploring consumer attitudes, feelings, desires or perceptions. It is always possible to construct hypothetical answers and ask people to agree or disagree, but these may not get at what really matters to prospective buyers.

Qualitative studies commence from the standpoint that there are consumer (or staff) attitudes and motivations to be explored for which the answers cannot be predicted. How customers feel about Brand A compared with Brand B; what attributes and values are perceived as adhering to Brand A and not Brand B; what sort of people are thought most likely to buy Brand A rather than B, and so on. To understand and communicate positioning and branding values, qualitative research is usually essential for larger companies (see, for example, the case study on Travel Inn in Part Six).

Most qualitative studies commence with exploratory or open-ended research in which small samples of targeted individuals are asked to express their views. This may be done on a one-to-one basis or in a focus group where interaction between individuals is part of the research process. The interviewer or focus group leader is typically an experienced researcher, often with some training in social psychology. He is responsible for introducing the subjects for discussion and encouraging views but not imposing any preconceived ideas. What emerges, recorded for analysis on tape, is a discussion in consumers' own words concerning what matters to them. Summarizing an hour-long tape and producing two or three pages on the main attitudes emerging is much harder than it sounds and it involves considerable skills and experience.

By definition, individual and group sessions cannot be quantitative because the ideas are not tied down to structured questionnaires or based on adequate samples of the target group. They can be used to structure subsequent quantitative surveys, or they can be used in their own right to help marketing managers understand the ways in which existing and potential customers think, and what matters to them.

In recent years, given adequate continuous quantification of the main patterns of visitor behaviour and profiles using databases as explained above, qualitative research has been more widely used. It is expensive but relatively quick to implement and especially useful in designing advertising messages and brochure contents in ways best calculated to communicate with prospective customers in their own terms.

Primary and Secondary

Primary data, covering both quantitative and qualitative data, is a label applied to marketing research that is specifically commissioned by a business to contribute to its decisions. It requires the gathering of data not available from any other (secondary) source. For example, a survey commissioned by one airline to study the current attitudes of business travellers towards its own and other airlines competing on the same route, would be primary data.

Secondary data is information gathered originally for a purpose not related to the needs of a particular business, but which may be used by it as part of its market information system. All published sources, including government statistics, trade association surveys and commercial publishers' market surveys, represent secondary data.

Common sense dictates that it will always be quicker and cheaper to obtain and use secondary rather than primary data. For any decision requiring research information, initial investigation should always begin at the secondary level before proceeding, if necessary, with primary research. The more efficient a marketing information system is, the less need there may be to commission (and wait for) expensive new data.

Omnibus and Syndicated

Not only in travel and tourism, but also in consumer markets generally, there has been a growing tendency for market research companies to operate their own regular (continuous) sample surveys and sell space in them to a range of customers. Such surveys are known technically as 'omnibus' surveys because they are potentially open to all users. Where an organization seeks answers, say, to just four or five key questions, it may be possible to get access to a nationally representative sample of 2000 adults for a tenth of the cost of commissioning its own survey. For the price, a client would not only get answers to his specific questions but also fully cross-tabulated data, using profile characteristics, such as age and readership of media, which are a standard part of any 'omnibus' survey. The United Kingdom Tourism Survey (UKTS) is probably the best-known survey of UK tourism. Up to 2000 it was in fact a series of questions regularly asked on an MAI Research Ltd omnibus survey.

There are many other omnibus surveys available, covering not only adults but many segments, such as motorists, doctors, business travellers, frequent users of hotels and so on.

Syndicated surveys serve much the same purpose as omnibus surveys but are usually commissioned by a group of clients on a cost-sharing basis. The regular survey of customer value for money and satisfaction, co-ordinated for its members by the Association of Leading Visitor Attractions (ALVA) in the UK since the late 1990s, is an interesting example. Members not only share costs and receive details for their own attraction; they also gain access to relevant comparisons with competitor sectors in the context of overall trends in the attractions market.

Both omnibus and syndicated studies provide cost-effective forms of research, especially for smaller businesses, for whom the costs of an ad hoc survey would usually be prohibitive. By using such studies, firms can also obtain technical assistance from research agencies with the wording of questions and interpretation of results. The omnibus method is especially suitable for achieving quantified results would be possible with ad hoc surveys.

Retail and Consumer Audits

In many sectors of consumer goods marketing other than travel, the most common forms of continuous marketing research are consumer and retail audits. It is no accident that two of the largest international marketing research companies, AGB Ltd and A. C. Nielsen, have built their multinational operations on such audits.

Initiated as long ago as the 1930s for manufacturers of products sold through grocery/chemist retail outlets, retail audits are based on visiting shops and physically checking and analysing product stocks, purchases from wholesalers and consumer sales in a sample of retail outlets selected to represent the national pattern. Such audits, carried out at regular monthly or two-monthly intervals in grocery and chemist outlets, can measure the volume of sales by product type, the average sales price, the volume of stocks and the proportion of outlets with stock on display. Of course, most such data are now audited by computers rather than physical checks. The results collected in the sample of audited outlets can be 'grossed up' to project the estimated sales in the total number (universe) of outlets from which the sample was selected.

In travel and tourism various agencies have audited holiday bookings and brochure display for tour operators, using samples of retail travel agencies. For hotels and other forms of accommodation, room and bed occupancy studies in samples of accommodation units perform the same 'audit' function for the accommodation sector, and have been used reliably for many years.

Consumer audits follow the same basic principles of regular reporting from nationally representative samples, based in this case on panels of consumers who keep specially designed diaries, in which all purchases are recorded. Since the profile of the samples is known in detail through the process of selection and recruitment, recorded purchases can be extensively analysed by segmentation data. The use of diary panels to record travel and tourism behaviour has been used in the Netherlands by the Central Bureau for Statistics since 1980 to measure holidays of four or more nights away from home, and it is satisfied with the reliability of the methodology for that purpose. In France, using a sample of 20 000 adults, national tourism trends for visits of one or more nights a year have also been monitored monthly by diary panel methods since 1990. The Target Group Index (TGI) Survey operated by the British Market Research Bureau is currently the best-known diary panel omnibus style survey operating in the UK. It covers a wide range of consumer purchases of which travel, tourism and recreational activities are only a small part.

INTERNATIONAL MARKETING STRATEGY

Strategic Marketing Planning

For marketing purposes, strategic planning is the process by which an organisation: first, analyses its strengths and weaknesses in its current and prospective markets - "where are we now?"; second, identifies its aims and the opportunities it seeks to develop – "where do we want to get to?"; and, third, defines the strategies and costed programmes of activity to achieve these aims – "how do we get there?". Strategic decisions are always focused on the longer run, normally beyond three years.

Marketing strategy identifies and is designed to produce future sales revenue through the specification of market segments to be targeted, products to be developed and focussed on, and associated action programmes to realise the potential identified in these targeted product: market segments. Business strategy is not only about marketing, but all strategy for commercial organisations depends on its ability to persuade sufficient customers to buy enough of its products to secure a surplus of revenue over costs in the long run and to produce customer satisfaction. The key components of marketing strategy are:

Goals and objectives: the position or place in its chosen markets that an organisation seeks to occupy in a future period, defined in terms of sectors of business, target market segments, sales volume, product range, market shares and levels of profit.

Images, positioning and branding: where the organisation wants to be in terms of the market's (trade and consumer) perceptions of its products and values, including image and branding in relation to competitors.

Strategies and programmes: the specification of actions, including product development and investment, needed to achieve the goals and objectives set. Budget: what resources - human, technical and financial – are required to realise the goals.

Review and evaluation: procedures and systems permitting the appraisal of the extent to which goals were met in the context of overall market conditions (including competitors' activities) and external factors.

As **Middleton and Clarke** (2001) state: "strategy is essentially proactive in the sense that it defines and wills the future shape of the organisation as well as responding to changing industry patters, technology, market conditions and consumer needs."

Tactical Marketing Planning

Tactical decisions are always focused on the short run – from a few weeks to a maximum of one to one-and-a-half years – in which specific marketing campaigns are planned, implemented and evaluated. Tactics respond to market conditions and particularly to competitors' activities.

Tactical, or operational, marketing plans include:

- ***Objectives and targets:*** specified, quantified, volume and sales revenue targets and other specific marketing objectives to be achieved.
- ***Mix and budget:*** decisions on the marketing mix (product, price, promotion, place) and marketing budget.
- ***Action programmes:*** the implementation of marketing programmes and coordination of promotional activity to achieve specified targets.
- ***Monitoring and control:*** an effective system of monitoring the results of the marketing and the application of control procedures related to the agreed targets.

The Strategic Market-planning Process

Kotler, Hamlin, Rein & Haider (2002) define the strategic market-planning process for destinations as going through five stages that answer the following questions:

- Place audit. What is the current state of the community of the destination, and how does it compare to places in similar situations? What are the community's strengths/weaknesses, opportunities/threats? i.e., what is commonly termed the SWOT (strengths, weaknesses, opportunities, threats) analysis.
- Vision and goals. What do the community's businesses and residents want the community to be?
- Strategy formulation. What broad strategies will help achieve these goals?
- Action plan. What specific actions must be undertaken to carry out the strategies?
- Implementation and control. What must the community do to ensure successful implementation?

The Place Audit establishes what a destination is like and why. What **Kotler,** *et. al.,* call "hard" and "soft" attraction factors are assessed in a comparative context. Sorting these factors into a SWOT analysis creates the basis for visions and goals. Economic and demographic factors are the basics but innovative and sensitive interpretation is needed.

For most destinations successful positioning and targeting takes into account not only of tourist market trends but also the needs and desires of the resident population. Even finding a good fit with the local and tourist markets is not enough – the destination's competitors must be identified and assessed, with such assessment being made for each market segment. **Kotler,** *et. al.,* quote the example of Dubai – "the desert's most exciting city". In the early period of its build up to spectacular success – tourist arrivals doubled between 1999 and 2003 to close to 5mn - its marketing message was:

"It has spectacular beaches but is not Australia; it is one of the most secure cities but is not Singapore; it has opulent city hotels and superb beachside resorts but is neither Jakarta nor Bali. It has world-class shopping but is not Hong Kong."

Called the sunshine destination, Dubai offers tourists a unique holiday adventure with five star leisure facilities, beautiful beaches, Arabian hospitality plus the modernity of a fast track, bustling metropolis. It may not accord to what many would term a "responsible" destination but it has pursued a highly successful tourism development and marketing policy and strategy in fulfilment of the objectives established by its government.

Relative to other destinations, a place can be better, broadly the same or weaker. If a destination is assessed to be a superior competitor, it needs to protect its position, though if it is outstandingly attractive this may lead to excessive demand growth possibly eroding its competitive advantage through overcrowding..

Where a destination is assessed to be a peer competitor, strategic options are for intensified competition or cooperation. This latter approach – termed co-operatition - can be a means of sharing the market between two destinations and reducing the costs of competitive marketing.

A weak competitor will need to establish a new strategy and positioning.

Strategic planning is a long-term process so a clear understanding of likely future trends and developments that will impact the destination is needed. In considering Asian destinations, **Kotler,** *et. al.,* draw particular attention to the following: funding for regional and community programmes, globalisation, reducing financial resources, environmental forces and regulations, information technology and demographic changes (e.g., lifestyle changes, rise in the elderly population, decentralization from national to local levels, integration between Southeast Asian nations).

In assessing a destination's competitive position, an "outsider-in" approach is needed in order to identify which of its characteristics represent:

- a major strength
- a minor strength
- a neutral factor
- a minor weakness
- a major weakness

Competitive positions are determined both by outside factors beyond local/regional influence and location characteristics that specific local actions can influence. The destination's long-term strategic approach should be sought to maximise the leverage of its major strengths and to improve its notable weaknesses. The "hard" and "soft" factors assessed in the strengths and weaknesses assessment can be presented in matrix form according to the five-scale degree of importance noted earlier in this paragraph.

It may be necessary to develop such an analysis and matrix separately for each major segment being evaluated since not all the attraction factors will have the same meaning for each group. It will then be necessary to choose the factors of central significance to each segment and allocate importance values to these individual factors. In this way a performance: importance matrix can be developed per the model adopted from **Kotler,** *et. al.,* (2002) below.

For each factor, a rating should be assessed and entered in the matrix, based on, say, a numerical score from 1 (low) to 10 (high) for each of the performance and importance axes. When ratings are combined, four possibilities emerge. Where performance is lacking but the factors are important for the target market (cell A), critical improvements are indicated; where both performance and target market importance are strong (cell B) the need is to continue the value-adding process. Cell C indicates areas where the destination is performing poorly but which are not of high importance to target customers, so low priority is given for any action. In cell D, the destination is doing well but the factors of low importance so care should be taken not to over-invest.

Performance >> Importance V V	Low 1 2 3 4 5	High 6 7 8 9 10
High 10 9 8 7 6	A. Concentrate here	B. Keep up the good work
Low 5 4 3 2 1	C. Low priority	D. Possible overkill

Source: after Kotler, Hamlin, Rein and Haider (2002)

Fig. 8.1. Performance-Importance Matrix

Even if a destination has a major strength, its value in strategy is whether it represents a comparative advantage to the destination over a competitor in respect of the target market segment. What is important is for the destination to have greater relative strength for factors considered important by the selected target segment. A place does not need to correct all its weaknesses or promote all its strengths, because factors vary in importance to different target markets. The destination should fully understand which strengths and weaknesses most affect the perceptions and behaviour of its targets. The resulting analysis becomes a major basis for developing destination marketing plans.

The next step is to identify a destination's opportunities and threats. An opportunity is where the destination has "a fairly good chance to achieve a competitive advantage" (**Kotler,** *et. al.*, 2002) while threats come from unfavourable trends or developments in the environment that would erode its competitiveness. Each opportunity and threat has to be evaluated according to the probability of occurrence and the degree of advantage/ harm its occurrence would have for the destination. By assembling a picture of the major opportunities and threats facing a specific destination, its overall attractiveness can be assessed:

- Ideal: high in opportunities and low in threats,
- Speculative: high in both major opportunities and threats,
- Mature: low in major opportunities and threats,
- Troubled: low in opportunities and high in threats.

Again, a helpful way to conduct this type of analysis is to use a grid with opportunities and threats on the axes and numerical ratings given from 1 to 10 for minor to major.

Carrying out the SWOT analysis and an examination of the key issues facing the destination enables strategic planners to develop a clear and full picture of the situation. However while many types of development and marketing action may be indicated from these analyses, they need to be consistent with a coherent overall vision so that these possible actions can be prioritized. Vision development calls for planners to solicit input from the destination's residents as to how they want their community to be in 10 or 20 years time – possibly through the circulation for comment of two or more possible scenarios (**Kotler,** *et. al.*, 2002). A crude example might consider zero growth through a moratorium on new tourism development, managed quality growth based on a strict development approvals process permitting only specific types of development, to unrestricted growth encouraging all types of tourism development. **Kotler,** *et. al.*, (2002) also point out that the development of a vision should go further than simple distinguishing between potential growth paths by factoring in issues such as:

- Which unique combinations of attraction factors should be targeted?
- Which are the destination's target markets?
- What are the short and long-term goals?
- What are the vision's operative prerequisites?

Once the "players" in the destination agree on a vision, it needs to be translated into specific objectives and goals ie clear statements about what the destination is aiming to achieve, and specific magnitudes and timescales for their achievement. Once the destination planning team has defined the vision, objectives and goals, it can translate these into strategies for accomplishing the goals.

Even in instances where a destination is found to have no obvious strengths, a strategy can be devised to create a competitive advantage. **Kotler,** *et. al.,* (2002) cite the examples of Varanasi and Sepang. The former has built international interest around events associated with the city's ancient and religious heritage – its 2,000-year-old history of knowledge and culture; while the latter has created a major event through the development of a world-class Formula One motor racing circuit, which attracts large international crowds for a small number of events BUT which is also serving to draw into Sepang other developments.

Strategy needs to be converted into an action plan with clear implementation responsibilities allocated – easier to do in small destinations than in larger ones! The action plan should list each action along with details of: who is responsible; how the action is to be implemented; what budget will be needed; and over what time frame will the actions be undertaken. A short-term horizon is needed for a tourism marketing action plan because of the need to be able to respond to the many influences on, and determinants of, a destination's tourism sector which cannot be anticipated when the initial pan is drawn up.

Strategy and implementation are the most important dimensions for a destination seeking to create a changed, relevant and strong tourism sector. The ability of a destination to succeed in these two dimensions varies and leads to what Kotler et al identify as four basic environments, as summarised in the following matrix.

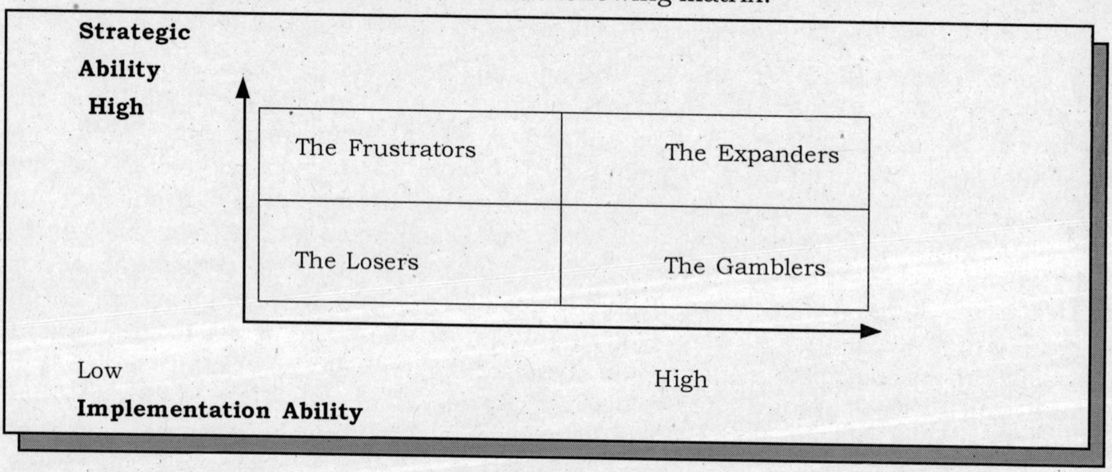

(**Source:** after Kotler, Hamlin, Rein and Haider (2002))

Fig. 8.2. Four Abilities Matrix

"Losers" are those destinations with inadequate capacity to take action in either the strategic or implementation dimension. Communities demand subsidy and compensation arguing on the basis of "justice" or "need". "Frustrators" possess strategic thinking capability but not the necessary implementation skills. The planners end up being frustrated. "Gamblers" have weak strategic ability but strong implementation capability. Success comes – unpredictably and only occasionally – from luck and hard work. Targeted marketing is rare because the strategic targeting of the appropriate segments has not been made. "Expanders" are destinations where both the strategic and implementation capabilities are well-developed. The norm in such destinations is for leadership prepared to support long-term strategies and stimulate sub-strategies and action plans.

Distinguishing between strategy and tactics

Middleton and Clarke (2001) identify three strategic concepts to assist in distinguishing between strategy and tactics: strategic business units (SBUs) and business portfolio analysis; product-market growth models; and corporate and product positioning.

Many large travel and tourism companies have a portfolio of businesses or SBUs, with separate management structures, profit and loss accounts and plans for the future. Within any such portfolio, performance and prospects will vary. Continuous analysis is conducted according to, *inter alia*:

- Share of market
- Market size, growth and stage of product life cycle
- Cash flow generation
- Return on investment
- Strength of competition

The Boston Consulting group matrix plots the first two of these factors. The vertical axis shows the rate of growth of the market in which the product is sold, while the horizontal one represents the market share of the product compared with its major competitor. The matrix is divided into four cells.

Corporate portfolios will comprise a mixture of:

- Relatively new product-market groupings with good shares of growth markets (*stars*)
- Profitable products with well-established shares of mature markets (*cash cows*)
- Products with weak presence in emerging high growth markets (*problem children*)
- Products with low shares of declining markets and poor profitability (*dogs*)

The marketing strategic response is to increase/maintain marketing support for *stars* (since the company may be forced to defend itself against competitors seeking a higher share of a lucrative market) and *problem children* (in order to gain a higher share of an attractive market), diverting funds from *cash cows* (where the low market growth makes it unattractive for competitors to target), and ignoring or terminating involvement with *dogs*.

		Market share – actual or relative (%)	
		High	**Low**
Product-market *Growth* (%)	**High**	**Star** (maintain marketing investment)	**Problem Child** (increase marketing support)
	Low	**Cash Cow** (divert profits to marketing for stars and problem children)	**Dog** (no marketing support; consider withdrawing product)

[***Source:*** after Kotler, Bowen & Makens (2003)]

Fig. 8.3. The Boston Consulting Group Matrix

Product-market growth models

Market conditions are constantly changing. Profitable product-market portfolios will usually be under constant competitive pressure, and it will be necessary to update and augment products continuously to match changing customer needs and market conditions. The options for strategic growth are incorporated in a four-box model devised by **Ansoff** (1987).

		← *Market* →	
		Existing	**New**
↕ ***Product***	**New**	**Product development** (introduce new product to present market)	**Diversification** (launch new product to new market)
	Existing	**Penetration** (modification and intensive promotion of existing product to present market)	**Market development** (reposition and target present product at new markets)

[***Source:*** Ansoff (1987)]

Fig. 8.4. The Ansoff Matrix

Middleton and Clarke (2001) cite examples from travel and tourism for each of the four strategies of the Ansoff model:

- ***Penetration*** – a hotel catering for the corporate traveller market decides to undertake an aggressive marketing campaign targeted at existing customer groups to increase market share.
- ***Product development***– a tour operator develops a new tour programme range which it markets to its existing market segments.
- ***Market development***– a Dutch holiday village operator sets up villages in new geographic markets (Center Parcs in the UK in the late 1980s).
- ***Diversification*** – an airline company decides to buy and brand a railway operating company, stepping outside its existing product-market portfolio (for example, Virgin Atlantic acquiring the rail operation it branded as Virgin Rail)

MARKET POSITIONING

Position is a form of market communication that plays a vital role in enhancing the attractiveness of a tourism destination. This article describes the different parts of the positioning process and applies it to the case of positioning a U.S. destination to Japanese visitors.

The World Travel and Tourism Council claimed that tourism was the world's largest industry in 1991 (World Travel and Tourism Council, 1991). The past few years have shown a steady increase in the volume of international travel, and along with this growth in travel, the number of tourism destination choices has also increased as many policy-makers have recognized the value of tourism to the economies of their regions. To some extent, this increased travel can also be attributed to an increase in advertising, as tourism marketers try to enlarge their share of the global tourism pie by promoting their destinations to specific target markets. For example in 1987, Canada and Australia decided to increase advertising in Japan and this resulted in an increase in Japanese visitors of 55% and 33% respectively (**Bailey,** 1992).

One of the most effective tools in tourism marketing is positioning. The objective of positioning is to create a distinctive place in the minds of potential customers. A position that evokes images of a destination in the customers mind; images that differentiate the destination from the competition and also as a place that can satisfy their needs and wants. Positioning is a communications strategy that is the natural follow-through of market segmentation and target marketing. Since market segmentation is based on the notion that different tourism destinations appeal to different types of tourists, target market segments must be selected before tourism marketers can begin to entice these potential customers. An effective positioning strategy provides a competitive edge to a destination that is trying to convey its attractiveness to the target market.

The purpose of this paper is to discuss the vital role played by positioning in tourism marketing and to present various approaches to positioning a tourism destination.

Positioning is more than just image creation. This important form of market communication helps to distinguish tourism destinations from similar destinations so that customers can choose the one that is the most attractive. Thus, true positioning differentiates a destination from its competitors on attributes that are meaningful to customers and gives it a competitive edge. However, this is a complex process that requires careful analysis of the attributes of destinations and the needs of the target markets. Selection of a positioning strategy that creates a distinctive place in customers' minds is essential in preventing the following pitfalls (**Lovelock,** 1991).

(1) The destination is forced into a position of competing directly with a stronger competitor. For example, a destination that is further from the source of its visitors may be relegated to a secondary or tertiary level of competition with destinations that are closer to the market.

(2) The destination's position is so unclear that its target market does not recognize the message that is being sent to them. This often happens when a destination tries to be all things to all people.

(3) The destination has no identity or has a negative image in customers' minds and does not create customer demand.

Effective Positioning

According to the basic principles of marketing, products and services are created to solve customer "problems" (i.e., to satisfy needs and wants) and provide benefits. Thus, to be effective, positioning must promise the benefit the customer will receive, create the expectation, and offer a solution to the customer's problem. If at all possible, the solution should be different from and better than the competition's solution set, especially if the competitors are already offering a similar solution.

Positioning should be a single-minded concept, an umbrella from which everything else in the organization flows. Properly targeted, single-minded positioning affects everything a destination does or stands for, not only advertising, but also all of its promotions. Positioning also affects policies and procedures, employee attitudes, customer relations, complaint handling, and the myriad of other details that combine to make the tourism experience. Tourism services compete on more than just image, differentiation, and benefits offered. There must be a consistency among the various offerings and it is the positioning statement that guides this consistency. Likewise, although positioning can be applied for an entire country, a given area, or a specific city, tourism officials should develop a consistent message if the country plans to use one market to generate business for another. There are two tests of effective positioning. First, the position must be believable in the tourist's mind. Second, the destination must deliver that promise on a consistent basis.

Positioning Intangibles

One of the biggest challenges faced by tourism marketers is that the product is largely intangible. Some would argue otherwise, because what is more important than the hotel room, the meal, the beach, the ocean, and the mountains? These are all tangible aspects of the tourism destination. However, these tangibles are what is being "sold", but not what is being "marketed". If we were selling beaches or mountains, what difference would it make where the tourist went, assuming a comparable level of quality?

'What we are marketing, of course, are intangibles. The tangibles are essential and necessary but as soon as they reach a certain level of acceptance, they become secondary. Because they are so difficult to differentiate, to be competitive, the intangibles have to be marketed. Even as tangibles, mountains and beaches have a measure of intangibility because they are experienced rather than possessed.

If tourism products are mostly intangible, they have to be marketed with tangible evidence. This is what is referred to as "tangibilizing the intangible." However, this is a complicated process. By emphasizing the concrete elements one may fail to differentiate oneself from the competition, and since the intangible elements are abstract, by emphasizing the abstract one compounds the intangibility. Thus, tourism destination positioning should focus on enhancing and differentiating abstract realities by manipulating the tangible clues.

Unfortunately, being aware of this need does not ease the problem. It is still difficult to find meaningful tangible evidence that supports intangible constructs. What must be done, is to create a "position" in the tourist's mind. That is why positioning relies heavily on target marketing. The mental constructs held by the target market must be known, as well as the tangible evidence that sustains them. Positioning, then, is a relative term. It is not simply how the destination is perceived, but how the perceived image performs in relation to competing images. It is the customer's mental perception which may, or may not, differ from the actual physical characteristics. It is most important when, the product is an intangible and there is little difference among the competition regarding the physical characteristics.

POSITIONING PROCESS

The positioning process consists of the various steps needed to develop an effective positioning strategy (Figure 1). This process must be continuous to keep up with changes in the environment including the changing needs of the customer and the competitors tactics. Developing a positioning strategy for a destination in the United States to attract visitors from Japan will be used as a test case to illustrate the steps in the positioning process.

Market Positioning

Market positioning is the first step and is defined as the process of identifying and selecting markets or segments that represent business potential, to determine the criteria for competitive success (**DiMingo,** 1988).

This must be based on a thorough knowledge of the needs, wants, and perceptions of the target market, along with the benefits offered by the destination. To do this, a few crucial questions must be answered. These are:

(1) What is important to the target market?

(2) How does the target market perceive the destination?

(3) How does the target market perceive the competition?

(4) What attributes should a destination use to differentiate itself to make the best use of its limited resources?

The reality of the matter is that if the target market does not perceive the image, the image does not exist. If the target market does not believe that what the destination has to offer is a benefit, it is not a benefit. If the target market does not believe that the benefit can be delivered, promises are meaningless. If the benefit is not important to the target market, it is not important. If the benefit is not perceived as being different from that of the competition, then differentiation has not succeeded. In short, images, benefits, and differentiation are solely the perception of the tourist, not the perceptions of tourism officials or the tourism marketer.

According to the former United States Travel and Tourism Administration, 3.2 million Japanese inbound travellers, who present a solid market for tourism destinations in the United States, generated $ 10.1 billion in tourism revenue for the U.S. in 1990. (United States Travel and Tourism Administration, 1991). The following shows the top ten ranked activities identified by Japanese visitors (**Bailey,** 1992):

(1) Sightseeing in cities

(2) Shopping

(3) Dining out

(4) Guided tours

(5) Visiting landmarks

(6) Taking pictures

(7) Beach activities

(8) Visiting theme parks

(9) Swimming

(10) Visiting galleries.

The three highest ranked activities (Sightseeing in Cities, Shopping, and Dining out in Restaurants) seem to provide an advantage to reasonably large cities where these are readily available. In addition, according to **Bailey,** (1992), Japanese persons who are planning to travel to the U.S., initially, do not have a specific destination to visit. Instead, they search for a trip that has several attributes similar to those listed below (**Bailey,** 1992):

(1) Some place where other people went

(2) Reasonable price.

(3) As many places as possible to cover.

(4) Minimum contact with local community.

(5) Perfect Japanese-like service.

(6) Good food.

(7) Absolutely free.

Combining these attributes with the top 10 activities listed above, one can get an indication of the needs of Japanese visitors. During the trip they like to go to places that have been previously visited by Japanese visitors and where they have opportunities for sightseeing, shopping, and dining. They are very concerned about personal safety, not interested in associating with the local community, and like to receive Japanese-style services.

Market positioning research also requires an evaluation of the image that customers have of a tourism destination. This can be used to identify the vital elements which comprise the benefits. The beauty of a destination, the architecture of a palace, and the historic artifacts in a museum are examples of attributes that may produce a benefit, or may be a tangible representation of an intangible benefit, but are not themselves the benefit. The benefit itself is what the attributes do for the visitor, for instance, a sensation of grandeur, an aura of prestige, or the gaining of knowledge. The credibility of these benefits may diminish rapidly if expectations are not fulfilled. Architecture is soon forgotten if the tour bus breaks down on the return trip. The impression of grandeur loses credibility if visitors feel that their personal safety is threatened. It is the fulfillment of expectations or the inability to, that creates the perception of deliverability for the tourist. Benefits, like positioning, exist in the mind of the customer and are determined only by asking the customer. Only after this information is obtained, can a destination match its strengths to the visitors' needs and the benefits sought. This knowledge will also provide a basis for the development of a credible differentiation strategy.

Psychological Positioning

This step utilizes communications to convey a destination's identity and image to the target market. It converts customer needs into images and positions a destination in the visitor's minds.

Psychological positioning is a strategy employed to create a unique product image with the objective of creating interest and attracting visitors. Since it exists solely in the mind of the visitor, it can occur automatically without any effort on the part of the marketer and any kind of positioning may result. Two very dissimilar destinations may be perceived as the same; two similar destinations may be perceived as different. What the marketer hopes to do is to control the positioning, not just let it happen. Moreover, failure to select a position in the marketplace, to achieve, and to hold that position may lead to various consequences, all undesirable, as pointed out earlier. There are two kinds of psychological positioning in marketing: objective positioning and subjective positioning. Each has its appropriate place and usage.

Objective Positioning

Objective positioning is concerned, almost entirely, with the objective attributes of the physical product. It means creating an image about the destination that reflects its physical characteristics and functional features. It is usually concerned with what actually is, what exists. For example, Colorado is mountainous and the French Quarter is in New Orleans. However, objective positioning need not always be concrete. It may be more abstract than these examples. The French Quarter is in New Orleans which is also "the birthplace of jazz."

Objective positioning can be very important and is often used in the tourism industry. If a destination has some unique feature, that feature may be used to objectively position the destination, to create an image, and to differentiate it from the competition. If objective positioning is to be used to position the U.S. among Japanese visitors or tour operators any of the unique scenic landmarks, such as the Grand Canyon or Niagara Falls, could be used to show the size and magnitude of these attractions. However, this needs to be linked with other attributes and expectations of the Japanese visitor including "seeing as many places as possible,"; and especially, "where others have been before."

Less successful objective positioning occurs when the feature is not unique. This is why many destination promotions with pictures of beaches fail to create a distinct image or successfully differentiate the product. Other unsuccessful approaches may include a picture of two people looking at a mountain that looks like any other mountain or lying on a beach that looks like any other beach. One of the first rules of effective positioning is uniqueness.

Subjective Positioning

Subjective positioning is concerned with subjective attributes of the destination. Subjective positioning is the image, not of the physical aspects of the destination, but other attributes perceived by the tourist, (i.e., they do not necessarily belong to the destination but to the tourist's mental perception). These perceptions and the resulting images may not necessarily reflect the true state of the destination's physical characteristics. They may simply exist in the tourist's mind and not all tourists' imaging agree with a particular perception or image. Using the previous example of the Grand Canyon or Niagara Falls, subjective positioning would emphasize the awe-inspiring feelings experienced at these natural attractions rather than their physical attributes. Thus, a visit to the Grand Canyon becomes a far greater experience than viewing the physical land formation. What the marketer hopes is that the people in the target market will agree on a favorable image whether or not the image is true. This is the test of effective subjective positioning.

Positioning Approaches

This is the final step in the positioning process, and there are several different approaches to positioning any tourism destination (**Aaker and Shamsby,** 1982).

'While psychological positioning creates an image, this positioning approach completes the picture, using visual and words, to reinforce what the destination does best and what benefits are offered. Tourism marketers may decide to select the most appropriate of the following approaches, depending on the information gathered during market and psychological positioning.

Positioning by attribute, feature or customer benefit. For this strategy, emphasis is placed on the benefits of the particular features or attributes of the destination. For example, Thailand promotes the friendliness of its people with the statement "The world meets in the land of smiles."

Positioning by Price Value

International destinations are not usually positioned on the basis of price because lower prices may be perceived as connoting lower quality. However, value offered to visitors can be effectively utilized as exemplified by Malaysia which claims "Malaysia gives more natural value." With this positioning statement Malaysia is appealing not only to the sense of value (more for the money) but also to its natural attractions.

Positioning with respect to use or application

Here a destination is positioned based on the reasons for visiting it. Bermuda positions itself to the American meetings market with "Sometimes you have to leave the country to get any work done" which promises productive meetings in a relaxed environment. Cancun, Mexico is positioned as "The meeting place for sun worshipers."

Positioning according to the users or class of users

In this case, positioning features the people who should visit the destination. Hong Kong appeals to the incentive travel market with the statement 'When they've reached the top, send them to the peak," referring to Victoria Peak, a major tourist site in Hong Kong: Fisher Island, a luxury residential development in Florida, positions itself as the place "where people who run things can stop running."

Positioning with respect to a product class

This technique is often used to associate a destination with experiences that are extraordinary and/or unique. For example, the Principality of Monaco is positioned as "The fairy tale that does not end at midnight," or holding a convention in Thailand is "Smooth as silk where the sky's the limit, or "If your looking for an ideal meeting place, here's one that's close to heaven" for Israel.

Positioning *vis-a-vis* the competition

This approach is used when it is necessary to meet the competition head-on; to bring out differences between destinations. This approach is not used frequently in international tourism destination marketing since it may involve negative statements about another country or region. However, it is regularly employed in product and services marketing. For example, Visa credit cards compete with American Express by showing examples of places from around the world that do not accept American Express and only Visa cards are accepted. Ritz-Carlton Hotels is a little more subtle when they say, 'After a day of competition, you deserve a hotel that has none."

Any of these approaches could be used to position the U.S., the minds of Japanese visitors. For example, since Japanese visitors want to go where other Japanese tourists have already been, positioning according to users or a class of users may be appropriate. By developing a creative campaign, an operator can market the fact that many Japanese visitors have been to the Grand Canyon, and were impressed by its awe-inspiring presence. This may include testimonials from previous visitors or tour operators who can make a direct appeal to the target market. However, since the feeling of awe is an intangible construct, positioning statements must show a tangible example to illustrate this feeling.

Positioning is the ultimate weapon in niche marketing. Stripped of all its trappings, positioning analysis answers the following questions:

(1) What position does a destination own now? (In the mind of the target market.)

(2) What position does the destination want to own? (Look for positions or holes in the marketplace.)

(3) Who must the destination outposition? (Manipulate what's already in the mind.)

(4) How can it be done? (Select the best approach that will work for the target market.)

Positioning is a valuable weapon for tourism marketers. To position successfully requires recognizing the marketplace, the competition, and tourists' perceptions. Positioning analysis on a target market basis provides the tools to identify opportunities for creating the desired image that differentiates a destination from its competitors and for serving the target market better than anyone else.

TRAVEL DISTRIBUTION SYSTEM

Travel distributors allow you to broaden your customer base far beyond the reach of your own limited marketing budget. They are particularly important to the inbound tourism industry as overseas consumers still rely heavily on the advice of local travel experts when planning their Australian holiday, particularly in long haul and emerging markets.

Travel distributors can also provide insights and advice on international markets and suggest changes or improvements to your product that will help you meet the needs of your target market.

Buying your Product

The travel distribution system covers all the channels through which an international traveller can buy your product. Other than approaching you directly, international travellers may book your product via:

Local travel agents

- Tour wholesalers/operators that market directly to consumers (direct sellers). Inbound tour operators or meeting planners
- Online portals or individual Internet booking engines.

Distribution channels and consumer purchasing behaviour varies from market to market so you will also need to understand the structure of the distribution system specific to your target markets. Tourism Australia's market fact sheets provide more detail on the distribution system - the way consumers purchase travel - in each market. When considering how best to distribute your product to international consumers, it is important to understand each channel and the relationships between companies within the distribution channel.

How the Distribution System Works

The travel distribution system has traditionally been very structured, with clearly defined functions for each role in the chain. However as technology and company mergers transform the tourism industry, there is an increasing amount of cross-over in the roles and functions of various sectors of the distribution system.

The traditional structure of the distribution system includes Inbound Tour Operators (ITOs) based in Australia, tour wholesalers based overseas and the international retail agents, the link to the international consumer. However, this varies considerably from market to market. In some countries, such as Japan, the system is very structured while in other markets a structured system has not developed. Market fact sheets available on Tourism Australia's corporate website outline consumer travel purchasing behaviour in each market, as well as providing a detailed description of the structure of the travel distribution system in international markets.

Company mergers around the world have prompted an increase in the cross-over of traditional distribution roles. Structured marketing agreements and cross-ownership are common relationships. For example, it is not uncommon for an inbound tour operator to be part of a larger company that also operates a wholesale arm in an overseas market, or for a travel wholesaler to also operate the travel agencies that sell its packages. As the traditional distribution system continues to evolve, it is important to clearly understand the structure of the companies that you work with and their relationships with other organisations.

The Internet

The Internet has also changed the way consumers research and book travel, impacting the traditional structure of the distribution system. Many travellers use the Internet as an information tool when researching holidays, however, personal advice and recommendations from travel agents are still important, especially for long haul journeys. The proliferation of 'last minute' websites to move surplus accommodation and fares has also changed consumer booking patterns, resulting in shorter lead times for bookings, even in some long haul travel markets.

As the travel distribution environment changes, companies will need to take a more integrated approach to international product marketing, considering all the distribution options available and the way that your targeted consumers book travel products. This will allow you to develop an effective mix of distribution partners to reach consumers.

What are Travel Distributors looking for?

Travel distributors seek product suppliers that can offer:

- Quality products and experiences,
- Reliability (consistent operating hours and regular schedules),
- Efficient operations and procedures,
- Friendly, helpful reservations staff,
- High levels of customer service,
- Stable operations,
- Pricing policies that consider all levels of distribution,
- Communication via email, toll free numbers and fax, and
- Fast and efficient turnaround and response times.

Building relationships and establishing your credentials takes time. Do not anticipate immediate results. The process of making key sales staff aware of your product, developing a new product range and brochuring a new product can take a minimum of 12-18 months.

ISSUES UNDERLYING THE CHANGES IN TOURISM DISTRIBUTION

Four underlying points help explain the 'revolutionary' speed of change in tourism distribution channels:

(1) The nature of distribution systems is one of the main ways in which the marketing of 'intangible' service products has always differed from the marketing of goods.

(2) While the digital revolution and the Internet are certainly changing the way that businesses are conducted and opening up alliances based on a depth of knowledge of customers that was previously unthinkable, the new ICT options are still only business tools and they do not change the principles underlying the consumer need for distribution channels or the trend to direct marketing. What ICT does is greatly increase the speed and convenience of purchasing for customers, and significantly reduce the cost at which access can be provided by businesses. The Internet in particular is attractive as a very fast, low-cost new channel of immediate value and immense potential. Concepts of access have always revolved around speed, convenience and cost, however, the new channel will replace some of the existing ones, just as electricity replaced gas for lighting purposes and telephones replaced letters around a century earlier.

(3) The compatible, low-cost hardware and software systems comprising the digital infrastructure that supports the Internet and e-commerce, did not just emerge in the

mid-1990s. It was developed globally over the last two decades of the twentieth century. E-commerce in its business-to-business form was pioneered by the airlines' global distribution systems. Such development reached a point around 1997/8 where there was a sufficient quantum mass of online businesses and customers, suggesting very rapid progress in the first year of the new century. Technical feasibility, now supported by practical availability and backed by massive industry investment, fully came together only at the end of the 1990s.

(4) Travel and tourism is one of the few 'pure' global information industries. Intangibility at the point of sale places great weight on the role of information provision and the industry is especially well placed to profit from the new developments in ICT. From exposure to advertising messages, through the selection of information and evaluation of options and prices; from the placing of a booking, payment and receipt of confirmation and tickets, right up to the point of departure on a visit, all the processes are conducted by exchanges of information. Currently, and increasingly, the exchanges take place between computers that also finalize the settlement of bills and store information about customers on databases.

Overall, the real distribution 'revolution' lies in the speed of the new processes and the lower costs that are now attainable by businesses that invest in the necessary infrastructure. Exchanges of information can be, and historically were conducted by letters, telephones and faxes, albeit slowly and at a far lower volume of transactions than big businesses require in the new millennium. Many such exchanges traditionally also involved intermediaries or 'middlemen,' such as retailers, because they added value to the basic processes, providing convenience and access at what was formerly an acceptable cost.

Right up to the 1990s a widespread myth persisted in marketing theory that, because services cannot be inventoried on shelves and in warehouses, distribution systems or 'channels' were actually less important in service industries than in others. Paradoxically, the inability in travel and tourism to create physical stocks of products is exactly the reason why the distribution process has now become so significant in the information age. It creates innovative opportunities and a flexibility that manufacturers must envy. Creating and manipulating the distribution systems that provide access for consumers is one of the principal ways to manage demand for highly perishable products, and distribution has become the primary area for seeking competitive advantage in both cost reduction and service improvement The importance of location and access Location, location was the traditional mantra for profitable tourism businesses. For most, small or micro-businesses with only one 'production unit', such as proprietor-owned guesthouses, small visitor attractions, equipment hire operators or indeed independent travel agents, the choice of location is still likely to be the most important business decision. A well-located small business can expect a good flow of customers to its area and past its doors. Product formulation, promotion and above all pricing have always been vital marketing considerations for small businesses, but not distribution. Traditionally, location is both place of production and the primary point of sale. As noted later, however, even the established distribution certainties of the smallest business are increasingly challenged and undermined by a combination of excess capacity in mature markets and the new opportunities provided by the Internet.

The fundamental requirement for well-located sites remains vital for large tourism businesses also. The more or less continuous search in the 1990s by international hotel companies for suitable development sites in the major cities of Europe provides some illustration of its importance.

But location of production units is seldom, if ever, a sufficient source of sales volume for bigger businesses; one or more distribution channels are required to provide supplementary points of sale away from the locations of service production and consumption. Apart from the opportunities opened up by the World Wide Web, the factors that focus increasing attention on developing distribution channels are:

- The growing size of businesses (greater production capacity has to be matched with more points of sale to generate the required volume of enquiries and bookings).
- The increasing number of units within a group or chain (under one ownership, or linked in strategic marketing alliances and co-operatives) that opens up distribution options.
- The greater distances that customers are willing to travel, especially international travel, and the need to provide reassurance through reservations that suitable accommodation and other facilities are available.
- The importance of reaching and drawing in more first-time visitors in order to make a business grow.
- The even greater need to provide the most convenient forms of access for repeat or 'loyal' customers.
- Growing competition for shares of markets where there is excess capacity in a destination.
- The need to sell capacity ahead of production to optimize business cash flow and operational planning.

The need to make maximum use of the sales promotion and tactical pricing opportunities afforded by modern distribution channels, especially in response to yield management programmes that identify periods where bookings are weak.

These eight factors, separately and combined, focus attention on the need to develop more efficient and cost-effective distribution systems that move the purchase decision away from the location of production towards places that prospective customers find more convenient, especially their own homes and offices.

As this chapter will indicate there are other good marketing reasons for developing distribution or access systems, especially cost reduction and control, protecting market share and matching competitors. But the overriding reason is usually to generate sales revenue additional to that which may be sustained solely by a good location. While, to some extent, additional expenditure on advertising or other communications is an alternative to developing points of sale, in practice there is a balance to be achieved between promotion and place. A massive demand generated by advertising would be lost, for example, if convenient points of access were not available to turn demand into sales. As modern distribution systems increasingly embrace both advertising and sales promotion functions, the balance has tilted strongly toward investment in distribution in the last decade.

GLOBAL DISTRIBUTION SYSTEM

System Name	Countries of	Airline	Agency Installation in total and by world areas	
AMADEUS established 1987	France, Germany, Spain, Sweden	Air France, Lufhansa, Ibaria, SAS	Approx. 48,000 agency Installation	c. 30,000 Installation in Europe, 6000 in N. America, 6000 in Caribean/Latin America, and 4000 in Far East/Australlia
GALILEO (APOLLO) established 1987	USA, UK, Netherlands, Italy, Switzerland, Greece, Belgium, Portugal	United Airlines, US Air, Air Chanada, BA, KLM, Swisar air, Olympic Airways, TAP	Approx. 48,000 agency Installation	c. 14,000 Installation in Europe, 15000 in N. N. America, 1600 in Caribean/Latin America, and 6000 in Far East/Australia
SABRE established 1987	USA	American Airlines (ABACUS Group of Asian, Airlines pined in 1998)	Approx. 48,000 agency Installation	c. 18,000 Installation in America, 6000 in Europe, 5000 in N. Caribean/Latin America, and 18000 in Far East/Australia
WORLDSPAN established 1990	USA and Far East	Delta, TWA North West Airlines	Approx. 18,500 agency Installation	c. 9000 in N. America, 7000 in Europe and 100 in Far East/Australia

Source: Data compilied with the support of Hotel Systems Support Services Ltd. based on Travel Distribution Report Vol. 7 No. 20 (2000) via Hotel Electronia Distribution Network (HEDNA).

Note: Although GDSa originated with airlines, under competition rules they are not permitted to favour particular companies and are essentially open to all airlines on the same terms and conditions.

GDS linked airline ticketing systems are used by over 800,000 travel agents; both domestic Australian travel agents like Flight Centre, American Express as well as International travel agencies like Carlson Wagonlit. Our GDS network distributes through SABRE, Apollo/WorldSpan, Amadeus, Galileo and Pegasus.

The GDS is a major sales channel for direct retail bookings through major travel websites. Accept real-time bookings from over 3,100 consumer travel websites, including Expedia, Travelocity, Travel Hero, Trip Adviser, Zuji, Orbitz and more. In the US, these sales channels have proven to be the most prolific source of bookings. Studies indicate that most travellers use the Internet to research travel options before booking. Over 40% of those buyers visit 3 websites — Expedia, Travelocity, and Orbitz. Perhaps more interesting, studies show that for every 1 booking made on those websites another 3 bookings were made by guests who contacted the property directly to book; either on their website or by phone. This would indicate that there are few advertising options available to match the power of this sales channel.

Australia has lagged behind the US in sales. The major websites have also neglected our market. In the coming months and years you can expect that to change. Already we see Expedia open an Australian Specific website. Simple Google searches now regularly display links to Trip Adviser and others on the first page. Clearly, the GDS will soon provide significant sales to all participants.

Reasonable Cost

Those familiar with inbound tourism expect to pay high commissions. Various Australian State and Federal Government Tourism bodies promote inbound tourism programs that cen be very expensive to maintain as well as cumbersome to manage. Normally, they require accommodations to give them fixed room allocations and +35% net rates with guarantees of lowest price. Most small operators would rather go bankrupt than pay those rates.

We have a better solution. Eliminates fixed allocations. Reduces commissions. Sell at whatever rate you like. You also have simple price controls that allow you to adjust the rate paid by guests on a channel by channel basis. We do not put you at disadvantage to please agents. You have total control.

Our GDS bookings cost you 15%, plus the travel agent has the option to bill an additional 10%. In fact, few agents bill the extra 10%. While that may seem like a lot, you have the option to charge more for these bookings and embed costs in the guest price.

Simple Management – It has to be Easy!

Managing GDS sales is simple because everything is integrated into the one system. As you take bookings from any source availability automatically changes for the GDS and all other sales channels. If you adjust rates, block out availability, change a description or image – all sales channels including the GDS are automatically updated.

LET US SUM UP

Marketing research is a formalized means of acquiring information to assist in the making of marketing decisions. It is a systematic design, collection, analysis and reporting of data and findings relevant to a specific marketing situation facing the company.

Market research is a continuous process. Among the variety of methods used, some seem to the widely resorted to because of their advantages over others. Research techniques can be grouped as:

- *Desk Research*
- *Field Research*
- *Sample Surveys*
- *Motivation Research*

Strategic planning is the process by which an organisation: first, analyses its strengths and weaknesses in its current and prospective markets - "where are we now?"; second, identifies its aims and the opportunities it seeks to develop – "where do we want to get to?"; and, third, defines the strategies and programmes of activity to achieve these aims – "how do we get there?". Strategic decisions are always focused on the longer run, normally beyond three years.

GDS linked airline ticketing systems are used by over 800,000 travel agents; both domestic Australian travel agents like Flight Centre, American Express as well as International travel agencies like Carlson Wagonlit. Our GDS network distributes through SABRE, Apollo/ World Span, Amadeus, Galileo and Pegasus.

CHECK YOUR PROGRESS

(A) True/False

(i) Marketing research is a continuous process

(ii) Tactical planning is short term.

(iii) Dubai called sunshine destination.

(B) Fill in the Blanks

(i) AMA stands for..................................

(ii) ICAO stands for ....

(iii) IATA stands for.........................

(C) True/False

(i) Strategic planning is a long-term process.

(ii) ITO stands for Inbound Tour Operator.

(iii) GDS stands for Global delivery services

LESSON & ACTIVITY

Browse the website and find out few travel agents operate online and give a brief description about the websites and services provided by those.

KEY WORDS

Marketing Research: A systematic design, collection, analysis and reporting of data and findings relevant to a specific marketing situation facing the company.

Strategic Planning: strategic planning is the process by which an organisation: first, analyses its strengths and weaknesses in its current and prospective markets.

Tactical Marketing Planning: Tactical decisions are always focused on the short run - from a few weeks to a maximum of one to one-and-a-half years - in which specific marketing campaigns are planned, implemented and evaluated. Tactics respond to market conditions and particularly to competitors' activities.

GDS: The GDS is a major sales channel for direct retail bookings through major travel websites.

QUESTIONS FOR DISCUSSION

(1) Explain different types of marketing research in tourism.

(2) Write short notes on (a) desk research (b) consumer research (c) motivational research (d) sample survey.

(3) Explain the different positioning strategies in tourism marketing.

(4) Write a short note on international marketing of tourism products.

(5) What is TDS? Explain.

(6) Explain the concept of GDS in details.

(7) Explain the various challenges in tourism distribution.

CHECK YOUR PROGRESS: MODEL ANSWER

(A) *(i)* T *(ii)* T *(iii)* T

(B) *(i)* American Marketing Association

(ii) International Civil Aviation Organisation

(iii) International Air Transport Association

(C) *(i)* T *(ii)* T *(iii)* F

❑ ❑ ❑

9

International Tourism-Growth, Future and Impact of Technology

Chapter Outline

- *Introduction*
- *Futures of Tourism*
- *Tourism Growth in Major Regions*
- *Transportation*
- *Technology & Tourism*
- *Tourism and Environment*

Learning Objective

At the conclusion of this lesson you should be able to understand:

- *Futures of tourism.*
- *Latest developments in the tourism industry*
- *Technology and tourism*
- *Development in transportation*
- *Tourism and environment*

"The fool wanders, a wise man travels."

— Thomas Fuller

INTRODUCTION

People have been travelling from one place to another since the primitive age when they were living in a small group and did hunting and gathering for their daily life. The movement of people has become clearer when nation-states emerged. They were moving within or across borders for various purposes such as travel, trade, migration, spread of cultural, and dissemination of knowledge and understanding ; hence, contributing to the development of human civilization.

As for recreation purpose, a lot of wealthy middle class people in Roman era were visiting Pompeii and Herculanem, seaside resorts, to escape from hot summer in Rome (**William,** 1998). Thus, tourism is not the recent phenomenon.

In this 21st century, tourism is growing very fast and plays an important role in the world economy. According to Tourism Highlight 2006 Edition, published by World Tourism Organization, international tourist arrivals and receipts world wide in 2005 was approximately 8oo millions and $680 billion respectively despite terrorism in US and Europe, tsunami in some part of Asia, SAR in China and Southeast Asia, and rising of oil price.

FUTURES OF TOURISM

(1) Sustainability in Tourism

Firstly, concerns arose over sustainability in tourism. Particular concern arose with regard to climate change, air travel and the true cost of fuel. At present air travel is the greatest source of emissions and there is therefore a move to implement sustainability strategies including issues such as training, more advanced technology, etc. Indeed, key predictions involved changes in trading, the further development and implementation of carbon offsets and radical technological changes such as a move towards biomass fuels and aircrafts powered by hydrogen, although such changes were predicted to be some time in the future. This was further developed with realisation of the tourism industry being at the height of the budget airline peak and predicted a move away from such practice in the future. Nevertheless, with the emergence of key markets of China and India, there is a conflict in interests, particularly in the UK as attention moves away from encouraging shorter haul travel destinations, while remaining open to the inevitability of continued demand for longer haul destinations and the detrimental effects such travel inevitably creates. Indeed, referring to the recent white paper on sustainability, Rok Klancnik (WTO) realised that tourism cannot avoid the development of aviation and the need to create and maintain public/private partnerships to prevent and mitigate climate change. He also highlighted a shift in media attention towards the ethics of tourism and highlighted the WTO's Global Code of Ethics that addresses issues from climate change through to sexual exploitation. The media therefore holds an ethical responsibility as they grab onto 'hot stories' that will sell. As ethics and sustainability is now an issue that can 'sell' and the majority of media support and give attention to ethical practices in tourism.

(2) Globalisation

Concentration through mergers and the development of partnerships Secondly, while tourism was noted to account for approximately 10% of global GDP, through globalisation powers are moved out from Governments into the hands of the private sectors that have increased access to knowledge and innovations. While there are distinct benefits to such practice, discussion noted such shifts contribute detrimental effects and problems with the environment, etc. Governments were recognised to be in a weak position as they are unable to exercise levels of control and the travel and tourism industry remains reliant upon international agencies and the EU (**Victor Middleton,** Consultant). Consequently, greater partnerships between both public and private sectors were highlighted as vital to future developments in travel and tourism. Greater Government regulation and intervention is required and Governments need to begin to listen to the importance of travel and tourism within the economic, social and environmental issues.

(3) Developments in Technology

Thirdly, attention turned to the importance of e-Tourism and the influences technological changes have on the structure of the tourism industry in bringing both opportunities and challenges. **Dimitrios Buhalis** explained that the Internet is changing industry structures, generating both opportunities and threats. Indeed, **Florence MacKay** (SABRE) noted the importance of the internet and dynamic packaging in tourism. Through the internet GDS's have moved to diversify, becoming open systems such as UNIX that have enabled faster growth and introduction of new processes. Indeed, while in the past tourism has emerged through mass marketing; developments in technology have initiated a move away from a 'one size fits all' and while mass marketing still commands a place in tourism, the need for diversity has led to increased market segmentation as technology becomes individual to tour operators.

(4) Consumer Centric Technologies and Accessibility

Fourthly, such developments in technology have led to an increased consumer-centric approach to tourism. Tourism businesses are moving to see tourists in a different perspective as focus moves away from mass marketing to addressing that which the tourists really want and wish for. Destinations are no longer the sole product *per se* as attention moves to providing activities such as shopping, spas, cultural events, etc. Tourism is becoming about going that bit further to understand what consumers want. Consequently, technology is moving to become consumer-centric and new avenues of distribution are realised. Focus lies in maximising distribution and accessing the diversity of consumers through technological developments. **Florence MacKay** (SABRE) acknowledged the importance of such technological development, investment and change as GDS and non-GDS content merge through the internet to meet demands of tourists who increasingly book flights, accommodation, tickets and research holidays, etc., online.

Young tourists and travellers were recognised as the most sophisticated users of IT and are able to take advantage of changing technologies as they optimize the potential of the internet to book holidays and engage with local economies directly. However, while youth tourism is always at the forefront of technology, changes constantly occur through generations as new and different technologies emerge.

Additionally, changing population demographics indicate a trend towards increasing numbers of older tourists and the various physical and environmental disabilities experienced by tourists. Concerns therefore arose over accessibility. While realising there are dangers in separating people into categories, Dr Graham Miller raised the issue that all tourists have accessibility issues at some point. Indeed, such is the increased concern over accessibility that the UK Government has highlighted this issue as key to the planning for the 2012 Olympics in London. Additionally, the School of Management at the University of Surrey is currently establishing a project called OSSATE: a 'one-stop shop' information source for accessibility requirements throughout Europe (http://www.ossate.org).

(5) Pressure on SMEs

Fifthly, such concerns over sustainability and the development of partnerships were related directly to SMEs as they face pressures to not only diversify, but to exist in a market with competing interests. While the travel and tourism industry is highly dependent upon such enterprises, they currently have little or no voice. Nevertheless, with regard to the previous theme, it was realised SMEs could take advantage of the internet and new technologies to compete with big brands. Indeed, many tourists, especially younger tourists, take advantage of such potentials as they access previously trapped SMEs.

(6) Innovation and Creativity Towards Competitive Advantage

Sixthly, it was realised there is an ever-increasing demand for new products in tourism. Lower cost no longer means low service and low quality. Rather, attention has moved towards providing high quality products for tourists. Tourism is now a mature industry and focuses on innovative, creative opportunities for travel as attention moves from how to what tourists are demanding. Products now focus on creating new and memorable experiences 'on the ground', on selling stories, on touching. Pressures of diversity demand new opportunities for travel. Examples discussed include opportunities for tourism for ethnic minorities in Cheshire, England, gangland tourism in Amsterdam and dark tourism to name but a few. Nevertheless, some warned that there are no new products as such, but new forms of packaging. Such change in direction was also felt to greatly benefit SMEs as they can fill the narrative of memorable experiences as they are part of them.

(7) Constant Crisis Management

Finally, in addition to the concerns above, it was recognised that tourism is also facing constant crisis management. Terrorism is not a new concept and while September the 11th is often acknowledged as the principle moment in such crisis, it was also recognised that prior events such as SARS and international terrorism, Asian Tsunami and the threat of avian flu continue to threaten tourism. There is a distinct unpredictability in everything and such events serve to reaffirm the importance of the worldwide tourism industry on both global and local economies. While some regarded youth travel as a source of dissipating concerns and creating opportunity to spread peace and understanding as there is a distinct lack of understanding why such crises are arising and therefore the industry should be seen as an opportunity to be together and understand each other. Nevertheless, such optimism was equalled with concern over the potential of such tourists to sow the seeds of negative impacts.

Sustainable tourism is a form of tourism that follows the principles of sustainability. Sustainable tourism in its purest sense, is an industry committed to making a low impact on the natural environment and local culture, while helping to generate income and employment for locals.

Global economists forecast continuing international tourism growth, ranging between three and six percent annually, depending on the location. As one of the world's largest and fastest growing industries, this continuous growth will place great stress on remaining biologically diverse habitats and indigenous cultures, which are often used to support mass tourism. Tourists who promote sustainable tourism are sensitive to these dangers and seek to protect tourist destinations, and to protect tourism as an industry. Sustainable tourists can reduce the impact of tourism in many ways, including:

- informing themselves of the culture, politics, and economy of the communities visited
- anticipating and respecting local cultures' expectations and assumptions
- contributing to intercultural understanding and tolerance
- supporting the integrity of local cultures by favoring businesses which conserve cultural heritage and traditional values
- supporting local economies by purchasing local goods and participating with small, local businesses
- conserving resources by seeking out businesses that are environmentally conscious, and by using the least possible amount of non-renewable resources

Increasingly, destinations and tourism operations are endorsing and following "responsible tourism" as a pathway towards sustainable tourism. Responsible tourism and sustainable tourism have an identical goal, that of sustainable development. The pillars of responsible tourism are therefore the same as those of sustainable tourism – environmental integrity, social justice and economic development. The major difference between the two is that, in responsible tourism, individuals, organisations and businesses are asked to take responsibility for their actions and the impacts of their actions. This shift in emphasis has taken place because some stakeholders feel that insufficient progress towards realising sustainable tourism has been made since the Earth Summit in Rio. This is partly because everyone has been expecting others to behave in a sustainable manner. The emphasis on responsibility in responsible tourism means that everyone involved in tourism – government, product owners and operators, transport operators, community services, NGO's tourists, local communities, industry associations – are responsible for achieving the goals of responsible tourism.

Responsible Tourism

Responsible Tourism can be regarded as a movement. It is more than a form of tourism (**Harrison and Husbands,** 1996) as it represents an approach to engaging with tourism, be that as a tourist, a business, locals at a destination or any other tourism stakeholder. It emphasises that all stakeholders are responsible for the kind of tourism they develop or engage in. Whilst different groups will see responsibility in different ways, the shared understanding is that responsible tourism should entail an improvement in tourism. Tourism should become 'better' as a result of the responsible tourism approach.

Within the notion of betterment resides the acknowledgement that conflicting interests need to be balanced. However, the objective is to create better places for people to live in and to visit. Importantly, there is no blueprint for responsible tourism: what is deemed responsible may differ depending on places and cultures. Responsible Tourism is an aspiration that can be realised in different ways in different originating markets and in the diverse destinations of the world (**Goodwin,** 2002).

Focusing in particular on businesses, according to the Cape Town Declaration on Responsible Tourism, it will have the following characteristics:

(1) minimizes negative economic, environmental, and social impacts;

(2) generates greater economic benefits for local people and enhances the well-being of host communities, improves working conditions and access to the industry;

(3) involves local people in decisions that affect their lives and life chances;

(4) makes positive contributions to the conservation of natural and cultural heritage, to the maintenance of the world's diversity;

(5) provides more enjoyable experiences for tourists through more meaningful connections with local people, and a greater understanding of local cultural, social and environmental issues;

(6) provides access for physically challenged people; and

(7) is culturally sensitive, engenders respect between tourists and hosts, and builds local pride and confidence.

Ecotourism

Ecotourism, also known as ecological tourism, is a form of Sustainable Tourism, differing by its focus on ecology. Ecotourism focuses on volunteering, personal growth, and learning new ways to live on the planet; typically involving travel to destinations where flora, fauna, and cultural heritage are the primary attractions.

Responsible ecotourism includes programs that minimize the negative aspects of conventional tourism on the environment, and enhance the cultural integrity of local people. Therefore, in addition to evaluating environmental and cultural factors, an integral part of ecotourism is in the promotion of recycling, energy efficiency, water conservation, and creation of economic opportunities for the local communities. Such changes have become a statement affirming one's social identity, educational sophistication, and disposable income as it has about preserving the Amazon rainforest or the Caribbean reef for posterity.

Coastal Tourism

Many coastal areas are experiencing particular pressure from sea change growth in lifestyles and growing numbers of tourists. Coastal environments are limited in extent consisting of only a narrow strip along the edge of the ocean. Coastal areas are often the first environments to experience the detrimental impacts of tourism. Planning and management controls can reduce the impact on coastal environments and ensure that investment into tourism products supports sustainable coastal tourism.

Community-based Management

There has been the promotion of sustainable tourism practices surrounding the management of tourist locations by locals or more concisely, the community. One of the main and important sites to promote tourism in developing countries is www. humanitour.com

This form of tourism is based on the premise that the people living next to a resource are the ones best suited to protecting it. This means that the tourism activities and businesses are developed and operated by local community members, and certainly with their consent and support.

Sustainable tourism typically involves the conservation of resources that are capitalized upon for tourism purposes, such as coral reefs and pristine forests. Locals run the businesses and are responsible for promoting the conservation messages to protect their environment.

Community-based sustainable tourism (CBST) associates the success of the sustainability of the ecotourism location to the management practices of the communities who are directly or indirectly dependent on the location for their livelihoods.

A salient feature of CBST is that local knowledge is usually utilized alongside wide general frameworks of ecotourism business models. This allows the participation of locals at the management level and typically allows a more intimate understanding of the environment. The use of local knowledge also means an easier entry level into a tourism industry for locals whose jobs or livelihoods are affected by the use of their environment as tourism locations. The involvement of locals restores the ownership of the environment to the local community and allows an alternative sustainable form of development for communities and their environments that are typically unable to support other forms of development.

Stakeholders

Stakeholders of sustainable tourism play a role in continuing this form of tourism. This can include organizations as well as individuals.

Non-governmental Organizations

Non-governmental organizations are one of the stakeholders in advocating sustainable tourism. Their roles can range from spearheading sustainable tourism practices to simply doing research. University research teams and scientists can be roped in to aid in the process of planning. Such solicitation of research can be observed in the planning of Cat Ba National Park in Vietnam another example is humanitour.com who encourage local people to start new businesses.

Dive resort operators in Bunaken National Park, Indonesia, play a crucial role but developing exclusive zones for diving and fishing respectively, such that both tourists and locals can benefit from the venture

Large conventions, meetings and other major organized events drive the travel, tourism and hospitality industry. Cities and convention centers compete to attract such commerce, commerce which has heavy impacts on resource use and the environment. Major sporting events, such as the Olympic Games, present special problems regarding environmental burdens and degradation. But burdens imposed by the regular convention industry can be vastly more significant.

Green conventions and events are a new but growing sector and marketing point within the convention and hospitality industry. More environmentally aware organizations, corporations and government agencies are now seeking more sustainable event practices, greener hotels, restaurants and convention venues, and more energy efficient or climate neutral travel and ground transportation.

Additionally, some convention centers have begun to take direct action in reducing the impact of the conventions they host. One example is the Moscone Center in San Francisco, California, which has a very aggressive recycling program, a large solar power system, and other programs aimed at reducing impact and increasing efficiency.

Tourists

With the advent of the internet, some traditional conventions are being replaced with virtual conventions, where the attendees remain in their home physical location and "attend" the convention by use of a web-based interface programmed for the task. This sort of "virtual" meeting eliminates all of the impacts associated with travel, accommodation, food wastage, and other necessary impacts of traditional, physical conventions.

Travel over long distances requires a large amount of time and/or energy. Generally this involves burning fossil fuels, a largely unsustainable practice and one that contributes to climate change, via CO_2 emissions.

Air travel is perhaps the worst offender in this regard, contributing to between 2 and 3% of global carbon emissions. Given a business-as-usual approach, this could be expected to rise to 5% by 2015 and 10% by 2050. Car travel is the next worst offender. Mass transport is the most climate friendly method of travel, and generally the rule is "the bigger the better" - compared to cars, buses are relatively more sustainable, and trains and ships are even more so. Human energy and renewable energy are the most efficient, and hence, sustainable. Travel by bicycle, solar powered car, or sailing boat produces no carbon emissions (although the embodied energy in these vehicles generally comes at the expense of carbon emission).

TOURISM GROWTH IN MAJOR REGIONS-FOCUS ON ASIA PACIFIC COUNTRIES

A variety of patterns have characterized recent international tourism trends for Asia and the Pacific in terms of receipts and the number of tourist arrivals. According to the World Tourism Organization, the value of worldwide tourism receipts was US$ 622 billion in 2004. Asia and the Pacific earned 20 per cent of that amount, or about US$ 124 billion. Tourism industry receipts in Asia and the Pacific showed an impressive yearly growth rate of 24 per cent as compared with the world growth rate of 10 per cent. However, this represented recovery for the region from a decline in 2003 (-9.4 per cent) owing to the effects of SARS.

In 2004, the total number of international tourists worldwide grew by 10.7 per cent to a total of 763 million arrivals. The annual growth rate for arrivals in Asia and the Pacific was 27.8 per cent, numbering 152.9 million international tourists, or about 20 per cent of the world total. North-East Asia recorded 29.5 per cent growth in international tourist arrivals and South-East Asia 30.6 per cent growth in 2004 after a decrease of 13.7 per cent in 2003. Arrivals in South Asia grew by 16.5 per cent in 2004 and by 12.4 per cent in Oceania.

While tourism demand in Asia and the Pacific recovered in 2004, receipts grew somewhat more slowly than the volume of arrivals. This is related to the changing patterns of travel, which have shown a trend towards higher frequency shorter-stay trips with reduced spending by tourists, as a result of increased intraregional tourism. This trend was compounded by more competitive prices due to the entry of new low-cost airlines offering additional domestic and sub regional routes. In terms of arrivals in 2004, China ranked fourth among the top 10 tourism destinations worldwide and Hong Kong, China, seventh. At the same time, in terms of international tourism receipts, China ranked seventh and Turkey eighth among the top 10 countries. Independent travel has been developing faster than conventional package tours, although many destinations, especially in South-East Asia, expect to benefit from the fast growth of the outbound Chinese tourism market.

The World Travel and Tourism Council (WTTC) has estimated the contribution of tourism to socio-economic development using the tourism satellite account methodology.

In 2004, travel and tourism worldwide was expected to generate total demand of US$ 5,490 billion with a direct impact that included 73.7 million jobs (2.8 per cent of total employment) and a contribution to gross domestic product (GDP) of US$ 1,542 billion (3.8 per cent of aggregate world GDP).

The travel and tourism industry also has an indirect effect on all other sectors of the economy. In 2004, travel and tourism worldwide accounted for US$ 1,289.8 billion (12.2 per cent) of all service and merchandise exports, US$ 802.3 billion (9.4 per cent) of global capital investment and US$ 265.3 billion (3.9 per cent) of government expenditure worldwide.

In 2004, the forecast for real growth in the industry worldwide was 5.9 per cent for total demand, 5.2 per cent for direct growth in GDP and 4.6 per cent for direct growth in employment. In terms of the regional distribution of total worldwide demand, North-East Asia, South-East Asia and South Asia ranked third, fourth and seventh respectively among the top nine regions in 2004. Compared with the world average for real growth of total demand in 2004 (5.9 per cent), all three main regions of Asia showed higher than average growth of demand: 10.4 per cent for South-East Asia, 9.9 per cent for South Asia and 6.6 per cent for North-East Asia.

The values for travel and tourism GDP showed a similar pattern. North-East Asia, South-East Asia and South Asia ranked third, fourth and seventh respectively in 2004. In terms of the GDP share, tourism in North-East Asia ranked fifth out of nine regions at 9.3 per cent, South-East Asia seventh at 7.4 per cent and South Asia ninth at 5.0 per cent. The GDP shares for the three regions were below the world average of 10.4 per cent.

WTTC has reported on total (direct and indirect) travel and tourism employment in terms of number of jobs for the top nine regions of the world. Tourism worldwide was expected to create almost 215 million jobs in 2004, with North-East Asia accounting for the biggest share worldwide, at almost 72 million jobs; South Asia ranked second, with about 30 million jobs, and South-East Asia fifth, with about 20 million. In terms of the share of tourism in total employment for 2004, the global average was 8.1 per cent. In terms of the share of tourism in total employment for Asia, North-East Asia recorded 8.5 per cent, South-East Asia 8.1 per cent and South Asia 5.2 per cent.

Prospects for Tourism Growth

The rich and unique cultures, diverse natural environments and standards of service will continue to make destinations in the Asian and Pacific region attractive to international tourists. It is clear that the tourism industries of many countries in the region have been remarkably responsive to recent trends in demand. The region should therefore be well placed to benefit from positive prospects for the expansion of tourism worldwide.

The prospects for tourism growth, however, will be driven by a number of factors, including globalization, the concomitant developments in transport and tourism-related infrastructure and the development of intraregional travel. At the same time, there are a number of factors that could hinder the development of tourism, for example, visa and cross-border formalities, as well as various unforeseen shocks, for example, natural disasters, health crises and security threats, that have a direct impact on tourist arrivals. This section considers these factors and concludes with an assessment of

TRANSPORTATION

The state of natural attractions and tourism management has been the focus of much research over the years. Tourism affects all aspects of the natural environment. There is a need to study the "environmental inter-relationships...especially in ecologically sensitive areas such as small islands, reefs, desert oases, and tropical habitats" as these areas most often offer the "greatest tourism potential" (**Inskeep,** 1987, p 120). Degrees of impact vary according to the number of tourists, the resilience of the ecosystem to the pressure wrought by tourism, time, the changing fashions in tourism, and the transformational nature of tourism itself (**Burns and Associates,** 1989).

Transportation links the various destinations and ferries people, goods, and services. Tourism is all about travel; and the role of transportation in its operation is vital. It is largely due to the improvement of transportation that tourism has expanded. The advent of flight has shrunk the world, and the motor vehicle has made travel to anywhere possible. This reality coupled with changing work patterns and innovative marketing has driven international mass tourism through the years.

Culpan (1987, p. 546) identified transportation modes and management as the "important ingredients of the international tourism system," acknowledging that linkage by air, sea and land modes is essential for the operations as well as the availability of support services such as fuel stations, auto repair, motels and rest facilities for land travel.

Advances in transportation have widely eased travel. It is attributed to the ease and accessibility of modern transport that has spurred the widespread growth of nature tourism within the United States and overseas (**Honey,** 1999). The increase in the number of visitors to what were once remote areas has resulted in degradation and damage of the resources prompting the need to re-evaluate the role of transportation in the exercise. Impacts of tourism development include soil erosion or compaction, clearance of vegetation to give way to roads and tourism facilities, recreation use of off-road vehicles, trail bikes, snowmobiles, horses, and even the trampling of pedestrians (**Buckley,** 1996). The careful planning of sensitive areas which includes the utilization of zoning to determine areas for facilities and tourist activities and to protect natural areas and discourage development, and the planning of roads, hiking and riding trails should be integrated into the natural.

Croall (1995, p. 1) was exhaustive in his criticism of what he called "the spectre of tourism" which he sees as slowly ruining erstwhile pristine landscapes, quaint communities, as well as polluting the air and water, trivializing cultures, and degrading life on this planet. He puts the blame on poor or lack of visitor management and the level of accessibility of the destination area. Accessibility and tourism activities have broken barriers and opened formerly off-the-beaten-track areas to visitors through aggressive marketing of some far-off paradise with the availability of transport.

Transportation in tourism is most often seen as just part of the tourism system which is in charge of bringing the tourists to the destinations, a means of getting around the place and leaving it once the duration of the trip is over. **Page and Lumsdon** (2004) contend that the transportation system of a tourist destination has an impact on the tourism experience which explains how people travel and why they choose different forms of holiday, destination, and transport. The improvement in transportation modes plus low fares has increased the accessibility of areas once considered off-the-beaten-path. Access to tourism sites vary according to the nature of the site, the state of infrastructure, and the efficiency of the public transport system.

The OECD (1988 as cited in Button, 1993) came out with a table outlining the major impacts of transportation on the environment. For land transportation, the rail and roads impact wildlife and habitat when these pass through natural areas, creating divisions in an otherwise contiguous plain. Emissions from road and air transport are the common sources of greenhouse gases and industrialization has not helped much in curtailing the sources. "The transport sector is responsible for over a quarter of the world's primary energy use, and for about 54 percent of all world oil consumption" (**Peters,** 2000, p. 110). Air and noise pollution accounts for the engine noise from planes, motor vehicles, construction, overhead cable cars, as well as human voices and footfalls (**Buckley,** 1996).

Access and Modes

Tourism and accessibility may be linked to the level of degradation of the destination. Issues arising from this include the concept of carrying capacity, impacts per capita, and visitor management. How these issues are managed is reflective of the type of tourism being advocated by the operator, the community as well as the government. Accessibility can make or break a destination. There are two streams of argument here: one involves the number of visitors and the other involves number of visitors per capita.

The first contend that too much access brings in a bigger number of people that can increase the level of degradation, decrease the experience, and impact the natural state of the resources. The second argument takes into consideration the ratio of visitors to the host population and the level and type of impacts created.

On the issue of carrying capacity, **Inskeep** (1987) acknowledges the fact that areas such as small islands, arid and coastal lands, reefs, mountains and lakes are vulnerable to tourist overuse and overdevelopment and proposes that carrying capacity should be a part of the comprehensive regional and site-specific analysis and planning process. And "it is important to distinguish between capacity based on tourist acceptability and that predicated on environmental deterioration because the two may not be the same" (**Inskeep,** 1987, p. 121).

Fennell (2003) and **Honey** (1999) cited the experience of the Galapagos Islands in Ecuador wherein the increase in access started a chain of problems: in the 1970s access to the islands was through cargo ships from Ecuador's main port in Guayaquil which plied the islands every three months or so but the growing popularity of the islands as a nature enclave spurred the boating business to expand from just five small boats in the early 70s to forty-two by 1980; and when the United States military base on Baltra accommodated regular commercial airlines, visitor number quickly grew to unsustainable proportions as crowding on trails and the monitoring of visitor movement became inefficient with the lack of qualified guides.

Immigration escalated as higher paying jobs were on hand which led to the introduction of new species such as goats and rats which in turn endangered the species endemic to the island (**Honey,** 1999). Ratio of visitor to host population should be kept at a level wherein the community is comfortable with the level of influx of visitors and there is no conflict regarding resources.

Many researches have covered the problems of areas wherein the local community has been alienated by the tourism development in their area. Worse, aside from being banned from using the beaches as these are for the exclusive use of hotel guests, oftentimes locals suffer power and water shortages just so that hotels have air conditioning and running water at all times.

An increase in visitor number means a lot of things: congestion on the roads and trails, increase in pollution level (both noise and air), more trash to contend with, insufficient infrastructure to support the increase, as well as the impacts on the environment and wildlife.

The telling disappearance of the golden toad in the Monteverde Cloud Forest Reserve in Costa Rica is one case where numbers fell from 1,500 in 1987 to virtually zero within two years has been attributed to the increase in tourism of the area (**Honey,** 1999). Independent Digital (UK) Ltd. (2004) ran an article regarding how "cheap flights and a fascination with the environment" has contributed to the degradation of natural areas. It is so easy now to hop on a plane and reach one's destination within the day, factor in the cheap prices and a destination area is immediately swamped with visitors.

The modes we choose and how we travel are indicators of our level of awareness. Some tour operators give options to their clients while others just group them together to get the best out of a deal. As argued earlier, access to places would rather be organically developed or planned with the conservation of nature in mind. And the impacts of transportation on the environment have been an issue through the years. The Kyoto Protocol is seen as the instrument to force industrialized countries to reduce emissions, yet still has to prove its worth.

As with the arguments regarding economics, **Ozbay, K.** *et al.*, (2003) theorized that having a reliable and efficient transport infrastructure is a key factor in a region's economic welfare. They utilized several accessibility indexes such as **Hansen's** (1959), **Ingram's** (1971), and those of **Black** and **Conroy's** (1977) to check the performance of a transport network and came up with a conclusion that a region with good access ensures the efficient operations of manufacturing, retail, labour, and housing markets. The relation between being an economic success and accessibility is logical in the sense that the flow of goods and services are unhampered. This logic can be abused by governments willing to sacrifice the environment for steady cash flow. The question of sustainability and economic issues again enter the picture.

Day Trips and the Automobile

The impact of automobiles in tourism can be observed in the increasing number of daytrips and leisure travel. Most trips to the countryside are common and most utilize automobiles, which can take their toll on the resources. **Nelson and Wall** (1986) investigated the relationships of the changing transport network of Vancouver Island and confirmed the observations of **Rajotte** (1972) and **Lundgren** (1982) that established tourist destinations decline in importance once a more accessible destination is opened elsewhere. It was the extensive use of the automobile that initiated the changes on Vancouver Island, even the coastal liners and passenger trains gave in to the competition it posed.

Transport Strategies

Transport strategies reflect the values of those in the business. In **Farrell** and **Runyan** (1991, p. 31), different transport-tourism management approaches are suggested: one is "to 'harden' the resource by paving, fencing, restricting, or directing traffic or by other means to facilitate more intensive use"; others include regulation using land use, limiting/ prohibiting access— dependent on the nature of the site, pricing is also a much debated alternative, and the use of visitor traffic management schemes such as private-public transport linkages, speed limits, group size and characteristics, and marketing. Since transportation is a derived demand then knowing the target population would greatly help in determining the most suitable modes of transport for certain areas.

Another strategy utilized in transportation management includes the creation of land use policies, by regulating location, scale, density and design of activities, which have an impact on traffic flows. It can also be utilized to adjust urban development around the needs of the public transport system to create a balanced passenger demand. The promotion of no motorized and public transport is emphasized and the involvement of users is encouraged in decision-making and in mitigating the negative effects of transport.

Though land-use planning alone cannot resolve unsustainable transport patterns, it can help reduce the number of unnecessary trips, prevent activity fragmentation and provide opportunities for other more environment-friendly modes of transport (**Herala,** 2003). Finally, the issue on tourism sustainability and transport can be noted when access to attractions that give destinations their tourism appeal are either off-limits or limited (**Ayala,** 1996). Reasons vary from the need to rehabilitate due to too much stress because of heavy visitation to non-accommodation of tourists to preserve a site.

The fact that the automobile is one of the most unsustainable modes of transport, this move is indeed good news. For countries with a high level of car ownership and use, this could be an issue regarding freedom and rights. Though this issue may not be of much concern in Third World Countries (TWCs), special cases such as the "highway...built through the Metropolitan National Park in Panama City, [which is] the largest area of tropical rainforest within the boundaries of a city" and the use of wildlife safari vehicles in East Africa is worth investigating (**Mowforth and Munt**, 1998, p. 118). In the final analysis, it is how people travel, how the destinations are being packaged, and the stand of the governments on ecotourism.

TECHNOLOGY AND TOURISM

Information technology and the tourism industry components

As indicated above the tourism industry is made up of three major components: namely,

(i) Transport sector, which includes air, water and surface transport,

(ii) Accommodation sector, all types of establishments that offer lodging to visitors (Hotel, Motel, Guest houses, Caravans etc.)

(iii) Attraction sector which comprises manmade and natural attractions which are developed to satisfy visitors educational, recreational, aesthetic needs etc.

TRANSPORT SECTOR

Transport provides the essential link between tourism origin and destination areas and facilitates the movement of holidaymakers, business travellers, people visiting friends and relatives and those undertaking educational and health tourism. Before setting out on a journey of any kind, every traveller makes sure which Transport Company has a good safety record. To this effect, airplanes coaches and even taxis are equipped with good communication equipment. An Airplane flies with the help of modern information technology equipment which provides information ranging from weather, altitude and other information to the pilot to communication made during emergency by the pilot with other airplanes and air traffic control stations. In-flight entertainment is also a product of information technology, video games, video films are examples. In the case of buses/coaches and taxis, in many countries with developed tourism business, they are equipped with radio communication systems for various uses. For example, the driver or the tour guide updates the Tour Company headquarters about the progress of the tour throughout the touring period. This communication ensures the safety of tourists. Fast and easy information flow is of paramount importance to build confidence in the travelling public. In recent years, the confidence built due to the use of modern IT has been demonstrated by a tremendous increase in the number of travellers worldwide.

ACCOMMODATION SECTOR

In the accommodation sector also the contribution of information technology is prominent. Any individual or group wishing to travel to any part of the world now has an easy access to the accommodation service providers. A visitor can access an information about the kind of hotels at the destination, their ranges of product, the price and other relevant information without leaving his/her office or home. What one has to do is to ring up a travel agency and get the expert advice. This will help any visitor greatly as to where to stay during any kind of away from home. Here the information can be obtained aided by still or moving pictures in order to give an exact feature of an accommodation, facilities and services of one's choice. At a destination also visitors are at ease during their stay in every respect, in getting information about their business, family or other information back home. They are also at ease to relax with the videos and television entertainment programs, which nowadays are part and parcel of many accommodation units.

ATTRACTION SECTOR

In the case of attractions both manmade and natural attraction owners need to communicate or inform their customers and potential customers about their production. Information about the kind of attraction, where they are located and how to get there is of vital importance. The attraction owners particularly the national tourist offices discharge their duty of promoting their country's tourist attractions using the information technology products. Information through promotional videos, Internet web sites, television advertisements and travel documentaries are the main information dissemination tools.

Travel intermediaries and the role of information technology

One of the unique characteristics of tourism products is the need of the role played by the so-called travel intermediaries. These travel intermediaries are travel agents, tour operators, conference organizers booking agents etc. They are so important again because of the nature of the tourism product, perishablity and intangibility. This means service products including tourism, cannot be stored for a litter sale, and cannot be inspected for their quality before purchase respectively. This entails a very big effort for marketing and distribution of these products. Tourism product supply is fragmented both geographically and as product component, coupled with their relatively low capital volume; individual components cannot afford to market and distribute their product for the dispersed potential and actual customers on their own. Let us take an airline company as an example. An airline company, which flies many destinations, can have a representative but cannot have so many offices or product distribution channels in all routes it serves. Or, in Addis Ababa itself for example, Ethiopian Airlines has few offices to distribute and market its product. However, one can also buy Ethiopian Airline ticket from many other travel agencies in the city. One can imagine if the airline can run these many say sixty offices on its own which are usually with high fixed costs. This makes the travel agents an indispensable partner both in efficiently distributing and marketing the product and substantially reducing the cost of operation for the airline. As these are working on commission basis, the cost of operation for the airline is relatively low. These travel agencies are performing this indispensable task of being intermediary by the use of computers and computer reservation systems (CRS).

CRS (Computer Reservation System)

The airline CRS systems were the pioneers of computer applications in the 1950s and are now virtually indispensable to airlines because they enable their revenue streams to be maximized by efficient inventory control (an inventory in this context refers to an airline's stock of passenger seats that is available for sale). However, these days, hotel and car hiring companies by renting the service from the airline companies also employ these systems. The technology works by using computers of special kind and leased telephone lines. The travel agent is connected on line to the central host computer system or CRS. The host computer is almost always a mainframe with massive database attached. The mainframe host polls each travel agent terminal every second or so, to see if it has any messages to send (**Inkpen,** 1999). In this system it is possible that airliners, Hotels and car rental companies can talk to the travel agent and *vice versa.* This system contributes to a great extent in increasing sales volume and giving precise information on the availability and selling the products efficiently ensuring substantial profit gain.

GDS (Global Distribution Systems)

GDSs are systems which distribute reservation and information services to sales outlets around the world. Unlike the CRSs used solely by an airline or hotel chain, GDS distribute more than one CRS to users who are usually travel agents. GDSs were formed from the airlines of several CRSs, each of which had its airline backer. Once formed, there was a period of some consolidation and shakeout, after which four main GDSs emerged. These are Amadeus, Galileo, Sabre and World Span.

This world leading GDSs are switches or simply computers that are connected on the one side to many different supplier systems and on the other side to many end users. The end users of switch comprise travel agents with a single reservation system to support the sale of airline seats and related travel products such as hotel-and car hire, via a single computer terminal, usually a Personal Computer (**Inkpen,** pp. 107). All the GDSs are owned by a group of airline companies. Eleven carriers of different countries for example own Galileo and there are 500 participating airlines companies. GDSs require massive investment because they are extremely large computer systems that link several airlines and travel principals into a complex network of PCs, telecommunications and large main frame computers. It is not important here to go into the complex operation how these GDSs are working. However it is pertinent to say that GDS are the macro version of CRSs with a specialized and improved information technology for the distribution of Travel products.

Internet and Travel and Tourism

So far it has been dealt with an information technology where intermediaries, travel agents, tour operators, etc., are an indispensable part in the distribution and marketing of travel and tourism products, and as an important point of sale or product outlets. Here I will discuss about an information technology where the producer and the consumer are directly communicating, by putting the indispensability of travel intermediaries in question.

This is not met perfectly than through Internet, which is the latest product of information technology. This interactive information-supplying medium is user friendly and gives enormous information of all kind related to travel. Apart from supplying information on world leading and emerging tourist destination of all kind, it is now possible to book and buy holidays through Internet using plastic money. It gives information on all Airlines, Hotels and Car hire companies, which are in its database. Microsoft is a travel agent. Its Internet site branded Expedia is one of the most important examples of the new generation of travel intermediaries (**Inkpen,** pp.196). Distribution of travel and tourism products using the Internet has a substantial cost reduction advantage for providers of tourism services. The cost incurred by suppliers in receiving a customer booking is the one, which is costly. So, Internet gives a practical aid both in supplying information and receiving bookings or selling tourism products on the principal's behalf.

Marketing tourism products on the Internet is also possible. This is done through the page of the company's Internet site. Once the company got access to the Internet, it gets various opportunities. Of these, Electronic-mail (e-mail) is one. As a tourism product supplier, especially with business travel as a selected target market, it makes possible to communicate the person through his/her e-mail address wherever the client is. Unlike telephone communication, there is no need for the presence of the receiver of the message during message transmission. It also gives a typed copy of the message. E-mail communication medium is very cheap yet efficient and effective. On the other hand, marketing on the Internet has an advantage of being used by all company's of all sizes as long as they can establish their Web Site on the Internet.

Tourism Product Development, Research and Information Technology

So far the marketing and distribution of tourism products with the utmost use of information technology is being discussed. Now I will discuss the other dimension of information technology at use in travel and tourism products. Developing any product needs data input and discussion to confirm the viability of a product. Nowadays, it is quite possible to exchange data and hold discussions between producers and researchers or producers and marketers in any part of the world without leaving one's office. This is done by the use of the information technology called video conferencing. The technology works using PCs so as to enable people to meet one another. Television screens linked by high-speed telecommunication lines are used to hold discussion and assess the impact of conversation on participants. With this technology, live transfer of data and discussions are possible. Coupled with non-verbal communication where people look at each other's reaction, video conferencing creates virtual togetherness. It gives an opportunity to discuss new development plan, a research problem or a research finding. This medium of communication has substantial cost reduction both in time and cost of travel, as participants need not travel to meet each other face to face. Actually this is a technology which is not in widespread use, however, in a dynamic growth.

Facilitation and Information Technology

Facilitation is one important aspect of enhancing tourism business. Facilitation includes, issuing of visa, customs clearing and immigration check in ports. Lack of appropriate management in giving fast and efficient service to tourists in this area will deter the tourist flow substantially. Recently, development has come about in using electronic medium for facilitation purpose. An example on this subject is Australia; a country developed 'Automated Visa Application system' what is called ETAS (Electronic Travel Authority System). This system works with three inter-linked functions, each of which is supported by computers that are located in different parts of the world.

(i) A front-end ETA application processing system supported by travel agents chosen GDS or CRS. *(ii)* An international data collection and routing system based on a SITA Computer located in Atlanta, and *(iii)* a data base look-up and electronic funds transfer System supported by the Australian Immigration Department's computer in Sydney (**Inkpen,** pp. 52). Based on these networks the electronic visa, where nothing will be put on the applicant's passport will be processed for the traveller by an authorized travel Agent. The travel agent feeds its computer with all details of the traveller and transmits to Australia where the details appear on the Australia Immigration Department computer. At arrival the visitor will be checked in the immigration computer at Sydney Airport by simply entering his passport number. This system has proved to be efficient and time saving and had generated an immense tourist flow from year to year to Australia.

TOURISM AND ENVIRONMENT

Water Quality

The tourism industry impacts water quality through construction and maintenance of tourist infrastructure, recreational boating, and certain activities of the cruise industry. Tourist infrastructure increases the pressure on existing sewage treatment plants and can lead to overflows during peak tourist times. A more gradual impact is the leaching of nutrients from septic systems of tourists' waterfront homes, accelerating eutrophication of adjacent water bodies, and depleting dissolved oxygen supplies. The construction of tourist facilities and infrastructure also increases the amount of impervious surfaces, which in turn increases the amount of polluted runoff reaching water bodies.

The most significant problem from the standpoint of human health associated with recreational boating and water quality is the discharge of sewage into water bodies with limited flushing, where the discharge occurs near the location of shellfish beds. Diseases that can be potentially transmitted through human contact with fecal discharge and/or ingestion of contaminated shellfish include typhoid fever, dysentery, infectious hepatitis, and nonspecific gastroenteritis (**Seabloom, Plews, & Cox**, 1989, p.1).

Spills and discharges of oil and toxic chemicals are other impacts that recreational boats and the cruise industry can have, although such impacts are not necessarily significant. In 1997, recreational vessels were responsible for 535 reported oil spills, comprising 6.2% of the total spill incidents in U.S. waters. The cruise industry was responsible for an even smaller percentage, at 1.6% of total spills in U.S. waters (U.S. House of Representatives.

Air Quality

Most tourism-related air pollution comes from automobiles. Automobiles emit by far the most carbon monoxide of all transportation modes. In 1997, they emitted 26 million short tons of carbon monoxide, compared with 1.7 million short tons from Recreational marine vehicles and 1 million from aircraft (U.S. Environmental Protection Agency.

Habitat/Ecosystem Alteration and Fragmentation

Ecosystems and natural habitat can be damaged by tourist infrastructure, tourist activities, recreational boating, and the cruise industry. Recreational boats and cruise vessels can damage aquatic vegetation by cutting it with their propellers or otherwise damaging it when running aground. Wetlands have been destroyed in order to build tourist-related infrastructure, such as airports, roads, and marinas (**Andereck,** 1993, p. 29). For example, in Jamaica over 700 acres of wetlands have been destroyed since the 1960s for tourism development (**Bacon,** 1987, pp.105-6).

When snorkeling and hiking, tourists can damage ecosystems by littering, and trampling coral and vegetation. This type of damage is cumulative in nature. One or two tourists may not cause visible harm, but hundreds over time can do substantial damage.

Impacts on Wildlife

Wildlife can be adversely affected by the construction and maintenance of tourist infrastructure, and by tourist activities. Impacts from tourist infrastructure can be direct, such as when development in lower elevations of mountain resorts restricts the migratory range of certain wildlife, or indirect, such as when marine turtles are disoriented by automobile headlights and resort illumination (Gartner, 1996, p.125). The two primary ways in which tourist activities disturb wildlife are by altering their eating habits and feeding patterns, and by altering their habitat. Feeding patterns are altered directly by tourists feeding animals, and indirectly by littering, which encourages wildlife to scrounge for food (**Mathieson & Wall,** 1982, p.109). Wildlife habitat is altered by tourists' trampling and by the use of off-road vehicles (ORVs).

Aesthetic and Cultural Impacts

Tourism can diminish the aesthetic appeal of a destination through the construction of buildings that clash with the surrounding environment, creating "architectural" or "visual" pollution (**Andereck,** 1993, p. 30; **Mathieson & Wall,** 1982, p. 121).). The high-rise hotels along the coastal zone of Atlantic City and Miami are examples, as are several high-rise hotels in Jerusalem, whose construction arguably damaged the city's architectural beauty (**Bosselman,** 1978, pp. 26-7).

Impact on Gateway Communities Outside National Parks and Other Host communities

Tourism affects the natural landscape and character of "gateway communities," which are adjacent to national parks, and other significant tourist destinations. Development related to tourist activity can be detrimental to cultural and aesthetic aspects of these communities if undertaken in an indiscriminate and/or scattered manner. For example, Tusayan, the town near the south rim of the Grand Canyon is "dominated by a gaggle of fast-food restaurants, motels, and trinket shops along the highway and has been likened to a strip mall on the way to the Vatican" (**Whitman,** 1999, p. 19).

Positive Impacts

Despite its many adverse impacts, tourism can have positive impacts on both natural and artificially constructed environments, as well as on destination communities. In fact, tourism has motivated the preservation of such sensitive ecosystems as the Everglades National Park in Florida (**Andereck,** 1993, p.30). Furthermore, tourism that focuses on cultural and historic sites (sometimes referred to as "heritage" tourism) can be the impetus for the preservation and rehabilitation of existing historic sites, buildings, and monuments. For example, historic lighthouses and piers in Cape Cod, Massachusetts and historic buildings in Williamsburg, Virginia have been transformed and preserved for the purpose of tourism.

In addition, the economic benefits of tourism partially balance its negative environmental impacts. For example, gateway communities adjacent to national parks exist primarily because of the economic benefits of tourism. The parks attract more visitors to these communities, resulting in increased employment opportunities and an improved standard of living.

Upstream and Downstream Impacts

In addition to direct environmental impacts, impacts from tourism occur at every point along the supply chain. The "supply chain" with respect to service industries refers to all the actors involved in the provision of a service, including the consumer. The supply chain in the tourism industry consists of those industries that provide accommodations, provide transportation, make arrangements for travellers, and supply equipment. It also includes the tourists themselves. The degree of environmental impact of tourism can be influenced by factors along the supply chain. For example, a hotel can exert "upstream" influence on its suppliers to provide products that minimize environmental impacts, such as recyclable toiletries.

There are several existing initiatives within the private and nonprofit sectors to work with the lodging industry to reduce environmental impacts through supplier relations. The extent to which a hotel can leverage its suppliers depends upon several factors, including type of hotel (e.g., large chain or small independent) and type of supplies. Similarly, travel service providers can have "downstream" impacts by influencing tourists through education and provision of options to reduce resource use. For example, hotels can give guests the option not to have their linens washed daily, and cruise lines can limit the number of tourists that go ashore at sensitive destinations. Downstream influence through tourist education is seen most clearly with ecotourism, defined as travel and tourism that attempts to minimize impacts on the environment. Tour operators specializing in ecotourism influence their customers through provision of environmental guidelines before and during trips.

This is the present and future of tourism (in numbers):

	2003			2013		
World total	*Billion USD*	*% in total*	*growth*[1]	*Billion USD*	*% in total*	*growth*[2]
T&T personal interest	2135,9	9,9	2,2	3862,3	10,8	3,7
Business Travels	488,8	...	0,6	871,7	...	3,7
Government expenses	224,1	3,9	2,8	378,2	4,1	3,0
Capital investments	686,0	9,6	2,8	1398,6	10,1	4,3
Visitor exports	530,9	5,9	3,0	1332,1	6,0	7,1
Other exports	479,0	5,3	8,9	1187,0	5,4	7,2
T&T consumption	3252	...	2,1	6223	...	4,3
T&T demand	4544,2	...	2,9	8939,7	...	4,6
T&T industry GDP	1280,4	3,7	1,1	2279,2	3,8	3,6
T&T economy GDP	3526,9	10,2	2,0	6461,4	10,8	3,9
T&T inudstry labor force	67441,1	2,6	0,1	83893,6	2,8	2,2
T&T economy labor force	194562,0	7,6	1,5	247205,0	8,4	2,4

2003: real growth adjusted with inflation – %; 2004-2013: trend of real growth adjusted by inflation – % '000 jobs.
Source : WTTC, the 2003 Travel and Tourism Economic Research, www.wttc.com

LET US SUM UP

There are various development in the tourism industry like the concept of sustainable development, community based development, responsible tourism, eco tourism, sustainable tourism, crisis management etc. Recent time, there are movements across the world to reduce the negative impact of tourism industry on environment. At the same time, involvement of technology has also brought many changes in tourism industry like GDS, CRS, e-ticketing etc.

CHECK YOUR PROGRESS

(A) Fill in the Blanks

(*i*) SME stands for.................................

(*ii*) CRS stands for ....

(*iii*) NGO stands for ....

(B) True/False

(*i*) Responsible Tourism is a pathway towards sustainable tourism.

(*ii*) Eco Tourism is also a form of sustainable tourism.

(*iii*) Virtual tourism has no impact on the real tourist movement.

(C) Fill in the Blanks

(i) WTTC stands for................................

(ii) ORV stands for................................

(iii) Amadeus software used for................................

LESSON & ACTIVITY

Give an example of a tourist spot from your area and explain the environmental impact of tourism movement in that area.

KEY WORDS

Sustainable tourism: It is a form of tourism that follows the principles of sustainability. Sustainable tourism in its purest sense is an industry committed to making a low impact on the natural environment and local culture, while helping to generate income and employment for locals.

GDS & CRS: It is a system which distributes reservation and information services to sales outlets around the world. Unlike the CRS used solely by an airline or hotel chain, GDS distribute more than one CRS to users who are usually travel agents. GDS were formed from the airlines of several CRS, each of which had its airline backer. Once formed, there was a period of some consolidation and shakeout, after which four main GDS emerged. These are Amadeus, Galileo, Sabre and World Span.

Gateway communities: Communities which are adjacent to national parks, and other significant tourist destinations.

QUESTIONS FOR DISCUSSION

(1) Explain the latest developments in the tourist products.

(2) Write a note on future of tourism.

(3) How technology is related to tourism? Explain in details.

(4) Explain the impact of tourism on environment.

(5) What is sustainable tourism? Explain briefly.

(6) Write short notes on (a) GDS (B) CRS (c) e-Ticketing.

CHECK YOUR PROGRESS: MODEL ANSWER

(A) *(i)* Small Medium Enterprise
(ii) Computerised Reservation system
(iii) Non-Governmental Organisation

(B) *(i)* T *(ii)* T *(iii)* F

(C) *(i)* World Travel and Tourism Council
(ii) Off-Road-Vehicle
(iii) Airlines ticket booking.

❑ ❑ ❑

REFERENCES

(1) *International Tourism* by H.L. Bhattia.

(2) *Contemporary tourism: an international approach* – Chris Cooper & C.Michael Hail.

(3) *International cases in Tourism Management* – Susan Horner & John Susan Brooke.

(4) *The International Marketing of Travel and Tourism: A Strategic approach* by Francois Vellas & Lionel Becherel.

(5) Human Resource Management for Tourism, Hospitality and Leisure Industries: An International Perspective by Tom Baum.

(6) Adams, A. V., Middleton, J., & Ziderman, A. (1992). Market-based manpower planning with labour market signals. *International Labour Review,* 131(3), 261–279.

(7) Airey,A. (1998). Academic papers: Education for tourism — East meets West. *International Journal of Tourism and Hospitality Research,* 9, 7–18.

(8) Airey, D., & Frontistis, A. (1997). Attitudes to careers in tourism: An Anglo Greek comparison. *Tourism Management,* 18(3), 149–158.

(9) Airey, D., & Johnson, S. (1999). The content of tourism degree course in the UK. *Tourism Management,* 20(2), 229–235.

(10) Airey, D., & Nightingale, M. A. (1981). Tourism occupations, career profiles and knowledge. *Annals of Tourism Research,* 8(1), 52–68.

(11) Andriotis, K., Vaughan, D. R. (2004). The tourism workforce and policy: Exploring the assumptions using Crete as the case study. *Current Issues in Tourism,* 7(1), 66–87.

(12) Arthur, M. B., Hall, D. T., & Lawrence, B. S. (1989). *Handbook of career theory.* Cambridge:Cambridge University Press.

(13) Association of Graduate Careers Advisory Services. (2003). Sector briefings 2003: Tourism sector.

(14) Baum, T. (1988). Toward a new definition of hotel management. *The Cornell Hotel and Restaurant Administration Quarterly,* 29(2), 36–40.

(15) Baum, T. (1989). Managing hotels in Ireland: Research and development for change. *International Journal of Hospitality Management,* 8(2), 131–144.

(16) Belau, D. (2003). New threats to employment in the travel and tourism industry 2003. *Geneva: International Labour Organisation.*

(17) Bennison, M., & Casson, J. (1984). *The Manpower Planning Handbook.* Maidenhead: McGraw-Hill.

(18) Ben-Shem, T., & Avi-Itzhak, E. (1991). Work values and career choice in freshmen students: The case of helping verses other professions. *Journal of Vocational Behaviour,* 39(3), 369–371.

(19) Chartrand, J. M., & Camp, C. C. (1991). Advances in the measurement of career development constructs: A twenty year review. *Journal of Vocational Behaviour,* 39(1), 1–39.

(20) Cooper, C. (1991). *Progress in tourism, recreation and hospitality management.* London: Belhaven Press.

(21) Cooper, C., & Shepherd, R. (1994). Dimensions of the education-industry interface for tourism. *Industry and Higher Education,* 8(1), 36–45.

(22) Airey, D. (1979). Tourism education in the United Kingdom. *The Tourist Review,* 34(3), 13–15.

(23) Airey, D. (1994). Education for tourism in Poland: The Phare programme. *Tourism Management,* 15(6), 467–471.

(24) Airey, D. (1997). After 25 years of development: A view of the state of tourism education in the UK.

(25) In: E. Laws (Ed.), The ATTT tourism education handbook (pp. 9–12). London: *Tourism Society.*

(26) Botterill, D. (1996). Making connections between industry and higher education in tourism. *London: The National Liaison Group for Higher Education in Tourism.*

(27) Botterill, D., & Tribe, J. (2000). Guideline 9: Benchmarking and the higher education curriculum. *London: National Liaison Group for Higher Education in Tourism.*

(28) Bramwell, B. (1996). Sustainable tourism management education in Europe. *Tourism Management,* 17(4), 307–308.

(29) Bramwell, B., Goytia, A., & Henry, I. (1996). Developing sustainable tourism management education. In: G. Richards (Ed.), *Tourism in Central and Eastern Europe: Educating for Quality* (pp. 207–224). Tilberg: Tilberg University Press.

(30) Buhalis, D. (1998). Information technologies in tourism: Implications for the tourism curriculum.

(31) Paper presented at ENTER. International conference on information and communication technologies in tourism, Istanbul, Turkey.

(32) Burke, J. F. (1988). Teaching tourism in the USA. Paper presented at *International Conference for Tourism Educators,* Guildford, University of Surrey.

(33) Burns, P. (1992). Going against conventional wisdom. *Tourism Concern,* 3,8.

(34) Burns, P. (1995). Hotel management training in Eastern Europe. *Progress in Tourism and Hospitality Research,* 1(1), 53–62.

(35) Burton, P. (1988). Building bridges between industry and education. Paper presented at International conference for tourism educators, Guildford, University of Surrey.

(36) Busby, G. (1994). Tourism education or tourism training for the 1990s. *Journal of Further and Higher Education,* 18(2), 3–9.

(37) Busby, G. (1995). The changing role of staff development for travel and tourism lecturers. *Journal of the National Association for Staff Development in Further and Higher Education.*

(38) Busby, G., Brunt, P., & Baber, S. (1997). Tourism sandwich placements: An appraisal. *Tourism Management,* 18(2), 105–110.

(39) Cassels, D. (1994). Employer/educator partnerships: Harnessing employers' contributions. Paper presented at NLG conference, London.

(40) Cave, P. (1997). Placements in indus. *The National Liaison Group for Higher Education in Tourism.*

(41) Cave, P. (1999). Best practice in tourism placements. London: *The National Liaison Group for Higher Education in Tourism.*

(42) Charles, K. (1992). Career influences, expectations, and perceptions of Caribbean hospitality and tourism students; *A Third World perspective. Hospitality and Tourism Educator,* 4(3), 9–14.

(43) Charles, K. (1997). Tourism education and training in the Caribbean: Preparing for the 21st century. *Progress in Tourism and Hospitality Research,* 3, 189–197.

(44) Chen, S. C. (1990). The outline of higher level education in tourism in China. *Revue de Tourisme,* 45(4), 24–27.

(45) Chen, J. S., Chu, H. L. K., & Wu, WuChung. (2000). Tourism students' perceptions of work values:

(46) A case of Taiwanese universities. International Journal of Contemporary Hospitality Management, 12(6), 360–365.

(47) Chon, K. (1990). Toward a global perspective of hospitality education. *Hospitality and Tourism Educator,* 2(3), 10–11.

(48) Christie-Mill, R. (1978). Tourism education: Its development and current status with special reference to selected segments of tourism-related industries in Michigan. East Lancing:Michigan State University.

(49) Collins, S., Sweeney, A., & Green, A. (1994). Training for the UK tour operating industry: Advancing current practice. *Tourism Management,* 15(1), 5–8.

(50) Conlin, M. V. (1991). Credible higher education in tourism: A Caribbean example. Tourism: Building credibility for a credible industry. Proceedings of the Travel and Tourism Research Association twenty-second annual conference (pp. 227–232). Hyatt Regency Hotel, Long Beach, CA, June 9–13.

(51) Cooper, C. (1993). An analysis of the relationship between industry and education in travel and tourism. *Teoros International,* 1(1), 65–75.

(52) Cooper, C. (1997). A framework for curriculum planning in tourism and hospitality. In: E. Laws (Ed.), *The ATTT tourism education handbook,* (pp. 24–27). London: Tourism Society.

(53) Cooper, M. (1997). Tourism planning and education in Vietnam: A profile 1995–2010. *Pacific Tourism Review,* 1(1), 57–63.

(54) Cooper, C., & Messenger, S. (1991). Tourism education and training for tourism in Europe: A comparative framework. Paper presented at the international congress for education and training in tourism professions, Milan, Italy.

(55) Daniele, R., & Mistilis, N. (1999). Information technology and tourism education in Australia: An industry view of skills and qualities required in graduates. In: D. Buhalis & W. Schertler (Eds), *Information and Communication Technologies,* (pp. 140–150). Vienna: Springer.

(56) Davies, J. (1999). Language skills in the leisure and tourism industry. *Tourism,* 102, 20.

(57) Echtner, C. (1994). Entrepreneurial training in developing countries. *Annals of Tourism Research,* 22(1), 119–134.

(58) Echtner, C., & Jamal, T. (1997). The disciplinary dilemma of tourism studies. *Annals of Tourism Research,* 24(4), 869–883.

(59) Enghagen, L. K. (1990). Teaching ethics in hospitality and tourism education. *Hospitality Research Journal,* 14(2), 467–474.

(60) Evans, J. (1993). Tourism graduates: A case of over production? *Tourism Management,* 14(4), 243–246.

(61) Fayos-Sola, E. (1997). An introduction to TEDQUAL: A methodology for quality in tourism education and training. Madrid: *WTO.*

(62) Formica, S. (1996). European hospitality and tourism education: Differences with the American model and future trends. *International Journal of Hospitality Management,* 15(4), 317–323.

(63) Formica, S. (1997). The development of hospitality and tourism education in Italy. *Journal of Hospitality and Tourism Education,* 9(3), 48–54.

(64) Gamble, P. R. (1992). The educational challenge for hospitality and tourism studies. *Tourism Management,* 13(1), 6–10.

(65) Getz, D. (1994). Students' work experiences, perceptions and attitudes towards careers in hospitality and tourism: A longitudinal case study in Spey Valley, Scotland. *International Journal of Hospitality Management,* 13(1), 25–37.

(66) Go, F. (1994). Emerging issues in tourism education. In: W. Theobald (Ed.), Global tourism: The next decade. London: Butterworth Heinemann.

(67) Go, F. (1998). Globalization and emerging tourism education issues. Paper delivered to Tourism Education Exchange, University of Westminster.

(68) Go, F., & Mok, C. (1995). Hotel and tourism management education: Building a centre of excellence in Hong Kong. *Tourism Recreation Research,* 20(2), 46–57.

(69) Godau,A. (1991). Developing tourism managers ?the Friedrich List Hoschule in Dresden. *Tourism Management,* 12(3), 257–258.

(70) Goeldner, C. R. (1988). The evaluation of tourism as an industry and a discipline. Paper presented at International conference for tourism educators, Guildford, University of Surrey.

(71) Goodenough, R., & Page, S. (1993). Planning for tourism education and training in the 1990s: Bridging the gap between industry and education. Journal of Geography in Higher Education, 17(1), 57–72.

(72) Gunn, C. (1992). The need for multi-disciplinary tourism education. *World Travel and Tourism Review,* 2, 265–271.

(73) Franklin, Adrian. *Tourism: An Introduction.* London : Sage Publications, 2003.

(74) Khan, Mahmood, Michael Olsen, and Turgut Var (eds.). *VNR's Encyclopedia of Hospitality and Tourism.* New York : Van Nostrand Reinhold, 1993.

(75) Travel Industry Association of America. *Domestic Travel Market Report.* Washington, DC : TIA, 2007.

(76) Travel Industry Association of America. Tourism Works for America. Washington, DC : *TIA, annual.*

(77) Turner, Louis, and John Ash. *The Golden Hordes.* London : Constable, 1975.

(78) Walker, John. *Introduction to Hospitality,* 3d ed. Upper Saddle River, NJ: Prentice Hall, 2002.

(79) United Nations World Tourism Organization. Compendium of Tourism Statistics. Madrid : *UNWTO,* 2007.

(80) United Nations World Tourism Organization. Yearbook of Tourism Statistics. Madrid : *UNWTO,* 2007.

(81) United Nations World Tourism Organization. Tourism in a Globalized Society. Madrid : *UNWTO,* 2003.

(82) United Nations World Tourism Organization. Thesaurus on Tourism and Leisure Activities. Madrid : *UNWTO,* 2001.

(83) United Nations World Tourism Organization. Educating the Educators in Tourism. Madrid : *UNWTO,* 1996.

(84) United Nations World Tourism Organization. Concepts, Deûnitions, and Classiû cations for Tourism Statistics. Madrid : *UNWTO,* 1995.

(85) United Nations World Tourism Organization. Implications of the UNWTO/ UN Tourism Deûnitions. Madrid : *UNWTO,* 1995.

(86) Wall, Geoffrey, and Alister Mathieson. *Tourism: Changes, Impacts, and Opportunities.* Upper Saddle River, NJ : Prentice Hall, 2006.

(87) Young, George. *Tourism: Blessing or Blight?* Baltimore: Penguin Books, 1973.

❑ ❑ ❑